WHOLE LOTTA COUNTRY HITS

Project Manager: Donna Salzburg
Art Layout: Candy Woolley

CONTENTS

BECAUSE YOU LOVE ME

Words and Music by
KOSTAS and JOHN SCOTT SHERRILL

Verses 2, 3, & 5:
A
F♯m
E
C♯7/E♯
call what I've been through, there's some
3.5. See additional lyrics
F♯m
C♯m
D
things that I wish I did-n't do. And now I do the things I
To Coda
A/E
E
Bm/A
A
D/A
A
do be-cause you love me. And now that
cresc.
Bridge:
D
C♯m
you're in my life, I'm so glad I'm a - live;
mf
C♯7/E♯
F♯m
C♯
'cause you showed me the way. And I know now how good it can

D Esus E Bm/A A

be___ be - cause_ you love me.___

dim. *mp*

1. Bm/A A

2. Bm/A A *D.S.* 𝄋 *al Coda*

4. I be -

𝄌 *Coda*

Bm/A A Bm/A A

love me,___ be - cause_ you

A/D D6 A/D D6 Bm/A A

love me,___ be - cause_ you_ love me.

rit.

Verse 3:
Instrumental solo ad lib.
(To Bridge:)

Verse 4:
I believe in things unseen;
I believe in the message of a dream.
And I believe in what you are
Because you love me.

Verse 5:
With all my heart
And all my soul,
I'm loving you and I never will let go.
And every day I let it show
Because you love me.
(To Coda)

ACHY BREAKY HEART

(a/k/a DON'T TELL MY HEART)

Words and Music by
DON VON TRESS

what a fool I've been and laugh and joke a - bout me on the
fist can tell my lip. He nev - er real - ly liked me an - y -
A
phone. You can tell my arms go
way. Or tell your Aunt Lou - ise. Tell
back to the farm. You can tell my feet to hit the
an - y - thing you please. My - self al - read - y knows I'm not o -
E
floor. Or you can tell my lips to
kay. Or you can tell my eyes to

tell my fin - ger - tips they won't be reach - ing out for you no
watch out for my mind. It might be walk - ing out on me to -
A
more.
day.
But Don't tell my heart, my
ach - y break - y heart. I just don't think he'd un - der -
E
stand. And if you tell my heart, my ach - y break - y heart, he

A
To Coda
might blow_ up and kill this man. Ooh.
E
1
A
2
A
D.S. al Coda
CODA
A
man.

Don't tell my heart, my ach - y break - y heart. _ I just don't think he'd un - der -
E
stand. And if you tell my heart, my ach - y break - y heart, _ he
A
might blow _ up and kill this man. Ooh. _
E

A
E
A

Gtr. tuned down 1/2 step:
⑥ = E♭ ③ = G♭
⑤ = A♭ ② = B♭
④ = D♭ ① = E♭

ALMOST HOME

Words and Music by
KERRY KURT PHILLIPS
and CRAIG MORGAN

A
E
A2
A
A♭
E♭
A♭2
A♭
pair of old wool socks on his hands. The bank's
I heard Mom - ma hol - ler, 'Son, hur - ry up'. I was
D
D♭
sign was flash - in' five be - low. It was freez - in' rain and spit - tin' snow. He was
close e - nough for my old nose to smell fresh cob - bler on the stove, and
A
E
A
A♭
E♭
A♭
curled up be - hind some gar - bage cans.
I saw Dad - dy load - in' up the truck.
C#7
D
C7
D♭
I was a - fraid that he was dead. I gave him a gen - tle shake.
Cane poles on the tail - gate, bob - bers blow - in' in the wind. Since

C#7
C7
D
D♭
When he o - pened up his eyes, I said, "Old man, are you o -
Ju - ly of Fif - ty Five, that's as close as I've
E
E♭
A/B
A♭/B♭
E7
E♭7
kay?"
been."
He said,
"I just climbed out of a
𝄋 Chorus:
D
D♭
A
A♭
cot - ton - wood tree.
I was run - nin' from some hon - ey - bees.
D
D♭
Drip dry - in' in the sum - mer breeze
af - ter jump - in' in - to

E
E♭
D
D♭
Cal - i - co Creek.
I was walk - in' down an old dirt road,
A
A♭
F♯m
Fm
past a field of hay that had just been mowed.
Man, I wish you'd just left
To Coda ⊕ 1.
D
D♭
E
E♭
me a - lone,
'cause I was al - most home."

2.
A
A♭
E
E♭
2. Then he said, I was al - most home."
Bridge:
A
A♭
E
E♭
I said, "Old man, you're gon - na freeze to death. Let me
F♯m
Fm
D
D♭
drive you to the mis - sion." He said, "Boy, if you'd left me a - lone, right
E
E♭
D.S. 𝄋 al Coda
now I'd be fish - in'. I just climbed out of a

Coda
E
Eb
A
Ab
'cause I was al - most home.
(Al - most home.
F#m
Fm
D
Db
Man, I wish you'd just left me a - lone;
—)
E
Eb
D
Db
I was al - most home."
3
3
A
Ab
rit.

AMAZED

Words and Music by
MARV GREEN, AIMEE MAYO
and CHRIS LINDSEY

Amazed - 4 - 1

Am7 / A♭m7 — F / F♭

I can hear your thoughts, I can see your dreams.

Chorus:

D / D♭ — A / A♭

I don't know how you do what you do. I'm so in love with you.

Bm / B♭m — G / G♭

It just keeps get-ting bet - ter.

D / D♭ — A / A♭

I wan - na spend the rest of my life with you by my side

Bm / B♭m — D/A / D♭/A♭ — G / G♭

for - ev - er and ev - er.

F
F♭
G
G♭
Ev - 'ry lit - tle thing that you do,
ba - by, I'm a - mazed by you.
1.
2.
A
A♭
C
C♭
D
D♭
A
A♭
C
C♭
G
G♭
Chorus:
Dsus D
D♭sus D♭
N.C.
G
G♭
A
A♭
Ev - 'ry lit - tle thing that you do,
I'm so in love with you.
Bm
B♭m
D/A
D♭/A♭
G
G♭
It just keeps get - ting bet - ter.

Verse 2:
The smell of your skin,
The taste of your kiss,
The way you whisper in the dark.
Your hair all around me,
Baby, you surround me;
You touch every place in my heart.
Oh, it feels like the first time every time.
I wanna spend the whole night in your eyes.
(To Chorus:)

BAYOU BOYS

Words and Music by
TROY SEALS, EDDY RAVEN
and FRANK J. MEYERS

E7
A
ev - er since_ the first_ time I ain't
ev - er been_ the same._
I gave up_ on base - ball_ and
E
1. D
A
I threw down_ my glove,
I dis - cov - ered girls,_
and
I got in - to love._
2. D
A
wonder if_ he knows._
D
A
Sleep all_ day_ we'd
E7
A
run all_ night._
D
E
Chas - in' the lad - ies 'cause_ we knew_ they might._
We
D
A
raised a lot_ of hell,_ we
E7
A
made a lot_ of noise._
D
A
To Coda
Ev - 'ry - bod - y knew we_ were

E7
A
D
A
Ba - you boys,
ev- 'ry- bod- y knew we were
E7
A
D
A
Ba - you boys.
Instrumental
D.S. 𝄋 (no repeats) al
Coda 𝄌
E
A
D
A
E7
A
Coda
𝄌
E7
A
D
A
Ba - you boys.
Sleep all day, we'd
Instrumental
E7
A
D
A
run all night.
Chas - in' the lad - ies 'cause we knew

Additional Lyrics

2. Me and my friend Albo, he's the one who had the car,
We made all the dances, we made all the bars.
We told each other secrets and we wore each other's clothes,
One night I stole his woman and I wonder if he knows.

(Chorus)

3. Sweet Marie was dangerous with those dark, seductive eyes,
She had me sayin' "Maybe, babe," before I realized.
She loved me so deeply and I tried to hold on,
But changin' don't come easy when you been this way so long.

(Chorus)

THE BEST DAY

Words and Music by
CARSON CHAMBERLAIN and DEAN DILLON

D
E
turned off on that old dirt road, he looked at me and swore:
Chorus:
A
Amaj9
Dmaj7
D6
1.2. "Dad, this could be the best day of my life. I've been dream -
3. See additional lyrics
E
A
E
in' day and night a - bout the fun
we'll have.
we've had.
Just
A
A7
D
Bsus
B
me and you do - in' what I've al - ways want - ed to. I'm the luck -
D
E
E7/G♯
To Coda
3
i - est boy a - live. This is the best day of my

1.
A
A+
D
E
life."
2.
Bridge:
A
Bm
A/C♯
D
Dmaj7
life."
Stand-in' in a lit - tle room,_ back of the church_
E
A
D
Dmaj9
_ with our tux - es on.
Look-in' at him,_ I say,_ "I can't be -
E
D.S.𝄋 al Coda
lieve, son, that you're_
grown."
He said,

Verse 2:
His fifteenth birthday rolled around,
Classic cars were his thing.
When I pulled in the drive with that old Vette,
I thought the boy would go insane.
When you're in your teens, your dreams revolve
Around four spinnin' wheels.
We worked nights on end, 'til it was new again.
And as he sat behind the wheel, he said,
(To Chorus:)

Chorus 3:
"Dad, this could be the best day of my life.
I've been dreaming day and night of bein' like you.
Now it's me and her.
Watching you and Mom, I've learned
I'm the luckiest man alive
And this is the best day of my life."
(To Coda)

BREATHE

Words and Music by
STEPHANIE BENTLEY
and HOLLY LAMAR

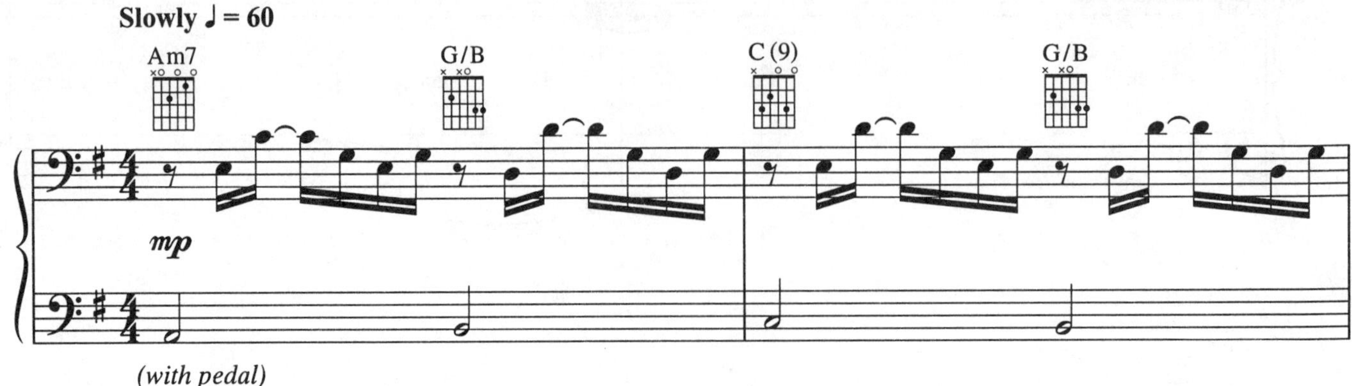

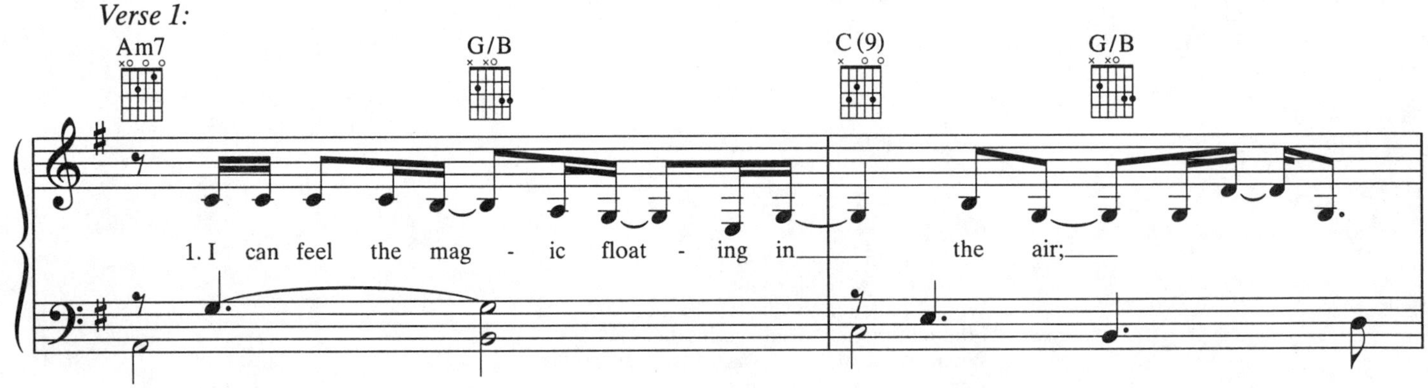

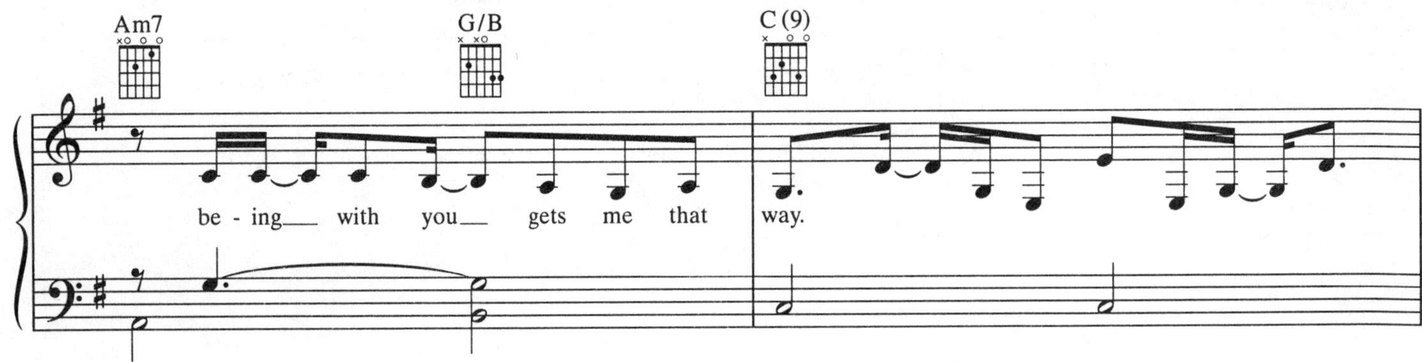

Am7
G/B
C (9)
G/B
I watch the sun - light dance a - cross your face and I've
Am7
Dsus
nev - er been this swept a - way.
Verses 2 & 3:
Am7
G/B
C (9)
G/B
2. All my thoughts just seem to set - tle on the breeze
3. In a way, I know my heart is wak - ing up
Am7
G/B
C (9)
when I'm ly - in' wrapped up in your arms.
as all the walls come tum - blin' down.
Am7
G/B
C (9)
G/B
The whole world just fades a - way, the on - ly thing I
Clos - er than I've ev - er felt be - fore and I know and you know

Am7
D
D7
hear is the beat - ing of your heart.
there's no need for words right now.
cresc.
'Cause I can feel you
mf
Chorus:
G
Am7
C (9)
D7sus
D7
breathe, it's wash - ing o - ver me and sud - den - ly I'm melt - in' in - to you. There's noth - in' left to
prove, ba - by, all we need is just to be caught up in the
G/B
touch, the slow and stead - y rush. And, ba - by, is - n't that the way that love's sup - posed
to be?
dim.
I can feel you
mp

1.
C(9)
G/B
Am7
D7sus
G
Am7
breathe.
cresc.
mf
Just
breathe.
C(9)
Dsus
D
G
Am7
C(9)
Dsus
2.
C(9)
G/B
Am7
D7sus
breathe.
cresc.
mf
Just
G
Am7
C(9)
Dsus
D
G
Am7
breathe.
C(9)
D7sus
G
Am7
Caught up in the touch, the slow and stead-y rush. And, ba-by, is-n't

C(9)
G/B
Am7
D7sus
D7
that the way__ that love's__ sup - posed__
to be?
I can feel you
dim.
mp
G
breathe.__
Just__
breathe.__
I can feel the mag - ic float - ing in__
__ the air;__
be - ing__ with you__ gets me that
way.
rit.

BURNIN' THE ROADHOUSE DOWN

Words and Music by
RICK CARNES and STEVE WARINER

A6
The band is heat - in' up and giv - ing ev -
er. One spark from that fid - dle bow could set
B9
'ry - thing they've got.
this place on fire.
E7
Some -
A6
bod - y check the ex -
It's so cool to be
A7
its in
here in the
D7
case a fire breaks
hot - test place in
out. We're
town.
A6
packed in tight,
Feels so right,
it's
F♯7
Sat - ur - day night, and we're burn
B9
- in' the road -
E7
house
A6
down.
N.C.
We're burn - in' it
Chorus:
D7
down.

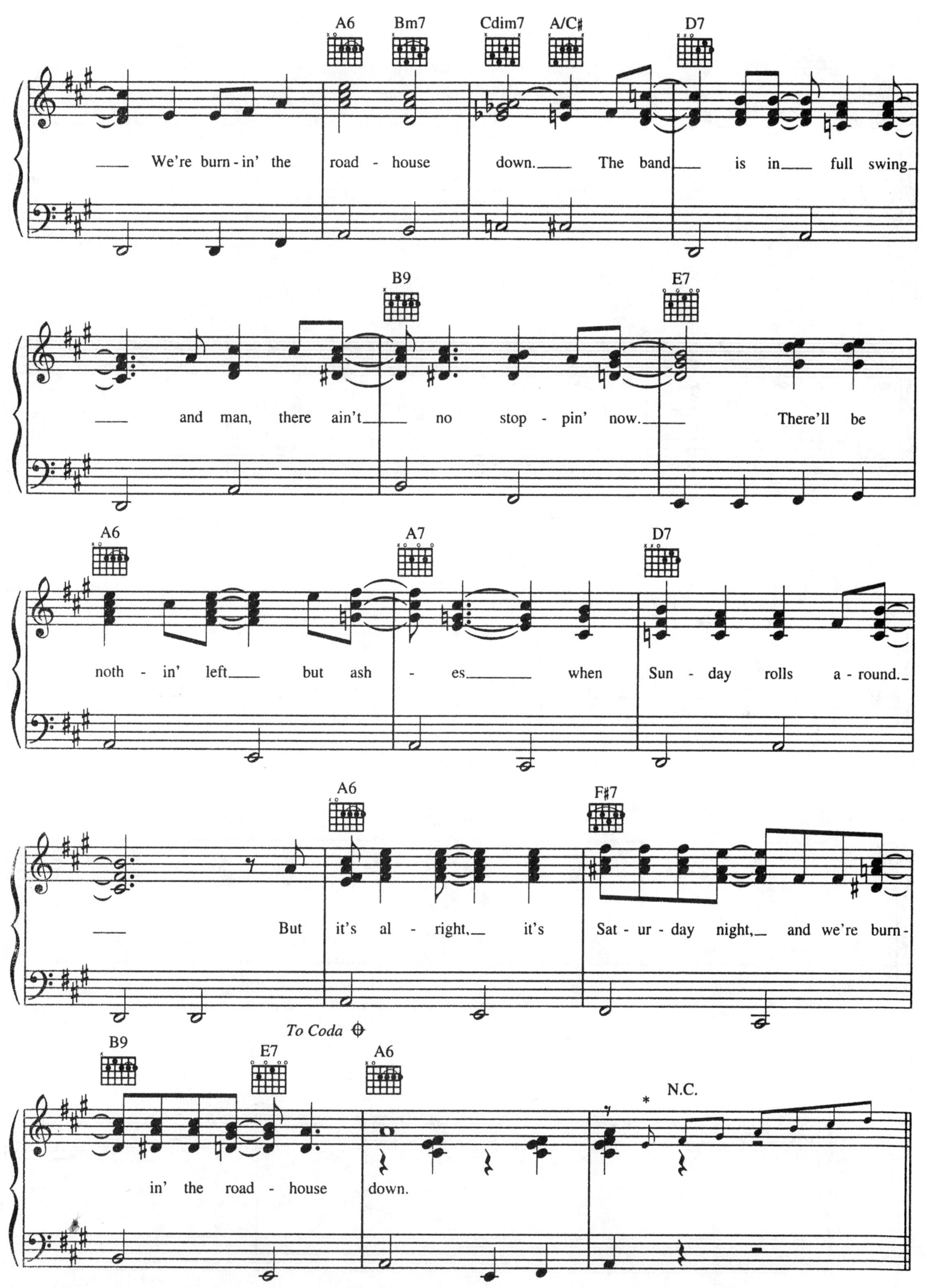

* Optional Instrumental solo in cue notes.

A6
A7
D7
A6
(Instrumental solo . . .
F♯7
B7
E7
A6
A7
D7
A6
. . . continue ad lib. solo . . .
F♯7
B7
E7
A6
D.S. 𝄋 al Coda
2. Yeah, it's a mob_
. . . end solo)
Coda
A6
down. They'll_ be sift - in' through the ash -

A7
D7
D♯dim7
es___ when Sun - day rolls___ a - round.___ But
A6
A7
F♯7
B9
E7
it's al - right,___ it's Sat - ur - day night___ and we're burn - in' the road - house
A6
down.
D7
A6
A♭
G
F♯
B9
F7
E7
A6

BUTTERFLY KISSES

Words and Music by
BOB CARLISLE and RANDY THOMAS

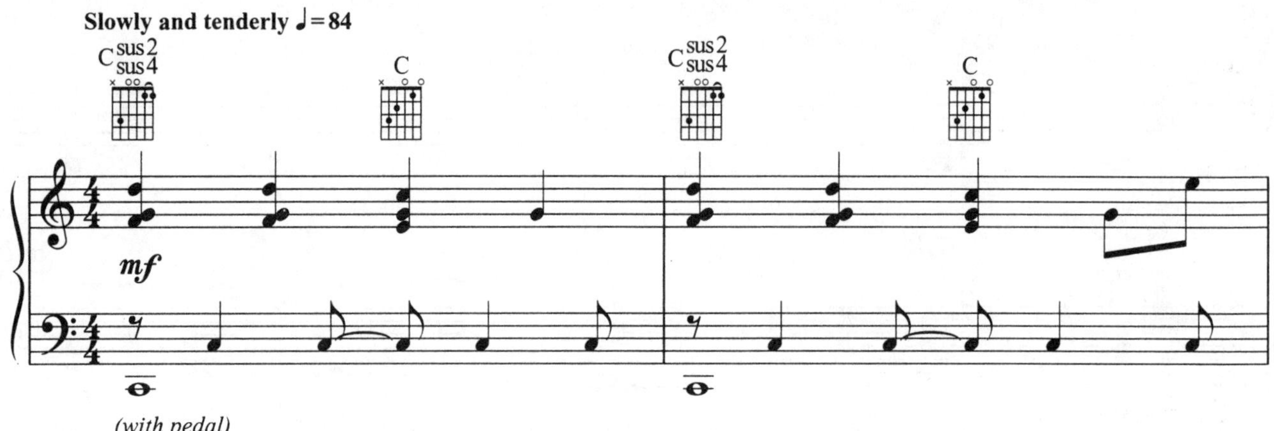

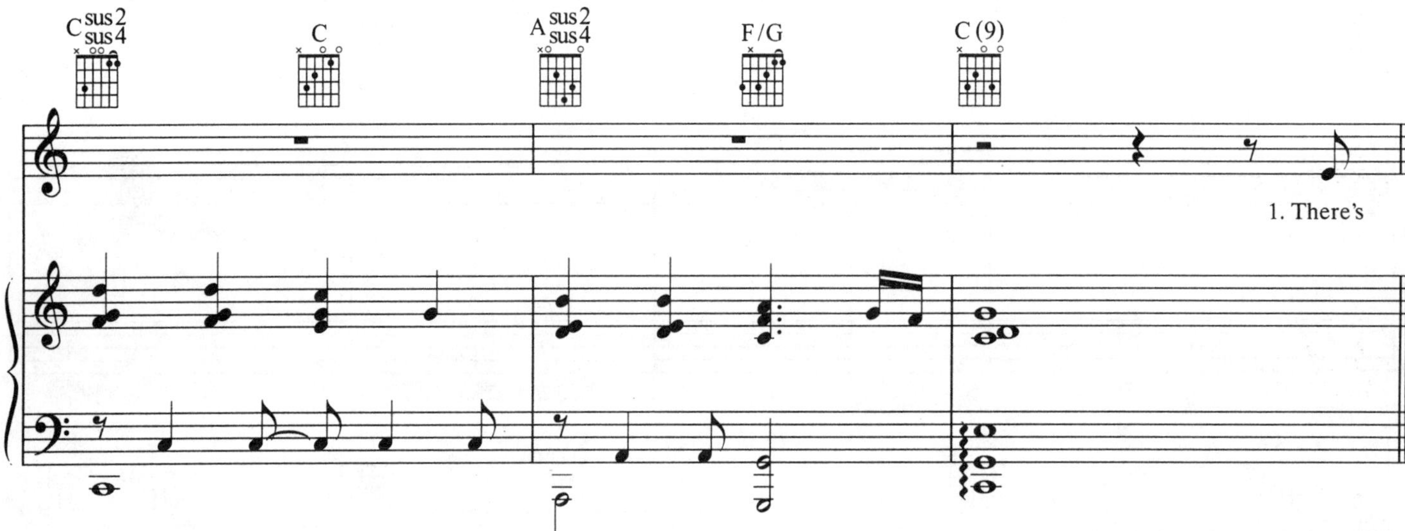

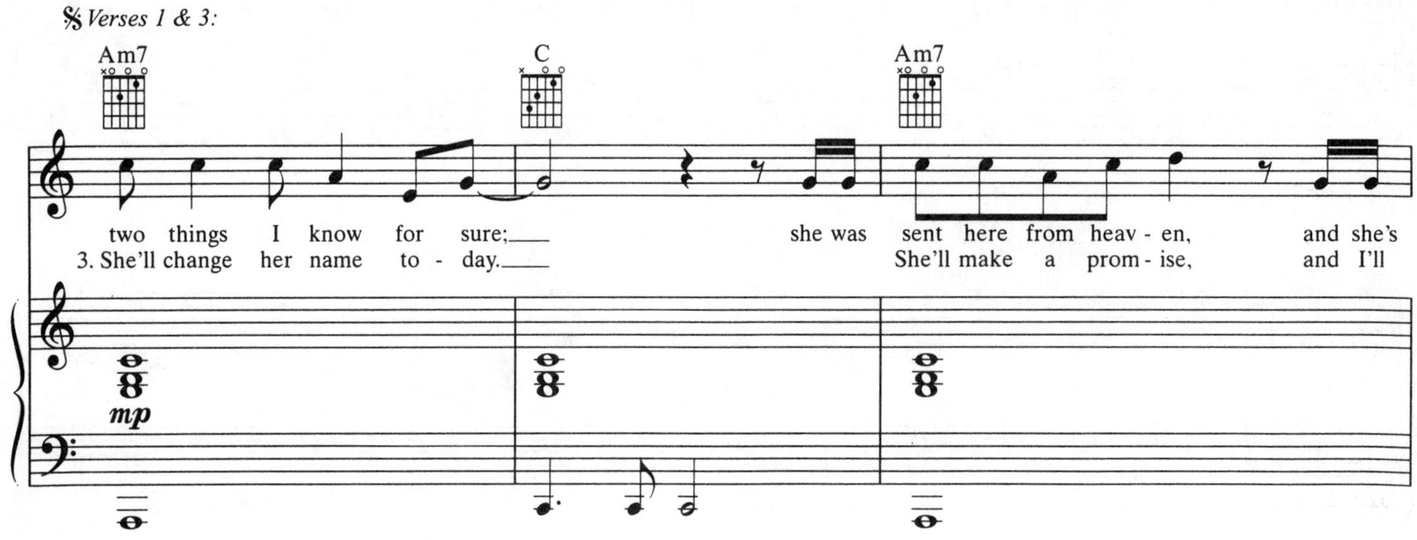

C Dm7 C/E F sus2 sus4 Gsus G

dad - dy's lit - tle girl. As I drop to my knees by her bed at night,
give her a - way. Stand - ing in the bride room just star - ing at her, she

Dm7 C/E F sus2 sus4 Gsus G F(9)/A G/B

she talks to Je - sus, and I close my eyes. And I thank God for all of the
asks me what I'm think - ing, and I say, "I'm not sure. I just feel like I'm los - ing my

C F(9)/A F/G

joy in my life, oh, but most of all, for
ba - by girl." Then she leaned o - ver and gave me

Chorus 1 & 3:

C sus2 sus4 C C sus2 sus4 C

but - ter - fly kiss - es af - ter bed - time prayer, stick - in'
but - ter - fly kiss - es with her ma - ma there, stick - in'

mf

Csus2 sus4
C
G/C
Asus2 sus4
Am
G
lit - tle white flow - ers all up in her hair.
lit - tle white flow - ers all up in her hair.
F(9)
C/E
"Walk be - side the po - ny, dad - dy, it's my first ride." "I
"Walk me down the aisle, dad - dy, it's just a - bout time." "Does my
F(9)
C/E
know the cake looks fun - ny, dad - dy, but I sure tried." Oh, with
wed - ding gown look pret - ty, dad - dy?" "Dad - dy, don't cry." Oh, with
F/A
G/B
C
Dsus
D
To Coda
all that I've done wrong, I must have done some - thing right to de - serve a
all that I've done wrong, I must have done some - thing right to de - serve her

F(9)
G7sus
Csus2 sus4
C
C(9)
hug ev-'ry morn - ing and but-ter-fly kiss - es at night.
mp
p
Verse 2:
Am7
C
Am7
2. Sweet six - teen to - day; she's look - ing like her ma - ma a lit - tle
mp
C
Dm7
C/E
F6 9
Gsus
G
more ev - 'ry day. One part wom - an, the oth - er part girl; to
Dm7
C/E
F(9)
G7sus
G
F(9)/A
G/B
per-fume and make - up from rib - bons and curls; try - ing her wings out in a

C(9)
F(9)/A
Gsus
great big world. But I re - mem - ber
Chorus 2:
Csus2 sus4
C
butter-fly kiss-es after bed-time prayer, stick-in' lit-tle white flow - ers all
mf
G/C
Asus2 sus4
Am
G
F(9)
up in her hair. "You know how much I love you, dad - dy, but if
C/E
you don't mind, I'm on - ly gon - na kiss you on the cheek this time." Oh, with

F/A G/B C Dsus D

all that I've done wrong, I must have done some-thing right to de-serve her

F(9) G7sus C sus2 sus4 C C sus2 sus4 C

love ev-'ry morn-ing and but-ter-fly kiss-es at night. (All the pre-cious

cresc.

Bridge:

E♭ Dm C sus2 sus4 C C sus2 sus4 C

time.) Oh, like the wind, the years go by. (Pre-cious but-ter-

f

E♭ Dm7 F/A G *D.S. 𝄋 al Coda*

fly, spread your wings and fly.)

dim.

Coda
F(9)
G7sus
F(9)/A
love ev-'ry morn - ing and but-ter-fly kiss-es._ I could-n't ask God_ for more,_ man,
G/B
A♭maj9
C/G
poco rit.
this is what love is.___ I know I've got_ to let_ her go, but I'll al - ways___ re-mem-ber_
poco rit.
freely
F(9)
G7sus
ev-'ry hug in the morn - ing and but-ter-fly kiss - es.___
freely
a tempo
C sus2 sus4
C
G/A
G7sus
C(9)
a tempo
rit. e dim.
mp

CHICKS DIG IT

Words and Music by
CHRIS CAGLE and CHARLIE CROWE

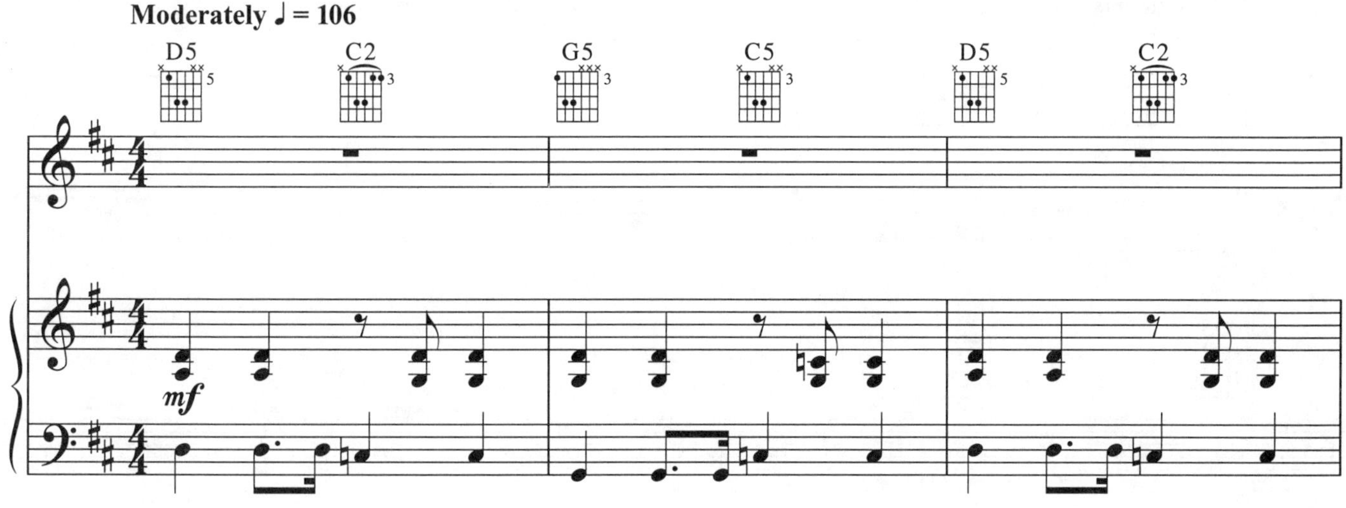

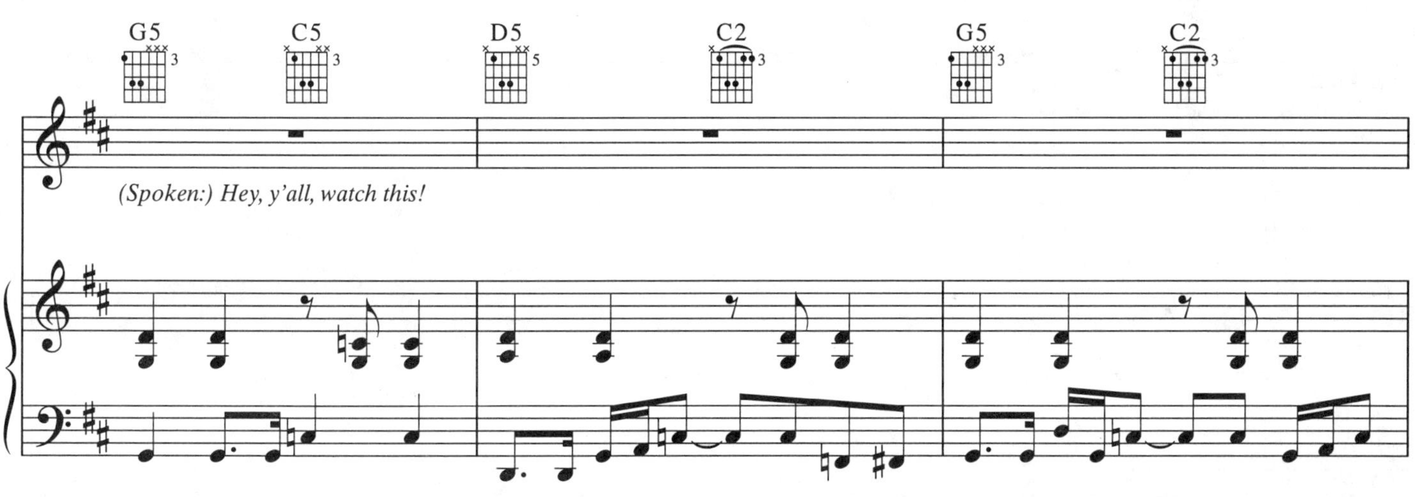

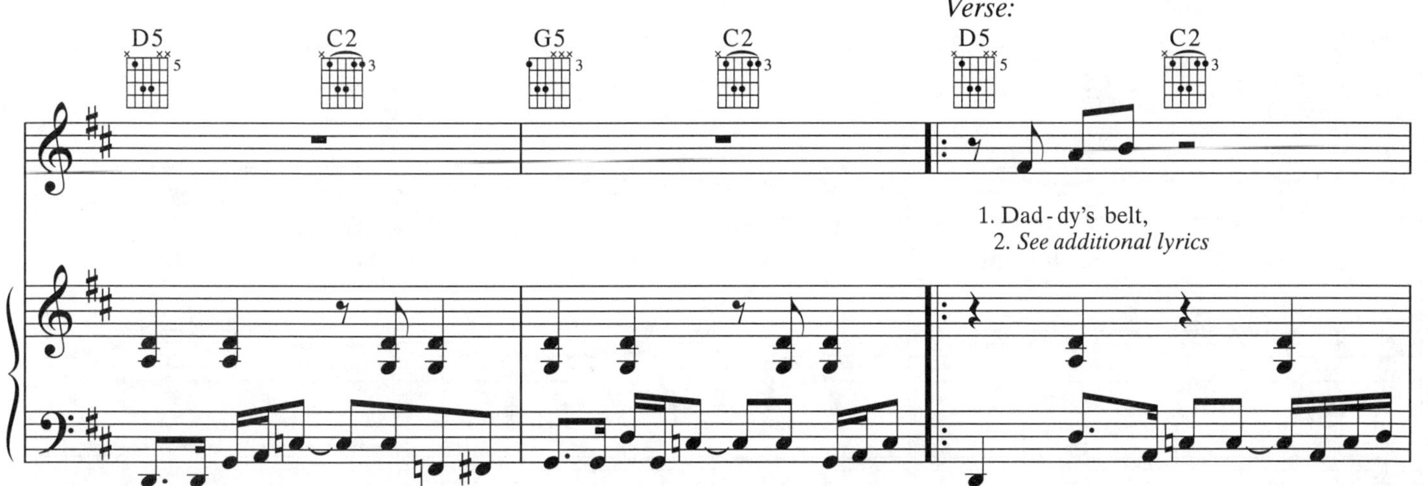

G5
C2
D5
C2
Mom - ma's drapes,
stand-in' tall on the back - yard shed, look-in'
cool in my Su-per-man cape.
I told the neigh - bor-hood girl, said,
"Hey, y'all, watch this!"
My fate was a bro - ken arm, and my
re-ward, one big *kiss.*
A
When Dad-dy asked me why I did it, I made him

Chorus:
A
C2
N.C.
D
A
laugh out loud when I told him 'cause the chicks dig it. Scars heal,
C
G
D
A
C
G
glo - ry fades, and all we're left with are the mem-'ries made, oh yeah.
D
A
C
G
C
To Coda
Pain hurts, but on - ly for a min - ute. Yeah, life is short, so go on and live
1.
G
D5
C2
G5
C2
it, 'cause the chicks dig it.

D5
C2
G5
C2
2.
G
it, 'cause the chicks dig it.
D5
C2
G5
C2
D5
C2
(Inst. solo ad lib....
1.
G5
2.
G5
D.S. % al Coda
...end solo)
Coda
G
C
G
it. It don't mat - ter if you lose or if you win it, hey, the chicks dig it.

Verse 2:
Black top road,
Learner permit,
Thought I was Earnhardt,
Drivin' fast, but I didn't see the ditch,
Took out a mailbox, then a fence and then a barn.
The police came and called my father,
But I met the farmer's daughter.
And when the judge asked me why I did it,
He threw the book at me when I told him,
"'Cause the chicks dig it."
(To Chorus:)

(On D.S.:)
Just throw caution to the wind, my friend,
Then sit back and watch your life begin, 'cause...
(To Chorus:)

CHATTAHOOCHEE

Words and Music by
ALAN JACKSON and JIM McBRIDE

C
G7
C
way down yon-der on the
(See additional lyrics)
Chat - ta - hoo - chee
it gets hot - ter than a
hoo - chie coo - chie.
G7
C
We laid rub - ber on the
Geor - gia as - phalt, we
got a lit - tle cra - zy but we
nev - er got caught.
F
C
Down by the riv - er on a
Fri - day night,
pyr - a - mid of cans in the
G7
C
F
pale moon - light.
Talk - ing 'bout cars and dream - in' 'bout wom - en,
D7
G
nev - er had a plan, just a
liv - in' for the min - ute.
Yeah,

C
way down yon - der on the Chat - ta - hoo - chee, nev - er knew how much that mud - dy wa - ter
G7
C
meant to me. But I learned how to swim and I learned who I was. A
To Coda
1.
G7
C
2.
D.S. al Coda
G7
C
lot a - bout liv - in' and a lit - tle 'bout love. lit - tle 'bout love.
Coda
G7
C
G7
C
lit - tle 'bout love, a lot a - bout liv - in' and a lit - tle 'bout love.
ritard.
N.C.
C
a tempo

Additional Lyrics

Verse 2: Well,we fogged up the windows in my old Chevy
I was willin' but she wasn't ready
So I settled for a burger and a grape sno-cone
I dropped her off early but I didn't go home

(To Chorus)

COME ON OVER

Words and Music by
SHANIA TWAIN and R.J. LANGE

Verse 1:
E
A
get a grip,
get a - way
some - where,
take a trip.
E
A
Take a break,
take con - trol,
take ad - vice
from some - one you know.
Chorus:
E
Come on o - ver,
come on in;
A
E
pull up a seat,
take a load off your feet.
Come on o - ver,
A
come on in;
you can un - wind,
take a load off your mind.
2. Make a wish,

Verse 2:
F
B♭
make a move, make up your mind, you can choose.
F
When you're up. when you're down, when you need
B♭
a laugh, come a - round.
Chorus:
F
Come on o - ver,
B♭
come on in; pull up a seat, take a load off your feet.
F
Come on o - ver, come on in;
B♭
you can un - wind, take a

F
load off your mind.
Oh,
B♭
oh.
F
Oh,
B♭
oh.
3. Be a win-
Verses 3 & 4:
F♯
ner, be a star, yeah, be hap - py to be who you are.
get a grip, get a - way some - where, take a trip.
B
F♯
Got - ta be your - self, got - ta make a plan, got - ta go
Take a break, take con - trol, take ad - vice

B
for it while you can, yeah.
from some - one you know.
cresc.
Chorus:
F♯
B
Come on o - ver, come on in; pull up a seat, take a load off your feet.
F♯
B
To Coda
Come on o - ver, come on in; you can un - wind, take a load off your mind.
F♯
B
F♯
B
D.S. al Coda
4. Get a life,

Coda
B
F♯
load off your mind, yeah.
Come on o - ver, come on in.
B
F♯
Yeah, come on, come on.
Oh,
B
oh.
N.C.
B
Oh,
oh.
F♯
B
N.C.
Oh,
oh,
come on in.

CONCRETE ANGEL

Words and Music by
STEPHANIE BENTLEY and
ROB CROSBY

C
G/B
Am7
G/B
C
G/B
D♭
A♭/C
B♭m7
A♭/C
D♭
A♭/C
Wear - in' the same dress she wore___ yes - ter - day,___ she hides the bruis - es with the
1.
Am7
C
G/B
Am7
G/B
B♭m7
D♭
A♭/C
B♭m7
A♭/C
lin - en and lace.___ Whoa.______
2.3.4.
Chorus:
Am7
G
C
G/B
Am7
G/B
B♭m7
A♭
D♭
A♭/C
B♭m7
A♭/C
nev - er born._ Through the wind___ and the rain,_ she stands hard___ as a stone_ in a world_
mf

C
G/B
Am7
G/B
C
G/B
D♭
A♭/C
B♭m7
A♭/C
D♭
A♭/C
that she can't rise a - bove.
But her dreams give her wings and she flies
Am7
G
C
D
B♭m7
A♭
D♭
E♭
to a place where she's loved.
Con - crete an - gel.
1.
D.S.𝄋
C
G/B
Am7
G/B
C
G/B
Am7
G/B
D♭
A♭/C
B♭m7
A♭/C
D♭
A♭/C
B♭m7
A♭/C
mp

Verse 2:
The teacher wonders but she doesn't ask.
It's hard to see the pain behind the mask.
Bearing the burden of a secret storm,
Sometimes she wishes she was never born.
(To Chorus:)

Verse 3:
Somebody cries in the middle of the night.
The neighbors hear, but they turn out the light.
A fragile soul caught in the hands of fate,
When morning comes, it'll be too late.
(To Chorus:)

Verse 4:
A statue stands in a shaded place,
An angel girl with an upturned face.
A name is written on a polished rock
A broken heart that the world forgot.
(To Chorus:)

COUNTRY AIN'T COUNTRY

Words and Music by
CARSON CHAMBERLAIN, CASEY BEATHARD
and TERESA BOAZ

G
A♭
been to col - lege and then law school since leav - ing his roots.
He said, "Now - a - days peo - ple trade heif - ers on line."
watch-ing crews turn the coun - ty road in - to four lanes.
D
E♭
Came home in a Lex - us, he
But dad ain't seal - ing deals with a
The old Sun - day drive has turned
G
A♭
D
E♭
G
A♭
left in a Ford.
hand - shake like be - fore.
in - to a chore.
Coun - try ain't
Coun - try ain't
Coun - try ain't
1.
A
B♭
D
E♭
D2
E♭2
D
E♭
coun - try no more.

2.3.
A
Bm
A
G
B♭
Cm
B♭
A♭
coun - try no more. No, coun-try ain't
A
D
D2
D
B♭
E♭
E♭2
E♭
coun - try no more. The back
Bridge:
G
D
A♭
E♭
for - ty was sold to make up for hard times, then
A
D
B♭
E♭
sold by the half - a - cre lot o - ver - night. The

G
A♭
D
E♭
hous - es went___ up and the trees were cut___ down.
A
B♭
D
E♭
There went__ the fin - est___ deer___ hunt - in' a - round.___ Lord,_
G
A♭
D/F♯
E♭/G
Em
Fm
ev - 'ry - one's lock - ing___ their__ doors____ 'cause_
G
A♭
A
B♭
To Coda
D
E♭
coun - try ain't coun - try__________ no more.____

G
D
A
D
A♭
E♭
B♭
E♭
G
F
D
G
A♭
G♭
E♭
A♭
D
D2
D
E♭
E♭2
E♭
D.S. 𝄋 al Coda
3. Now his
Coda
D
E♭
more.
There's no turn - in' back
and you

A
D
G
B♭
E♭
A♭
just can't ig - nore
that coun - try aint't
A
Bm
Bm/A
G
A
B♭
Cm
Cm/B♭
A♭
B♭
coun - try no more.
No, coun - try ain't coun - try no
D
D2
D
E♭
E♭2
E♭
more.
Yo - del
D2
D
E♭2
E♭
ay - hee.
rit.

COWBOY TAKE ME AWAY

Words and Music by
MARTIE SEIDEL and MARCUS HUMMON

Original key: F♯ major. This edition has been transposed up one half-step to be more playable.

Em D/F♯ G C D
grow some - thing wild and un - rul - y. I wan - na
Em D/F♯ G Em D/F♯ G
sleep on the hard ground in the com - fort of your arms on a
Em D/F♯ G C D
pil - low of blue bon - nets and a blan - ket made of stars. Oh, it
C G/B D
sounds good to me. I said, cow - boy,

G
G/B
Am7
D/B
7 fr
D
take me a - way. Fly this girl as high
Em
C
D
as you can in - to the wild blue. Set me
G
G/B
Am7
D/B
7 fr
D
free, oh, I pray, clos - er to
Em
C
D
heav-en a - bove and clos - er to you, clos - er to you.

C
G/B
G
C
G/B
G
C
G/B
G
Em
D
Em
D/F♯
G
I wan-na walk and not run.
I wan-na
Em
D/F♯
G
Em
D/F♯
G
C
skip and not fall.
I wan-na look at the ho - ri - zon and not see
D
Em
D/F♯
G
a build - ing stand - in' tall.
I wan-na be the on-ly one for

Em
D/F♯
G
Em
D/F♯
G
C
miles and miles ex - cept for may - be you and your
D
C
G/B
D
sim-ple smile. Oh, it sounds good to me. Yes, it sounds
C
G/B
D
G
G/B
Am7
D/B
7fr
so good to me. Cow-boy, take me a - way.
D
Em
C
Fly this girl as high as you can in - to the wild blue.

D
G
G/B
Am7
D/B
7fr
Set me free, oh, I pray,
D
Em
C
clos - er to heav-en a-bove and clos - er to you,
D/F#
D
G
G/B
Am7
C
To Coda
clos - er to you.
D
Em
C

D/F♯
D
G
G/B
Am7
G/B
D
Em
C
D/F♯
D
I said I wan-na
Em
D/F♯
G
Em
D/F♯
G
touch the earth, I wan-na break it in my hands. I wan-na
Em
D/F♯
G
C
D
D.S. al Coda
grow some - thing wild and un - rul - y. Oh, it sounds

CODA
G
G/B
G/A
G/B
D
Clos - er to you.
Instrumental ad lib.
Cow - boy, take me a - way,
clos - er to you.
Am
D/B
7fr
Em
C
Am7
1-3
4

COULD I HAVE THIS DANCE

Words and Music by
WAYLAND HOLYFIELD and
BOB HOUSE

A
A7
D
E
swayed to the mu-sic and held to each oth-er,
we moved to-geth-er, I knew for-ev-er,
D
E
A
E
I fell in love with you.
you're all I'll ev - er need.
Could
Chorus
A
D
I have this dance for the rest of my life? Would
E
D
E
you be my part-ner ev - 'ry night?

A
A7
D
Dm
When we're to- geth -er it feels so right. Could
A
To Coda
E7
A
1. D/E
I have this dance for the rest of my life? I'll
2. E
D.S. al Coda
Could
Coda
E9
E7
rest of my
A
A9sus
Bm7
E7sus
A
life?

THE DANCE

Words and Music by
TONY ARATA

The Dance - 3 - 1

C
D
was right.
How could I have known
that you'd ev - er
would fall.
Hey, who's to say?
You know I might
cresc.
Em
D/F♯
Chorus:
C
say good - bye?
have changed it all.
And now,
I'm glad I did - n't know
mf
D
Bm7
C
D
the way it all would end,
the way it all would go.
Our lives
C
D
Bm7
are bet-ter left to chance.
I could have missed the pain,
but I'd have had to miss
C
D
1.
G
C/G G
C/G G
D/G C/G G
D.S.
the
dance.
2. Hold-ing you,
dim.
mp

2.
G
C
D
dance. Yes, my life, it's bet-ter left to chance. I could have missed the pain,
Bm7
C
D
N.C.
but I'd have had to miss the dance.
rit.
a tempo
mp
Em
C
Dsus
D
8va
Em7(4)
Repeat ad lib. and fade

DADDY'S MONEY

Words and Music by
BOB DI PIERO, STEVE SESKIN
and MARK D. SANDERS

Moderately ♩ = 116

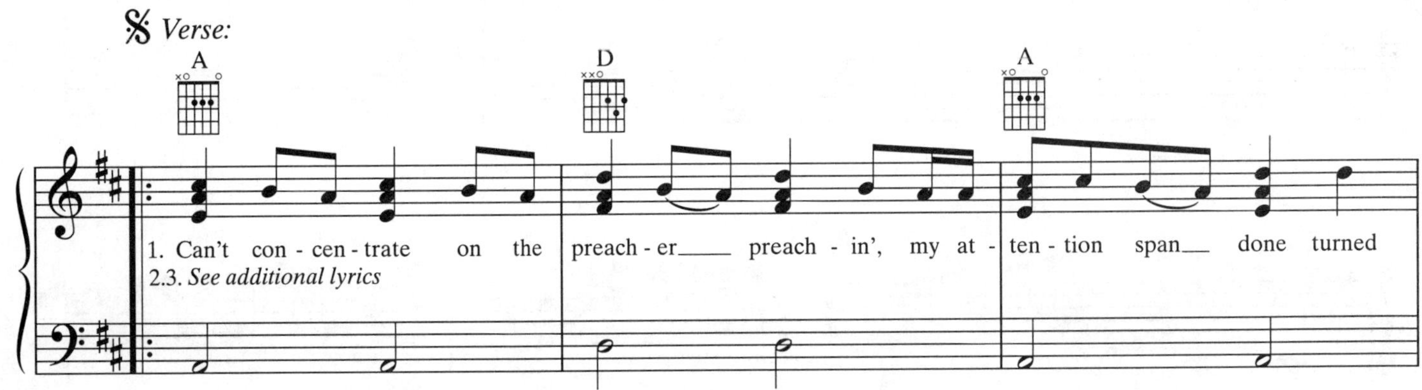

E7 A

up there in the choir loft. She's got her

Chorus:

D

dad - dy's mon - ey, her mom - ma's good looks, more laughs than a stack of

A

com - ic books. A wild i - mag - i - na - tion, a col - lege ed - u - ca - tion,

D

add it all up, it's a dead - ly com - bi - na - tion. She's a good bass fish - er, a

G

dy - na - mite kiss - er and coun - try as a tur - nip green. She's got her

A
To Coda
dad - dy's mon - ey, her mom - ma's good looks, and look who's look - in' at me.

1.
D

2.
D
G7

D

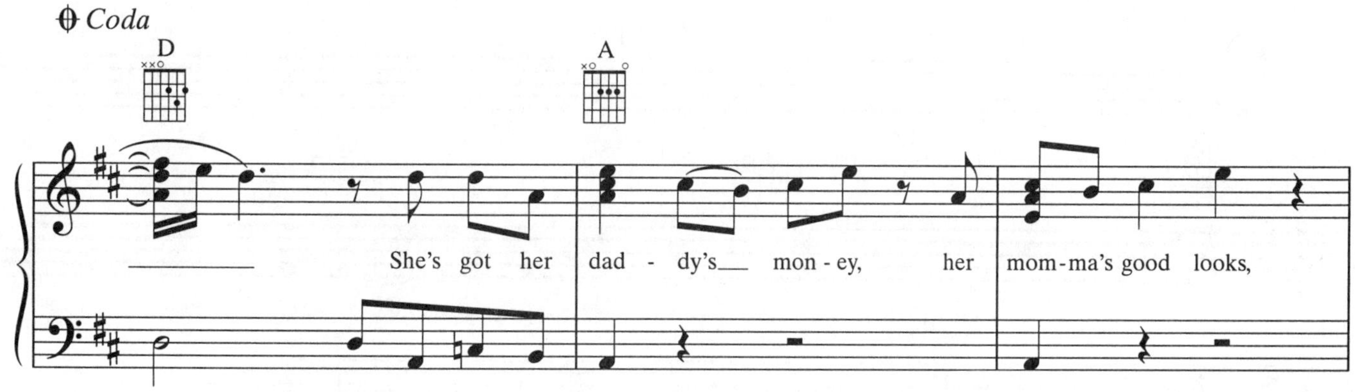

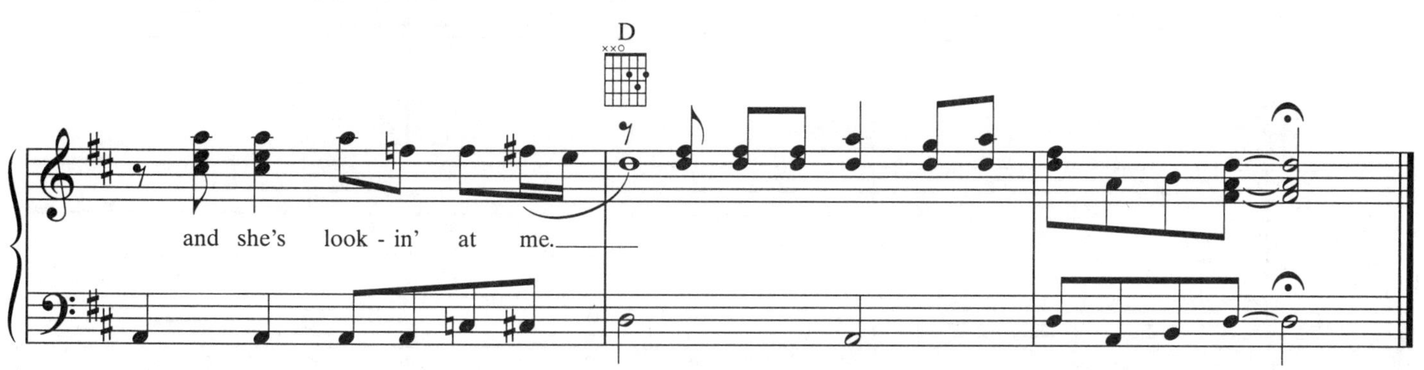

Verse 2:
Her second cousin was my third grade teacher,
I used to cut her grandma's grass.
Back then she was nothin' but knees and elbows,
Golly, did she grow up fast.
(To Chorus:)

Verse 3:
Lord, if you got any miracles handy,
Maybe you could grant me one.
Just let me walk down the aisle and say, "I do,"
To that angel with the choir robe on.
(To Chorus:)

DEEPER THAN THE HOLLER

Words and Music by
PAUL OVERSTREET and DON SCHLITZ

F
B♭
F
I come from the coun - try___ and I know I ain't seen it all _
back roads to the Broad - way shows, with a mil- lion miles be - tween, _
B♭
F
B♭
__ but I've heard that o - cean's salt - y and _ the stars _
__ there's at least a mil - lion love songs _____ that peo -
F
Gm7
3fr.
__ some - times they fall. ___________ And that would not _ do jus -
ple love to sing. ___________ And ev - 'ry one _ is dif -
Am7
B♭
tice to the way___ I feel for you _ so I had to sing _ a song _
f'rent and ev - 'ry - one's the same_ and this is just _ an - oth -

F/A
Gm7
3fr.
C7
a-bout all the things I knew.
er way of say-ing the same thing.
My love is
F
B♭
F
B♭
deep-er than the hol-er,
strong-er than the riv-er,
Dm
Gm7
3fr.
B♭
C7
high-er than the pine trees grow-ing tall up-on the hill. My love is
F
B♭
F
Am/E
Dm
pur-er than the snow-flakes that fall in late De-cem-ber and

Gm
3fr.
F/A
Bb
hon - est as a rob-in on the spring - time win-dow sill, and
C7
To Coda
F
Dm
long - er than the song of a whip-poor - will.
D.S. al Coda
Coda
From the
ritard.

YOU'RE STILL THE ONE

Words and Music by
SHANIA TWAIN and R.J. LANGE

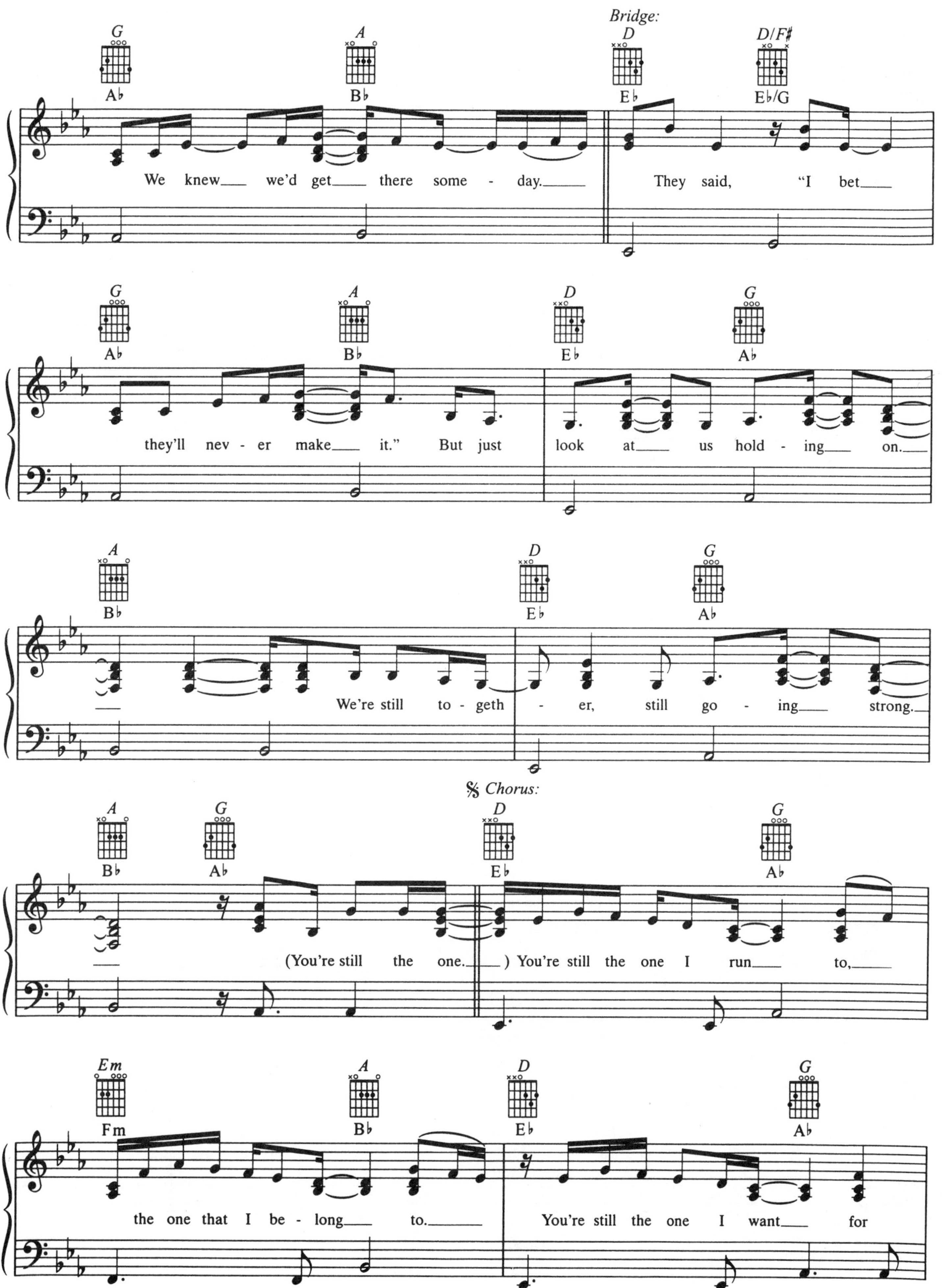
Bridge:
G A D D/F#
A♭ B♭ E♭ E♭/G
We knew we'd get there some - day.
They said, "I bet
G A D G
A♭ B♭ E♭ A♭
they'll nev - er make it." But just look at us hold - ing on.
A D G
B♭ E♭ A♭
We're still to - geth - er, still go - ing strong.
Chorus:
A G D G
B♭ A♭ E♭ A♭
(You're still the one.) You're still the one I run to,
Em A D G
Fm B♭ E♭ A♭
the one that I be - long to.
You're still the one I want for

Verse 2:
Ain't nothin' better,
We beat the odds together.
I'm glad we didn't listen.
Look at what we would be missin'.
(To Bridge:)

DON'T ROCK THE JUKEBOX

Words and Music by
ALAN JACKSON, ROGER MURRAH
and KEITH STEGALL

G
D
To Coda
G
- box.
Play me a coun-try song.
Verse:
N.C.
C7
G
1. Be-fore you drop that
mf
quar-ter,
keep one thing in mind;
A7
you got a heart - broke
hill - bill-y
stand-ing here in line.
D7
C
I've been down and lone - ly
G
C
G
ev - er since she left.
Be-fore you punch that
num-ber,

Verse 2:
I ain't got nothin' against rock and roll.
But when your heart's been broken, you need a song that's slow.
Ain't nothin' like a steel guitar to drown a memory.
Before you spend your money, babe, play a song for me.
(To Chorus:)

DON'T IT MAKE MY BROWN EYES BLUE

1.
F
Em7
F
G7
2.
F
F (G bass)
C
Don't It Make My Brown Eyes Blue.
Don't It Make My Brown Eyes Blue.
Am
Em7
F
C
Am
Em7
F
C
Tell me no se - crets, tell me some lies, give me no rea - sons, give me al - i - bies.
Am
Em7
F
C
Dm7
Em
F
F (G bass)
D. S. al Coda
Tell me you love me and don't let me cry, say an - y - thing but don't say good - bye.
Repeat and fade
Coda
F
Em7
F
Em7
F
F (G bass)
C
Am
Dm7
G7
don't it make my brown eyes, don't it make my brown eyes, Don't It Make My Brown Eyes Blue
And

DON'T TAKE THE GIRL

Words and Music by
CRAIG MARTIN and LARRY W. JOHNSON

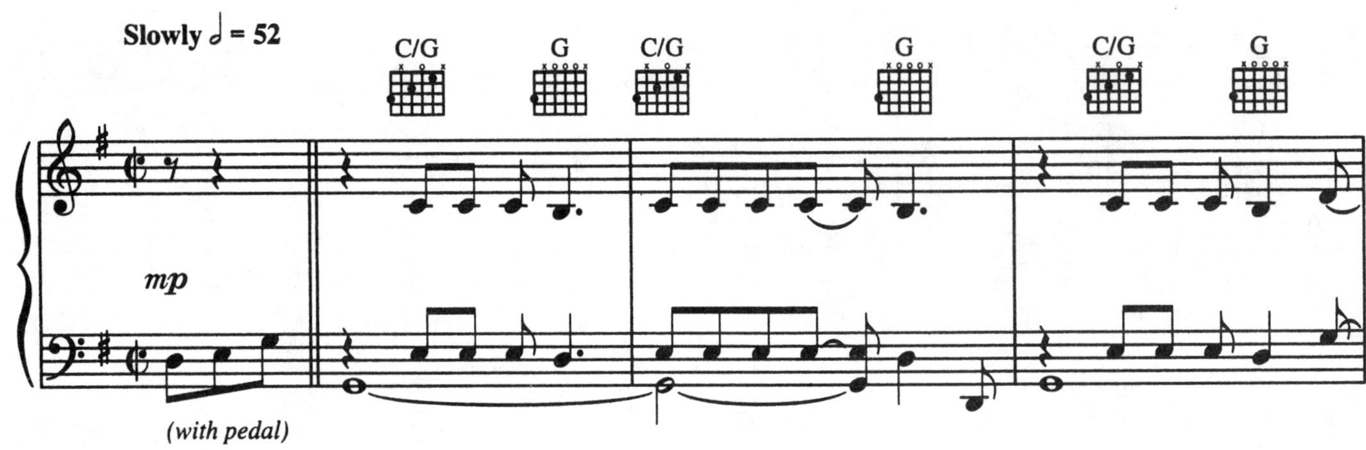

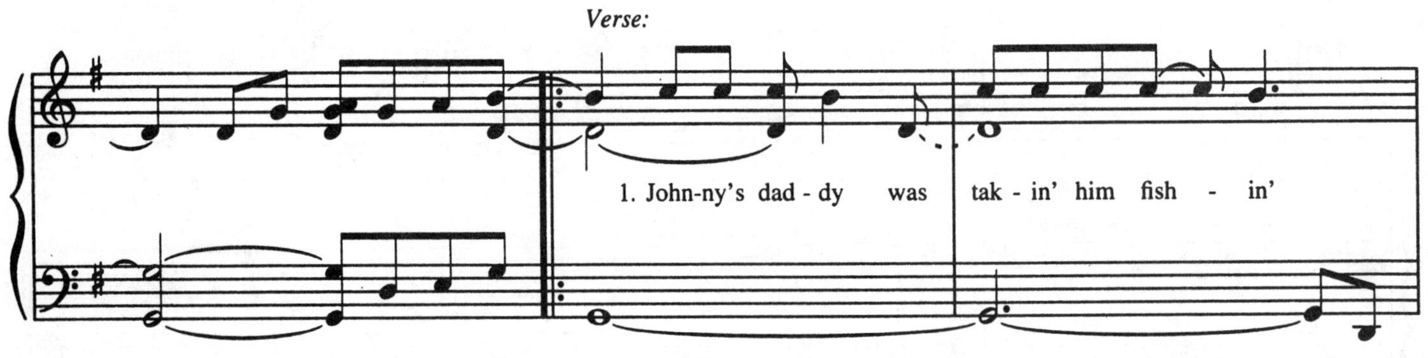

the front gate,
hold - in' a fish - in' pole.
Bm7
Cmaj7
Bm7
His dad looked down and smiled,
said, "We can't leave her be - hind.
Cmaj7
Am7
G/B
Son, I know you don't want her to go, but
Cmaj7
D7sus
G
Am/G
G
some-day you'll change your mind."
And John - ny said,
"Take Jim - my John - son,

Am/G
G
Am/G
G
take Tom-my Tomp - son,
take my best friend,
Bo.
Am/G
G
Am/G
G
Am/G
G
Am/G
G
Take an - y - bod - y that you want as
long as she don't go.
Am7
Take an - y boy in the world,
Dad - dy, please,
Cmaj9
D7sus
G
C/G
G
don't take the girl."

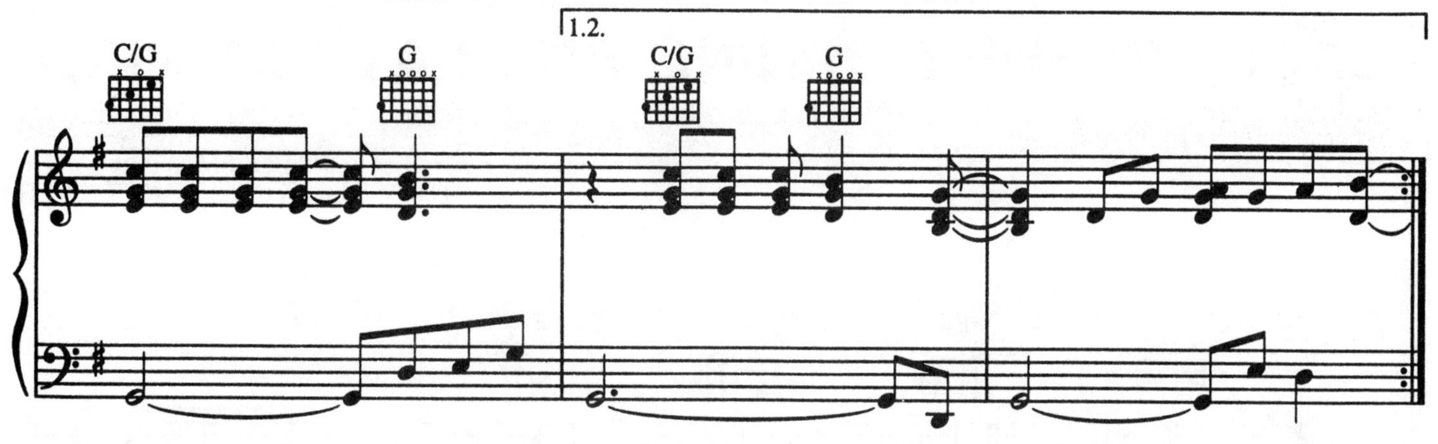

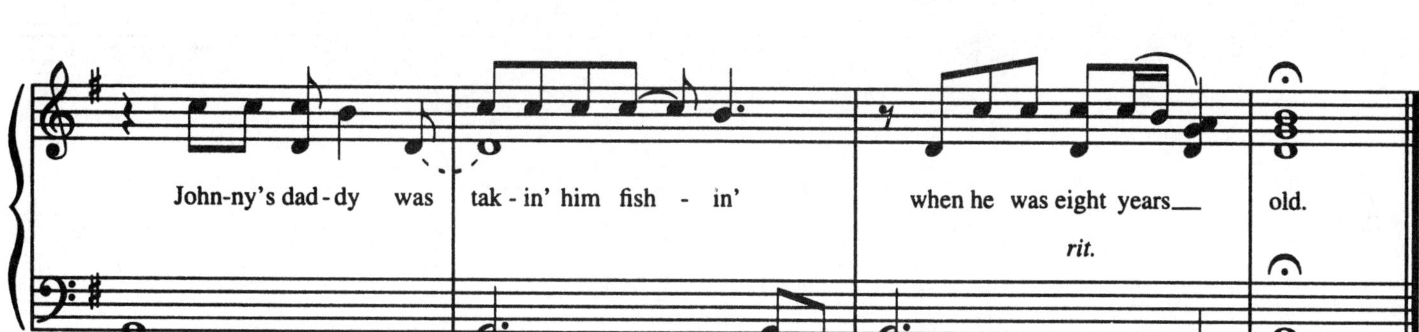

Verse 2:
Same ol' boy, same sweet girl, ten years down the road.
He held her tight and kissed her lips in front of the picture show.
A stranger came and pulled a gun and grabbed her by the arm.
Said, "If you do what I tell you to, there won't be any harm."
And Johnny said,
"Take my money, take my wallet, take my credit cards.
Here's the watch that my grandpa gave me, here's the keys to my car.
Mr., give it a whirl, but please, don't take the girl."

Verse 3:
Same ol' boy, same sweet girl, five years down the road.
There's gonna be a little one and she says, "It's time to go."
Doctor said, "The baby's fine but, you'll have to leave
'Cause his mama's fadin' fast," and Johnny hit his knees.
And then he prayed,
"Take the very breath you gave me, take the heart from my chest.
I'll gladly take her place if you'll have me.
Make this my last request.
Take me out of this world, God, please, don't take the girl."

EARLY IN THE MORNING AND LATE AT NIGHT

Words and Music by
TROY SEALS and FRANK MEYER

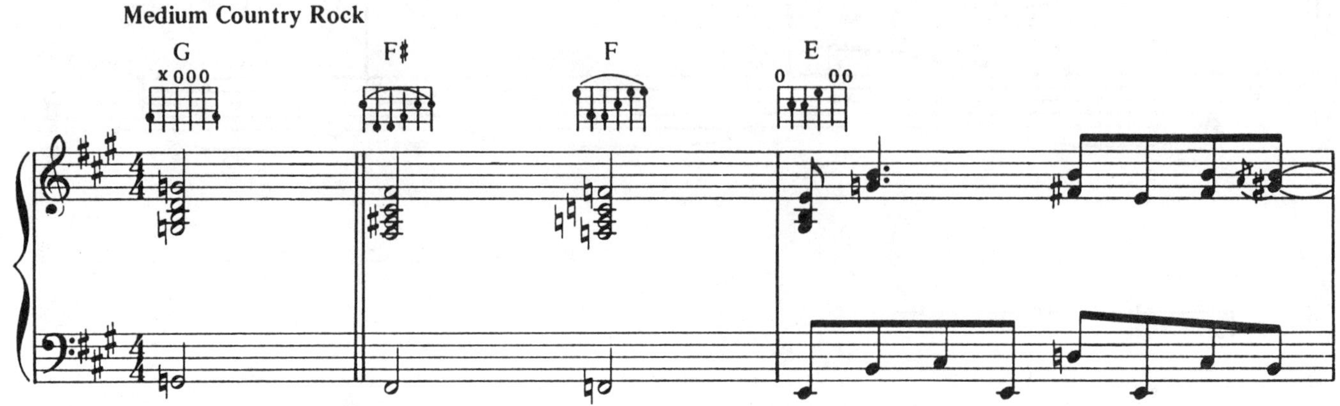

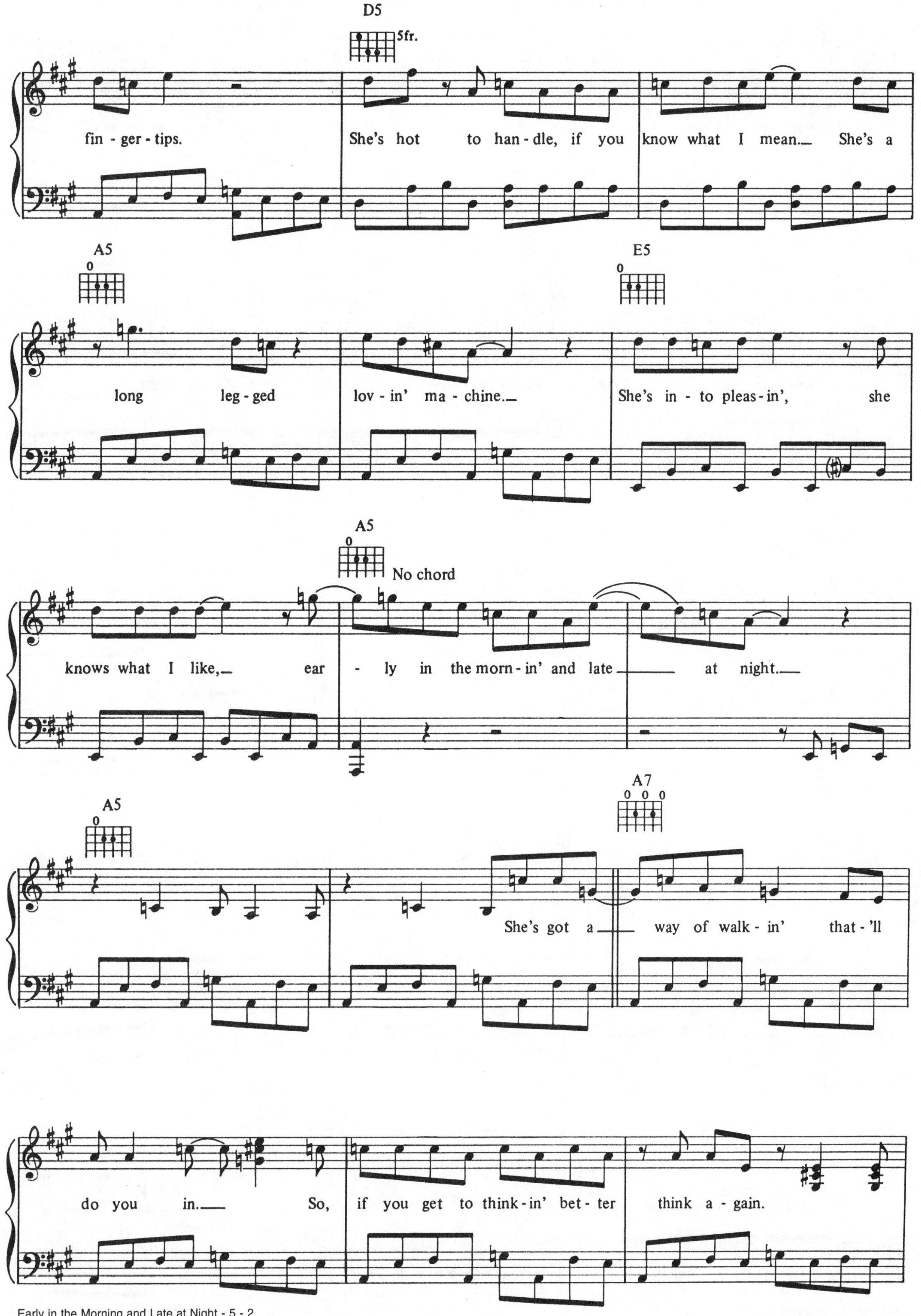
D5
5fr.
fin - ger - tips.
She's hot to han - dle, if you
know what I mean. She's a
A5
long leg - ged
lov - in' ma - chine.
E5
She's in - to pleas - in', she
knows what I like, ear
A5
No chord
- ly in the morn - in' and late
at night.
A5
She's got a
A7
way of walk - in' that - 'll
do you in. So,
if you get to think - in' bet - ter
think a - gain.

D7
A7
No harm in look-in', if you un-der-stand; she's a one man wom-an, I'm a
E7
one wom-an man. There's no doubt a-bout it when she holds me tight
A5
N.C.
A7
ear-ly in the morn-in' and late at night. Ear-ly in the morn-in' we rock,
late in the eve-nin' we roll. We're
E7
A7
in it right from the start, heart, bod-y and soul.

A7
She's cook-in' up a mess of moves,
E7
keeps a lot of love spread on the men - u.
She's got a man with a
A7
bit ap - pe - tite,
ear - ly in the morn - in' and late at night.
1. D7
A7
Sax Solo ad lib
D7
E7

2.
E7
N.C.
She's hot to han - dle, if you know what I mean.
E7
D
D♯
E
She's a long leg - ged lov - in' ma - chine.
E7
She's in - to pleas - in', she knows what I like. I like it
A
N.C.
A5
ear - ly in the morn - in' and late at night.

FALLIN' OUT OF LOVE

Words and Music by
JON IMS

C/G
G
G6
G(9)
G
So, you swal - low hard. May - be you
D/E
Em7
D/E
Em7
C(9)
drive all night, try - in' to fig - ure out where the whole
D
G/D
C/D
D
thing start - ed go - in' wrong. And in the
Dm7
C/D
Dm7
C/D
G/C
C
si - lence, some - thing be - gins to un - rav - el
cresc.

G/C
C
G/A
F♯m7/A
Em7/A
F♯m7/A
You nev - er knew him like you'll be know - ing him now.
C(9)
D
Fall - ing out of
Chorus:
C
D
Bm7
love and back in - to your life, pull - in' your heart out from un - der the knife,
Em7
Am7
D
G/D
D
clos - ing the door on all the dreams you used to know.

G6/9
G(9)
C/G
G
G/B
Cmaj7
Fall - ing out of love and back on your feet,
D
Bm7
Em7
turn - ing a - way from that dead end street, oh, and find - ing out that
Am7
Em7/B
Bm7
Cmaj7
C/D
1.
G6/9
G(9)
noth - ing feels as good as let - ting go.
dim.
G
D/E
Em7
D/E
Em7
D.S.
mp
2. That's when he

Verse 2:
That's when he calls you up out of the blue one day,
And you know he thinks he's talkin' to the girl that you used to be.
So, when you tell him he's just a memory,
Ain't it funny how his voice cracks when you're sayin' goodbye?
And in the silence, something begins to unravel.
He never knew you like he'll be knowing you now.
(To Chorus:)

FALL INTO ME

Words and Music by
DAN E. ORTON and
JEREMY STOVER

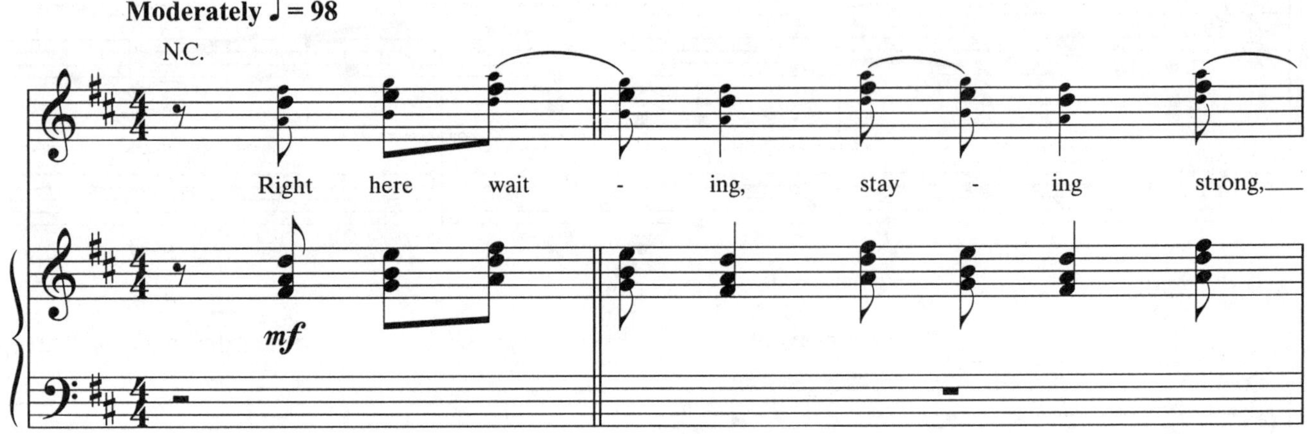

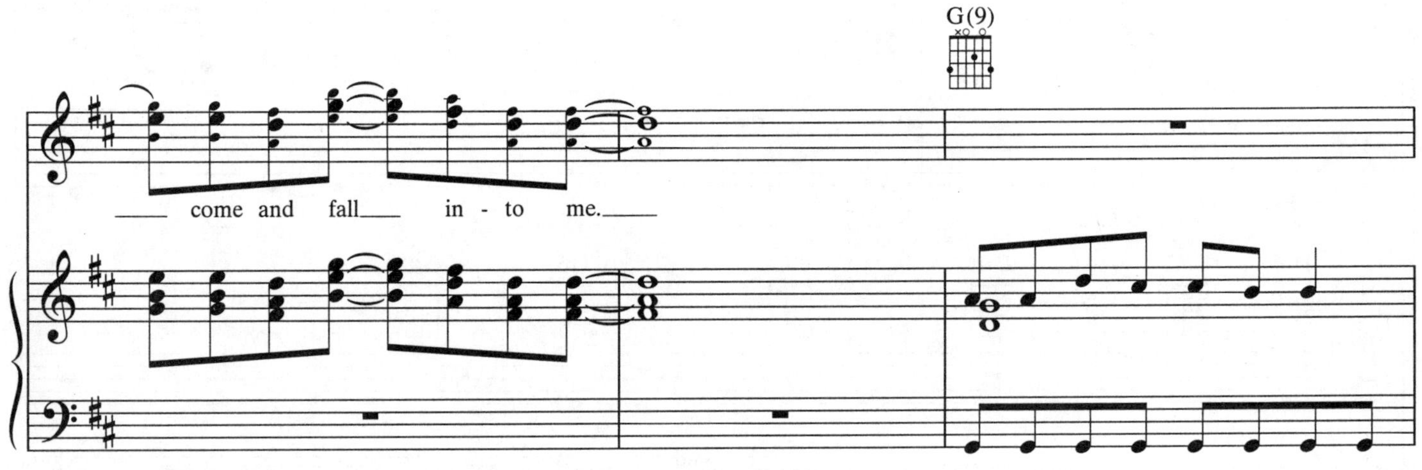

Verse:
G2 Asus Bm7 G2
1. You say you've turned it off, hid your heart up - on a shelf, scared of what it might cost to
2. I'll fol - low an - y road, an - y - where to get to you. I'll o - pen up my soul, if
Asus Bm7 G2 Asus Bm7
take it down for some - one else. 'Cause lov - ing him, you lost too much of your - self. Ba - by, can't
that's what you need me to do. Now, ba - by, it's your move. All you've got to do is be - lieve
Esus E G2 Esus E
you see that he's not me.
in love, just be - lieve in us.
Chorus:
G2 N.C. D A Bm7 G(9)
And I need you to know you can fall in - to me, that my arms

D
A
Bm7
G(9)
D
A
are wide o - pen and will always be right here wait - ing, stay - ing strong.
To Coda
1.
Bm7
G(9)
D
A
Bm7
G2
Come and fall in - to me.
2.
D
A
Bm7
G(9)
D
A
Bm7
G(9)
Esus
E
G(9)
Just be - lieve in love, just be - lieve

Esus E G2 N.C.

D.S. 𝄋 al Coda

in us. Ba - by, I need

𝄌 *Coda*

D A Bm7 G(9)

Come and fall in - to me.

D A Bm7 G(9) D A

Ba - by, fall in - to me.

Bm7 G(9) D A G2

FOREVER AND EVER, AMEN

Words and Music by
PAUL OVERSTREET and DON SCHLITZ

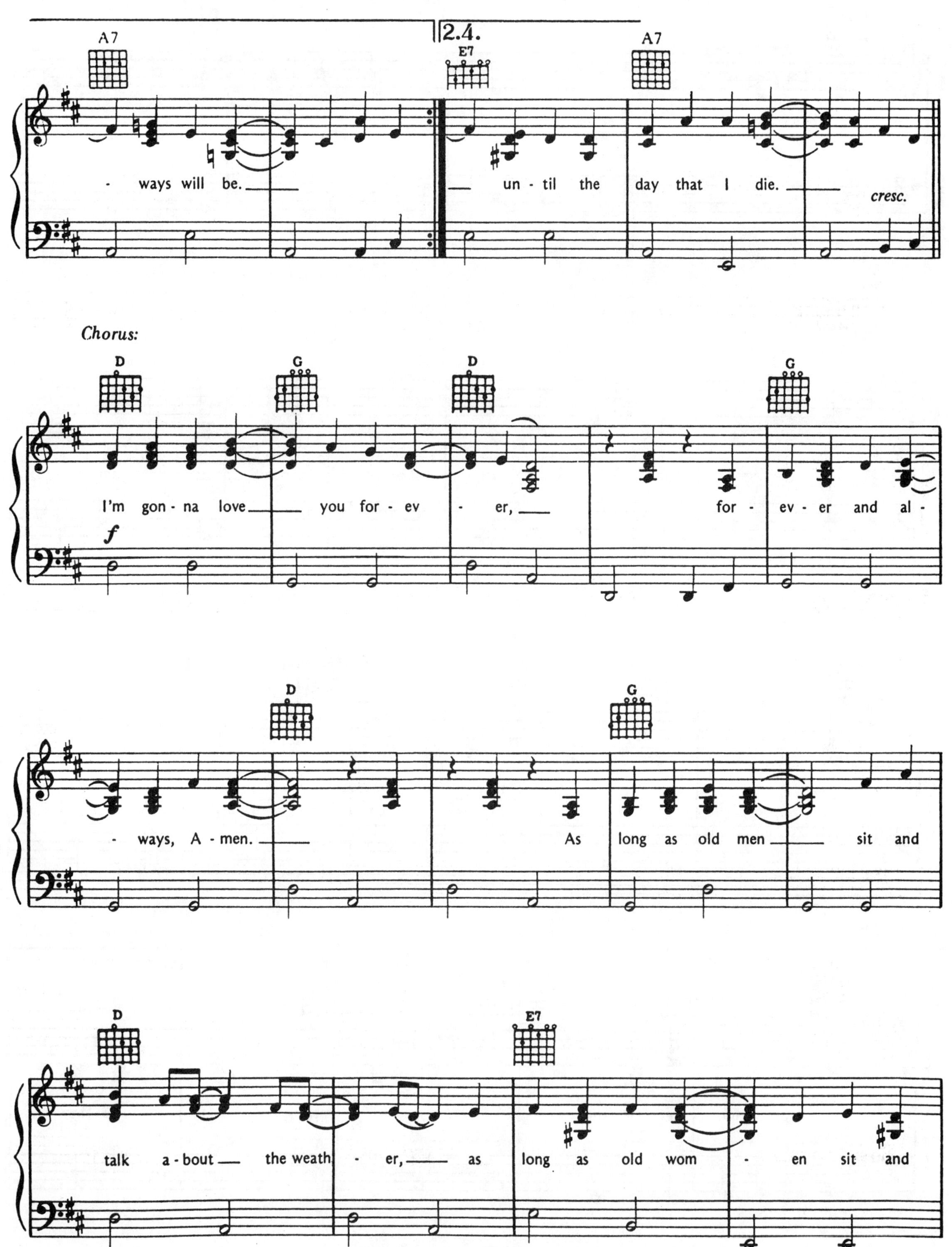
2.4.
A7
E7
A7
- ways will be.
until the
day that I die.
cresc.
Chorus:
D
G
D
G
I'm gon - na love you for - ev - er,
for - ev - er and al -
f
D
G
- ways, A - men.
As long as old men sit and
D
E7
talk a - bout the weath - er, as
long as old wom - en sit and

A7
D
G
talk a-bout old men. If you won-der how long I'll be faith-
D
G
-ful, I'll be hap-py to tell you a-gain.
just lis-ten to how this song ends.
E7
G
A
D
I'm gon-na love you for-ev-er and ev-
G
E
A
D
1.
D.S.
-er, for-ev-er and ev-er, A-men.
3.They say
dim.

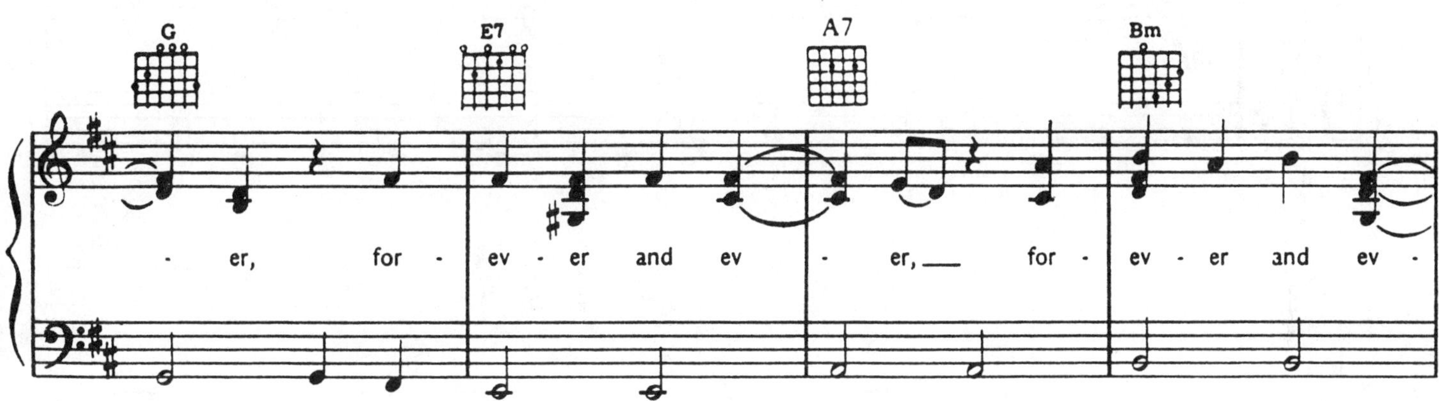

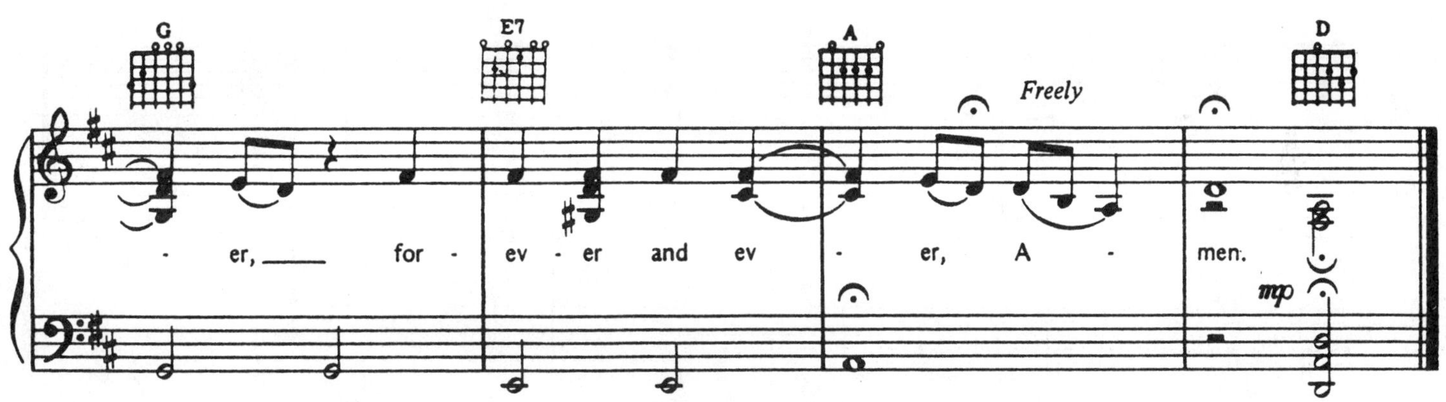

Verse 2:
You're not just time that I'm killing.
I'm no longer one of those guys.
As sure as I live, this love that I give
Is gonna be yours until the day that I die.
(To Chorus:)

Verse 3:
They say time takes its toll on a body,
Makes a young girl's brown hair turn gray.
Well, honey I don't care. I ain't in love with your hair.
And if it all fell out I'd love you any way.

Verse 4:
Well, they say time can play tricks on a memory,
Make people forget things they knew.
Well it's easy to see it's happening to me.
I've already forgotten every woman but you.
(To Chorus:)

FOREVER AND FOR ALWAYS

Words and Music by
SHANIA TWAIN and R.J. LANGE

* Original recording down a 1/2 step in F♯.

D
G
A7sus
C
me when you hold me.
I can still hear the words you whis-
pered when you told me
I can stay right here for - ev -
er in your arms.
And there ain't no way
I'm let - tin' you go now.
And there ain't no way

A7sus
C
D
Em7
and there ain't no how, I'll nev - er see that day.
G(9)/B
Am
D
Chorus:
G
'Cause I'm keep - ing you for - ev -
C
G
er and for al - ways.
We will be to - geth -
C
D
er all of our days.
Wan - na wake up ev - 'ry morn -

Am C *To Coda* 𝄌 G

ing to your sweet___ face, al - ways.___

G(9)/B Em7

C D

1. 2. *D.C. al Coda*

𝄌 *Coda*

G

I'm keep - ing you___ for - ev - er and___ for

C
G
al - ways.
We will be to - geth - er all of
C
D
Am
our days.
Wan - na
wake up ev - 'ry morn - ing to your
C
D
Am
sweet face.
I'm
keep - ing you for - ev - er and for
G
G(9)/B
al - ways.

Verse 2:
In your heart,
I can still hear a beat for everytime you kiss me.
And when we're apart,
I know how much you miss me,
I can feel your love for me in your heart.

And there ain't no way
I'm lettin' you go now.
And there ain't no way
And there ain't no how,
I'll never see that day.
(To Chorus:)

Verse 3:
In your eyes,
I can still see the look of the one who really loves me.
The one who wouldn't put anything else
In the world above me.
I can still see the love for me in your eyes.

And there ain't no way
I'm lettin' you go now.
And there ain't no way
And there ain't no how,
I'll never see that day.
(To Chorus:)

FORTY HOUR WEEK

(For a Livin')

Words and Music by
DAVE LOGGINS, LISA SILVER
and DON SCHLITZ

Moderately

E

mf

There are

E B

peo - ple in this coun - try who work hard ev - 'ry day,
see them ev - 'ry morn - in' in the fac - t'ries and the fields,

E A E

but not for fame or for - tune do they strive.
in the cit - y streets and the qui - et coun - try towns,

B
E
A
But the fruits of their la - bor are
work - in' to - geth - er like
worth more than they're paid.
spokes in - side a wheel.
And it's time a few of
They keep this coun - try
them were rec - og - nized.
turn - in' a - round.
Hel - lo,
Hel - lo,
De - troit au - to work - er. Let me thank you for your time.
Kan - as wheat field farm - er. Let me thank you for your time.
f
mf

E
A
E
You work a for - ty - ho - ur week for a liv - in'
You work a for - ty - ho - ur week for a liv - in'
B
E
just to send it on down the line.
just to send it on down the line.
A
E
Hel - lo, Pitts - burgh steel mill work - er. Let me
Hel - lo, West Vir - gin - ia coal min - er. Let me
f
mf
A
E
A
thank you for your time.
thank you for your time.
You work a for - ty - ho - ur week for a
You work a for - ty - ho - ur week for a

E
B
liv - in'
just to send it on down the line.
liv - in'
just to send it on down the line.
E
B
This is for the one who swings the
This is for the one who drives the
A
E
ham - mer, driv - in' home the nail; for the
big rig up and down the road; for the
B
A
one be - hind the count - er, ring - in' up the sales;
one out in the ware - house, bring - in' in the load;

E
C♯m
3fr.
for the one who fights the fi - re; the
for the wait - ress; the me - chan - ic; the po -
G♯m
3fr.
A
B
one who brings the mail;
for ev - 'ry - one who works
lice - man on pa - trol;
for ev - 'ry - one who works
C♯m/B
1. F♯m/B
B
be - hind the scenes
You can
be - hind the scenes
2. F♯m/B
E/B
F♯m/B
with a spir - it you can't re - place

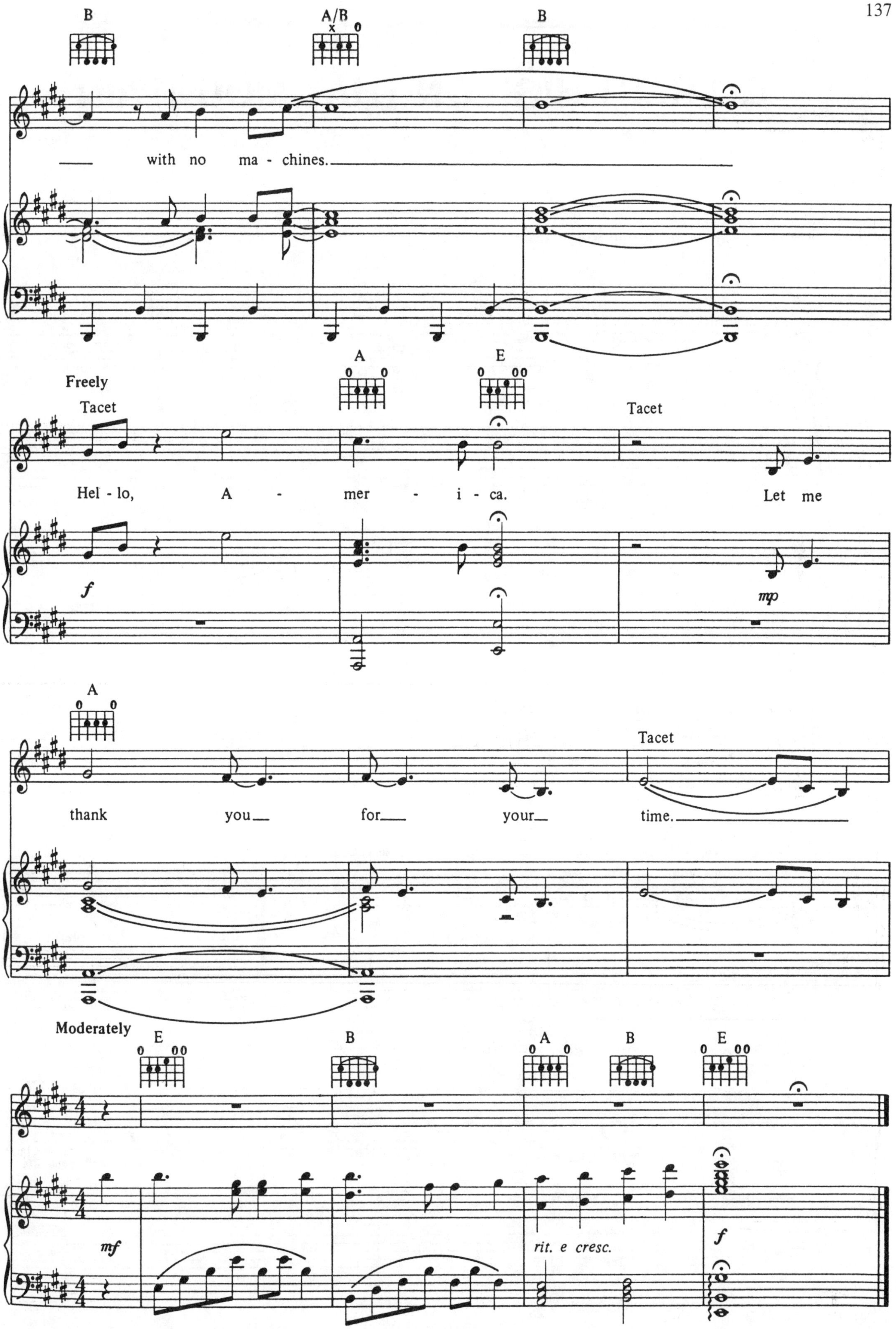

B A/B B

— with no ma - chines.

Freely

A E

Tacet

Hel - lo, A - mer - i - ca.

f

Tacet

Let me

mp

A

thank you for your

Tacet

time.

Moderately

E B A B E

mf

rit. e cresc.

f

GO REST HIGH ON THAT MOUNTAIN

Words and Music by
VINCE GILL

G
D
A7sus4
A7
to face the dev - il. You're no stran - ger to the
D
D
G
D
D/F♯
rain. Go rest high on that moun - tain. Son, your
G
D
G
3
work on earth is done. Go to heav - en a - shout -
D
G
D
A
1.
D
3
in', love for the Fa - ther and the Son. Oh, how we

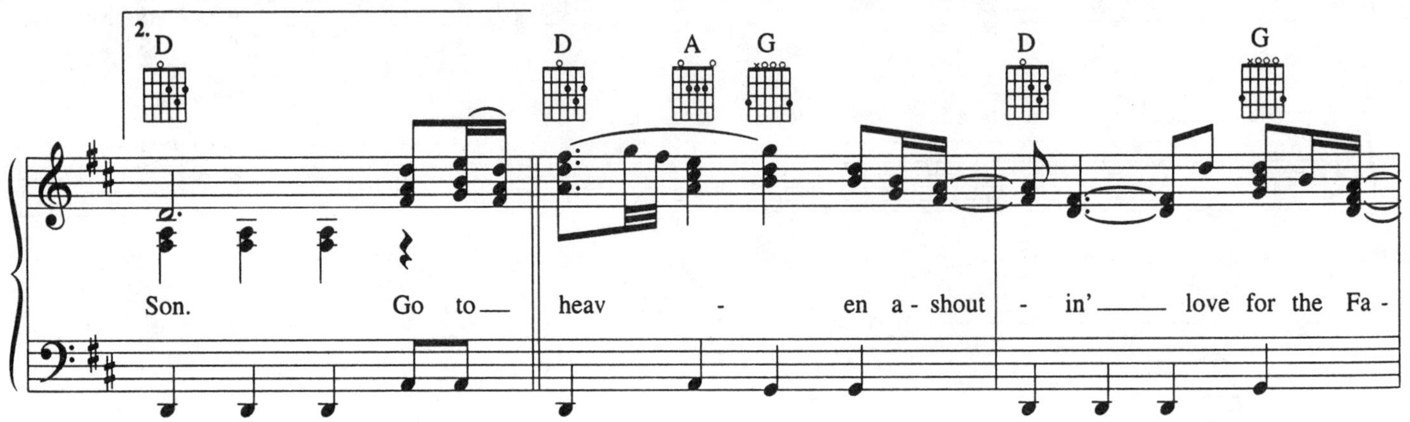

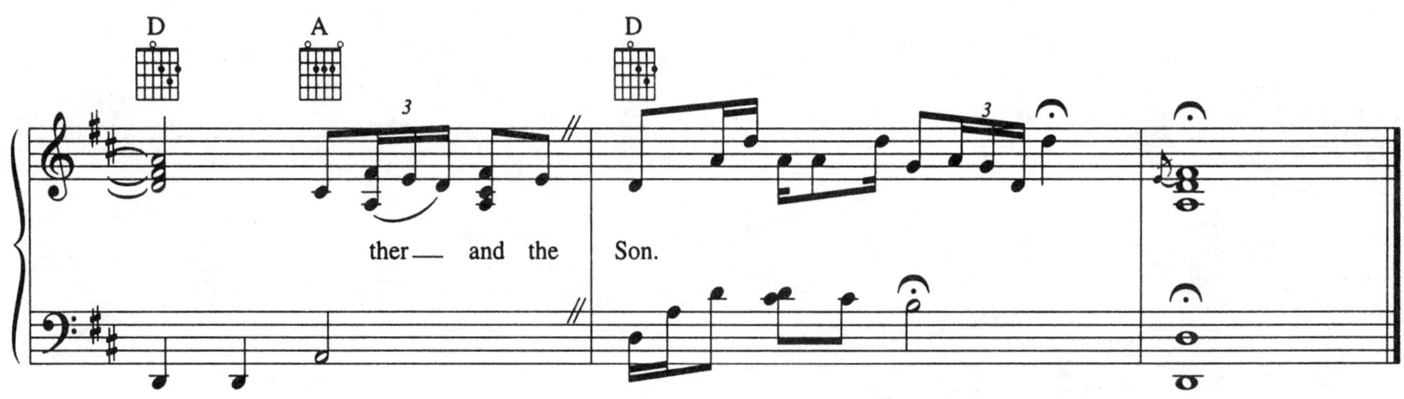

Additional lyrics

2. Oh, how we cried the day you left us,
   We gathered 'round your grave to grieve.
   I wish I could see the angels' faces
   When they hear your sweet voice sing.
   (To Chorus)

GOD BLESS THE U.S.A.

Words and Music by
LEE GREENWOOD

F Am7

thank my luck - y stars to be liv - in' here to - day, 'cause the

Gm7 Dm Bb

flag still stands for free - dom and they can't take that a - way. And I'm

Chorus

C/E Bb/D F

proud to be an A - mer - i - can where at least I know I'm free. And I

Dm
F/A
Bb
Am7
stand up; next to you and de - fend her still to - day. 'Cause there
Gm7
F/A
Bb
Gm7/C
ain't no doubt I love this land God bless the U S
F
Am7
Bb/F
F
Bb/F
A
(2.) From the
Verse
F
Bb/F
lakes of Min - ne - so - ta, to the hills of Ten - nes - see, a -

Gm7
Eb7
C7
cross the plains of Tex - as, from sea to shin - ing sea, From
F
Am7
De - troit down to Hous - ton and New York to L A Well, there's
Gm7
Dm
Bb
D. S. al Coda
pride in ev - 'ry A-mer- i - can heart, and it's time to stand and say That I'm
Coda
F
Bb
Gm7/C
Dm
Bb
God bless the U S A And I'm

Chorus
C/E
Bb/D
F
proud to be an A-mer-i-can where at least I know I'm free, and I
C/E
Bb/D
F
won't for-get the men who died, who gave that right to me. And I'd glad-ly
Dm
F/A
Bb
Am7
stand up next to you, and de-fend her still to-day. 'Cause there
Gm7
F/A
Gm7
Am7
Bb
C7
F
ain't no doubt I love this land God bless the U S A

A GOOD DAY TO RUN

Words and Music by
BOBBY TOMBERLIN and
DARRYL WORLEY

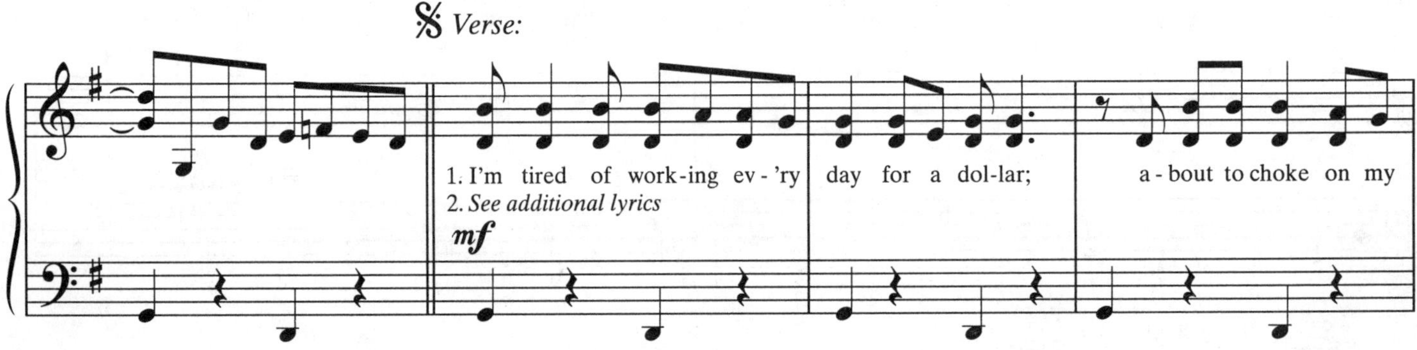

D
C
G
con - clu - sion: I can't make a move too fast.
D/F♯
Em
A
It was writ - ten in the sky to - day
C
G
D/F♯
Em
D
by the morn - ing sun. It sure looks like a good day to
cresc.
Chorus:
G
C
D
G
run. 1.2. Wide o - pen down a two - lane high - way; it's a - bout time that some things went my way.
f
3. Inst. solo ad lib....
C
D
G
Throw-ing trou-bles out to the wind, and I'm pray-ing that they nev-er catch up a - gain.
...end solo

Verse 2:
My baby's been working as a cashier;
She didn't get a vacation this past year,
But now it won't be long.
We don't need no destination,
Just a tank of gas and a good clear station
Playing our favorite song.
There's some places that we ain't been,
Some things that we ain't done,
And it sure looks like a good day to run.
(To Chorus:)

GOOD OLE BOYS LIKE ME

Words and Music by
BOB McDILL

Am
G
Am
Dad - dy came in to kiss his lit - tle man, with gin on his breath and a
smell of Cape Jas - mine through the win - dow screen, John R. and the wolf - man kept me
G
F
G
Bi - ble in his hand, he talked a - bout hon - or and things I should know, then he'd
com - pan - y by the light of the ra - di - o by my bed, with
F
G
stag - ger a lit - tle as he went out the door.
Thom - as Wolfe whis - per - in' in my head.
I can still
C
C/B
Am7
C/G
F
Em
hear the soft, south - ern winds in the live oak trees;

Dm7
G
C
C/B
Am7
C/G
F
Em
and those Wil-liams boys, they still mean a lot to me, Hank and Ten-
Dm7
G
F
G
Am
nes-see. I guess we're all gon-na be what we're gon - na be.
F
G
1 C
To Coda
So what do you do with good ole boys like me?
2 C
G
F
Well, me?

G C G F C

When I was in school I ran with the kid down the street,

F G C G

and I watched him burn him - self up

F C F G

on bour - bon and speed. But I was

Am G Am

smart - er than most and I could choose, learned to talk like the man on the six

G
F
G
o'-clock news.
Whe
I was eight-een, Lord,
I hit the road,
but it
F
G
D.S. al Coda
real-ly does-n't mat-ter how far I go.
I can still
CODA
Am
F
G
me.
Yeah, what do you do with good ole boys like
C
me?

GOOD HEARTED WOMAN

Words and Music by
WILLIE NELSON and WAYLON JENNINGS

F
liv - ing to - day;
him back home a - gain.
But she nev - er com - plains of the
Lord knows she don't un - der - stand him, but
F7
Bb
bad times or bad things he's done, Lord.
she does the best that she can.
C7
She just talks a - bout the good times they've
'Cause she's a good - heart - ed wo - man;

F
had and all the good times to come.
she loves her good - tim - in' man.
Chorus:
She's a good - heart - ed wo - man in love with a
F7
Bb
good - tim - in' man.
She
C7
loves him in spite of his ways that she don't un - der - stand.

Through tear - drops and laugh - ter, they'll
F7
Bb
pass through this world — hand - in - hand,
C7
a good - heart - ed wo - man lov - in' her good - tim - in'
F
1.
2.
D.S. and Fade
man.
She's a

GOOD MORNING BEAUTIFUL

Words and Music by
TODD CERNEY and ZACK LYLE

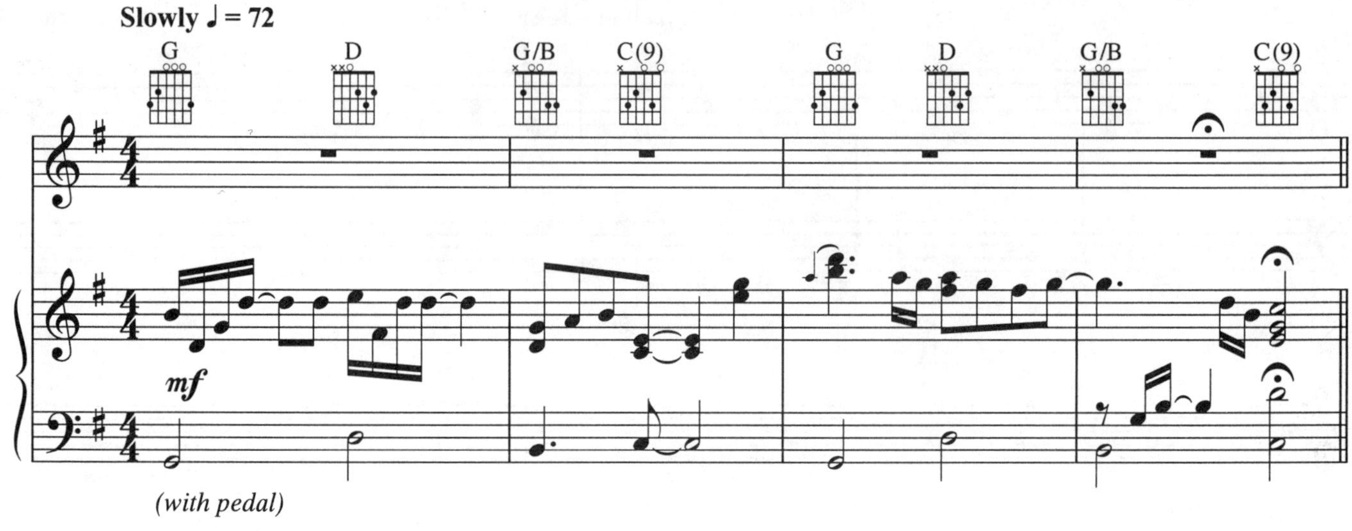

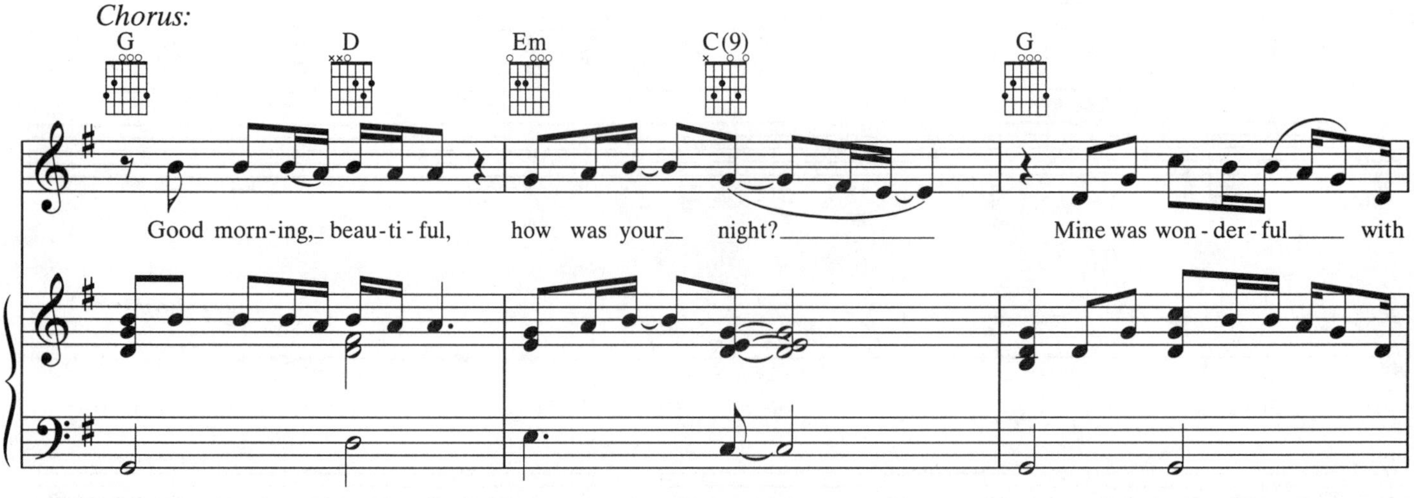

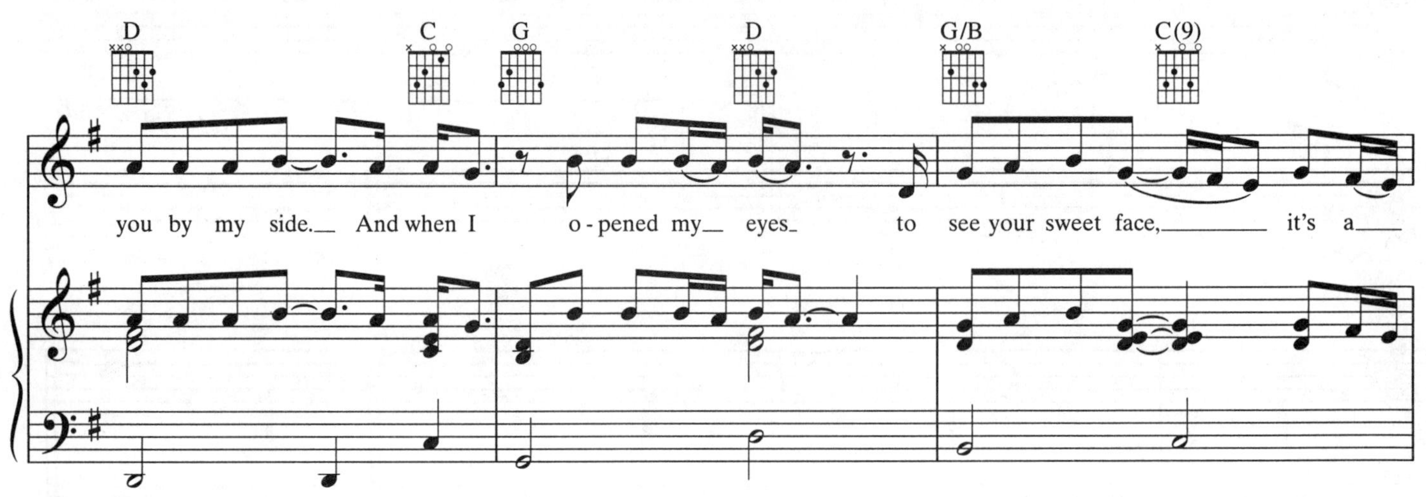

Am D G
good morn-ing, beau - ti - ful__ day.__
Verse:
C
I could-n't see__ the light,______
G/B Am7 G Am7 G/B
I did-n't know day from night,_____ I had no rea - son to care.______
C G/B Am7
But since you came_ a - long,_____ I can face_ the dawn,_______ 'cause I know you'll be there._
Chorus:
D C G D Em C(9)
1. Good morn-ing,_ beau-ti - ful, how was your_ night?______
2. (Inst. solo ad lib....

G
D
C
G
D
Mine was won-der-ful with you by my side. And when I o-pened my eyes to
To Coda
1.
2.
G/B
C(9)
Am
D
Am
D
see your sweet face, it's a good morn-ing, beau - ti - ful day.
Bridge:
G
D/F♯
Em7
C
G/B
...end solo)
I nev - er wor - ry if it's rain - ing out - side,
D.S. al Coda
Am7
G/B
C
D
C
'cause in here with you, girl, the sun al - ways shines.

Coda
Am7
D
Em7
A7
good morn - ing, beau - ti - ful day.
Am7
D
G
D
Good morn - ing, beau - ti - ful day.
a tempo
G/B
C(9)
G
D
Good morn - ing, beau - ti - ful.
1.2.3.
G/B
C(9)
4.
G/B
C(9)

HAVE I TOLD YOU LATELY

Words and Music by
VAN MORRISON

Cm7
Bb
Eb/F
ease my trou-bles that's what you do.
1. For the
2. Instrumental
Bb
Dm7
Eb
Eb/F
morn - in' sun in all it's glo - ry greets the
Bb
Dm7
Eb
Eb/F
day with hope and com-fort, too.
Ebmaj7
Dm7
You fill my life with laugh - ter and some-how you make it bet - ter,

Cm7
Eb/F
Bb
Cm7
Bb/D
ease my trou-bles that's _ what you do.
Solo ends
Ebmaj7
There's a love that's di-vine
and it's yours and it's mine _
Dm7
_ like the sun.
Cm7 Dm7 Ebmaj7
And at the end of the day
Dm7
we should give thanks and pray _ to the one, _
1
Eb/F
to the one. _ Have I

2
Eb/F
Bb
Dm7
to the one.
And have I told you late - ly that I
Eb
Eb/F
Bb
Dm7
love you?
Have I told you there's no one else a -
Eb
Eb/F
Ebmaj7
bove you?
You fill my heart with glad - ness,
Dm7
Cm7
Eb/F
take a - way my sad - ness,
ease my trou-bles that's what you

Bb
Cm7
Bb/D
Ebmaj7
do.
Take a - way all __ my sad - ness,
Dm7
Cm7
Bb
Cm7 Bb/D
fill my life __ with glad - ness,
ease my trou-bles that's __ what you do.
Ebmaj7
Dm7
Take a - way all __ my sad - ness,
fill my heart with glad - ness,
Cm7
Eb/F
Bb
ease my trou-bles that's __ what you do. ____
6
rall.

HAVE YOU FORGOTTEN?

Words and Music by
WYNN VARBLE and DARRYL WADE WORLEY

C(9)
We did - n't get to keep 'em by back-ing down.
If it was up to me, I'd show it ev - 'ry day.
D
C(9)
They say we don't re - al - ize the mess we're get - ting in.
Some say this coun-try's just out look - ing for a fight.
Am7
G/B
1.
C
Be - fore you start your preach - ing, let me ask you this, my
Af - ter nine - e - lev - en, man, I'd
Dsus
D
To Next Strain
2.
C
Dsus
friend: 1. Have you for - got - have to say, that's right. 2. Have you for - got -

Chorus:
G
D
(1. 2.) ten how it felt that day to see your
(3.) ten all the peo - ple killed?
C
Dsus
home - land un - der fi - re and her peo - ple blown a - way? Have you for - got -
Some went down like he - roes in that Penn - syl - va - nia field. Have you for - got -
G
D
ten when those tow - ers fell, we had
ten a - bout our Pen - ta - gon, all the
C
Dsus
D
neigh - bors still in - side, go - ing through a liv - ing hell?
loved ones that we lost, and those left to car - ry on?
And you
And we
Don't you

To Coda
1.
C
Dsus
say we should-n't wor - ry 'bout bin La - den.
vowed to get the ones be - hind bin
tell me not to wor - ry 'bout bin
Have you for - got -
G
C(9)
2.
Dsus
ten?
La - den.
Have you for - got-
G
C(9)
G
C(9)
ten? (Guitar solo...
...end solo) I've
Bridge:
D
C(9)
been there with the sol - diers who've gone a - way to war.
And you can

Am7
G/B
C
Dsus
D.S. % al Coda
N.C.
bet that they_ re-mem-ber___ just what they're fight - ing for. 3. Have you for-got-
Coda
Dsus
D
Am7
G/B
La - den.___
Dsus
G
C(9)
Have you for-got - ten?___ Have you for-got-
G
C(9)
G
ten?___ Have you for-got - ten?___
rit.

HELP ME UNDERSTAND

Words and Music by
CHRIS FARREN, STEVE MAC and
WAYNE HECTOR

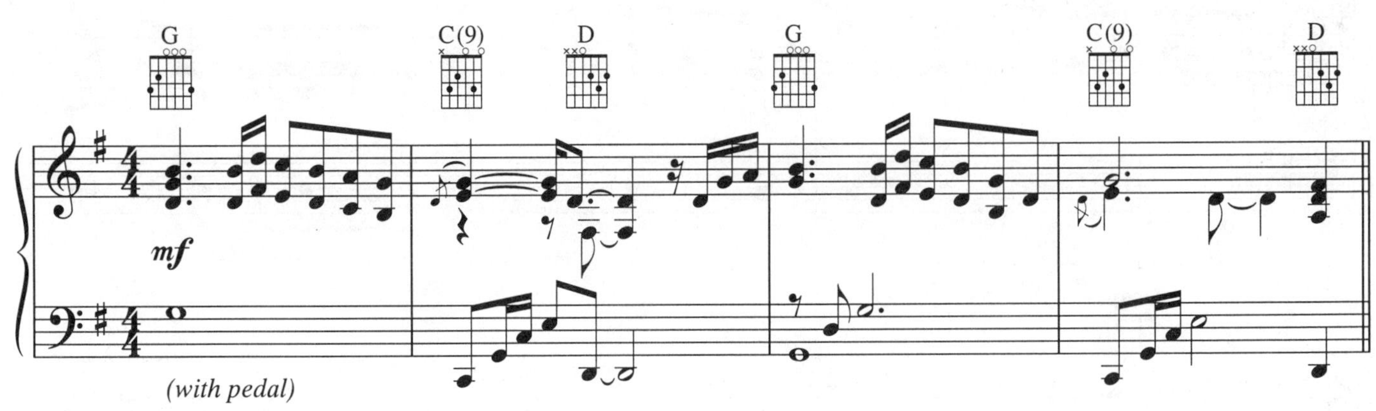

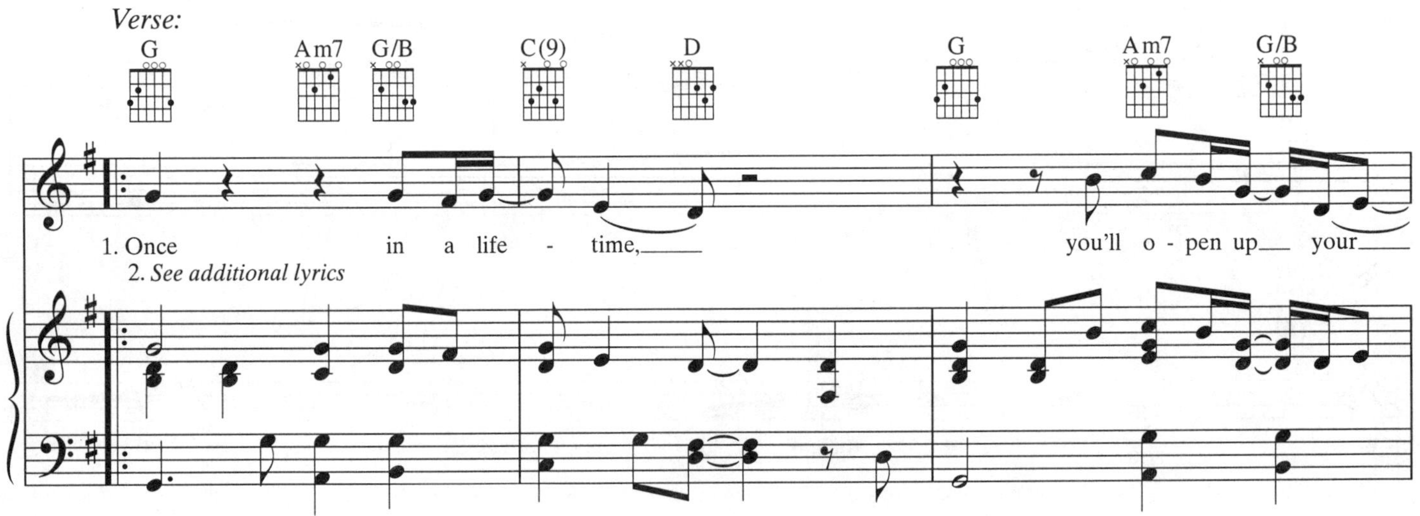

G
Am7
G/B
C(9)
D
you'll swear to nev - er be a - part
You
C
D/C
C
Am7/D
D7
think your love's on sol - id ground, then out of the blue, it all comes tum - b'ling
Chorus:
G
Am7
G/B
C
D
down. Who's gon - na hold me to - night when I'm feel - ing lone -
G
Am7
G/B
C
D
ly? Who's gon - na show me the light? 'Cause I need to know.

Em D C G/B

With all the things we've got, how can love just stop?

To Coda 𝄌 1.

Am7 G/A Am7/D G Am7 G/B

Tell me, some-bod-y help me un-der-stand.

2.

C(9) D Am7/D D

2. And my help me un-der-stand

Bridge:

F(9) G/F

why I'm not a part of your

F(9) G/F F G C/E

plan, and you don't need me an-y-more. Help me un-der-

Verse 2:
And my picture in your locket,
What will you do with it now?
All our friends and all our memories,
Tell me how we sort them out?
What's yours is yours,
What's mine is mine.
Is that all that's left
After all this time?
(To Chorus:)

HEY, GOOD LOOKIN'

Words and Music by
HANK WILLIAMS

Moderate country swing ♩ = 72 (♫ = ♩³♪)

CHORUS

C

1. Hey, HEY, GOOD LOOK-IN' What _ cha got cook-in' How's a-bout cook-in' some-thin' up _ with me _
2. (I'm) free and read-y so we _ can go stead-y How's a-bout sav-in' all your time _ for me _

D7 G7 C G7 C

Hey, sweet ba-by, Don't _ you think may-be We could find us a brand new rec - i - pe _
No more look-in', I know _ I've been took-en How's a-bout keep-in' stead-y com-pan-y _

D7 G7 C C7 F

I got a hot rod Ford and a
I'm gon-na throw my date book _

C F C F

two dol - lar bill and I know a spot right o - ver the hill__ There's so - da pop and the

o - ver the fence and find me __ one for five or ten cents_ I'll keep it 'til it's_

D7 G7

danc - in's__ free, so if you wan - na have fun come a - long with me__

cov - ered with age _____ 'Cause I'm writ - in' your name down on ev - 'ry page_

C D7

HEY, GOOD LOOK-IN' What __ cha got cook-in' How's a - bout cook - in'

HEY, GOOD LOOK-IN' What __ cha got cook-in' How's a - bout cook - in'

G7 1 C 2 C F C

some-thin' up__ with me. ________ 2. I'm

some-thin' up__ with me. ________

HONKY TONK MAN

Words and Music by
JOHNNY HORTON, TILLMAN FRANKS
and HOWARD HAUSEY

A7
I love to give the girls a whirl to the mu - sic of an old juke - box.
E
B
But when my mon - ey's all gone; I'm on the tel - e - phone,
E
sing - in', "Hey, hey, ma - ma, can your dad - dy come home?"
E7
Well now, I'm liv - in' wild and dan -
pret - ty lit - tle girl and a

B
A7
g'rous - ly, but I've got plen - ty of com -
jug of wine, well, that's what it takes to make a
E7
B
pa - ny. When the moon comes up and the sun goes down,
honk-y - tonk time. With the juke - box moan - in' those honk - y - tonk sounds,
A7
E7
I can't wait to see the lights of town.
I can't wait to lay my mon - ey down.
'Cause I'm a honk - y - tonk
E
man,
and I can't seem to stop.

A7
I love to give the girls a whirl to the mu - sic of an old
E
juke - box.
But when my mon - ey's all gone;
B
I'm on the tel - e - phone, sing - in',
E
"Hey, hey, ma - ma, can your
dad - dy come home?"
1.
Well, now, a
2.

From the Touchstone Motion Picture "CON AIR"

HOW DO I LIVE

Words and Music by
DIANE WARREN

F♯m7
G♯m7
C♯m7
Em7/A
ba - by, you would take a - way ev - 'ry - thing good in my life. And tell me
𝄋 Chorus:
D
A
G
F♯m7
now, how do I live with - out you? I want to know. How do I breathe with - out
Bm7
Em7
G(9)
you, if you ev - er go? How do I ev - er, ev - er sur - vive?
To Coda
1.
F♯m7/B
How do I, how do I, oh, how do I live? 2. With - out you,
2.
F♯m
How do I, oh, how do I live?

Bm7
F♯m7
F♯m7/B
If
G♯m7
C♯m7
F♯m7
you ev - er leave,
ba - by, you would take a - way ev - 'ry - thing.
G♯m7
C♯m7
F♯m7
Need you with me.
Ba - by, 'coz you know that you're ev - 'ry - thing
G♯m7
C♯m7
Em7/A
D.S.𝄋 al Coda
good in my life.
And tell me

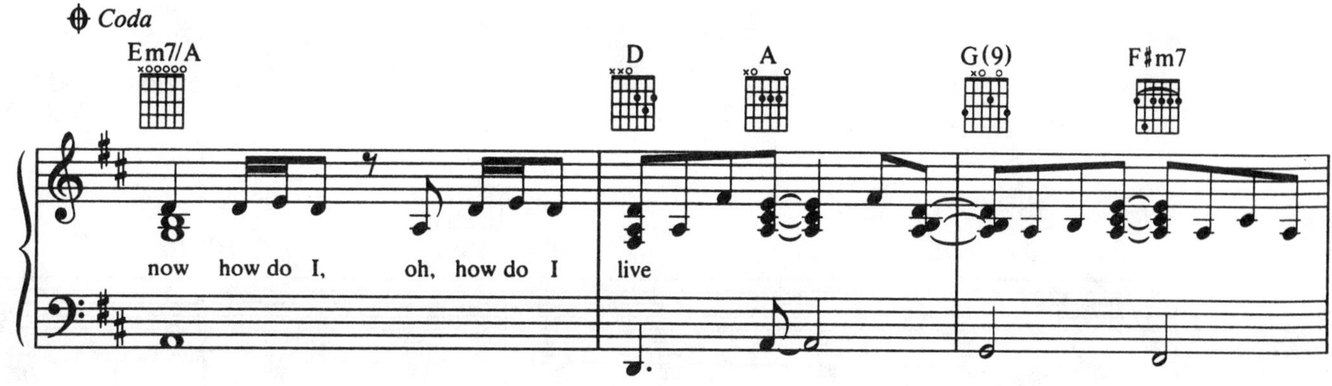

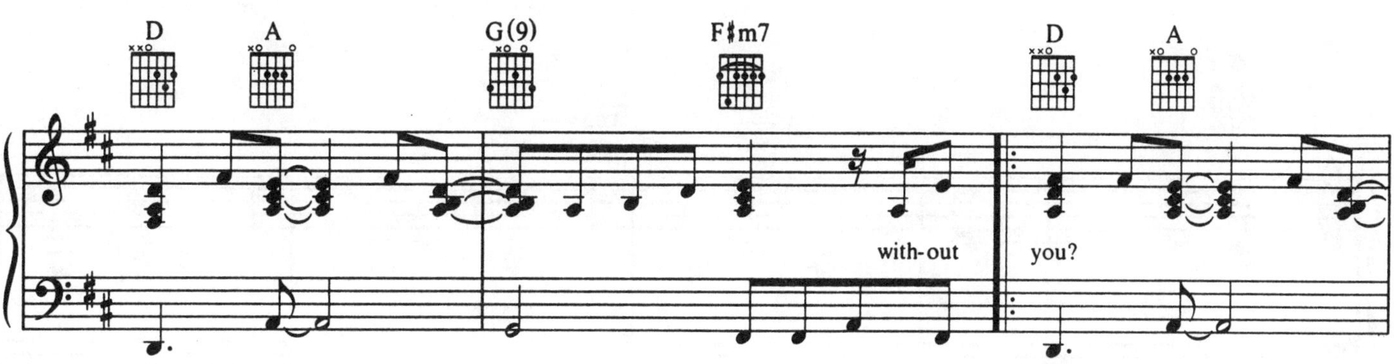

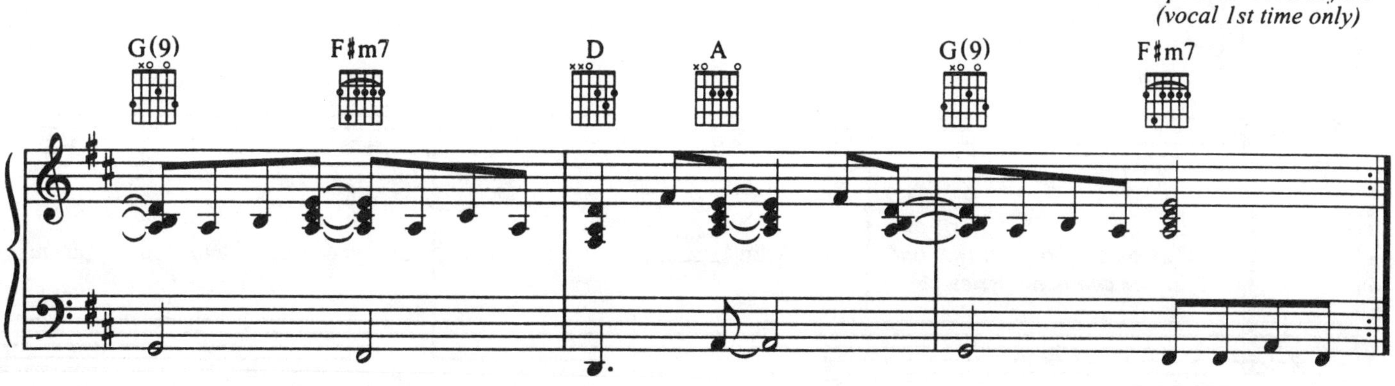

Verse 2:
Without you, there'd be no sun in my sky,
There would be no love in my life,
There'd be no world left for me.
And I, baby, I don't know what I would do,
I'd be lost if I lost you.
If you ever leave,
Baby, you would take away everything real in my life.
And tell me now...
(To Chorus:)

HERE I AM

Words and Music by
TONY ARATA

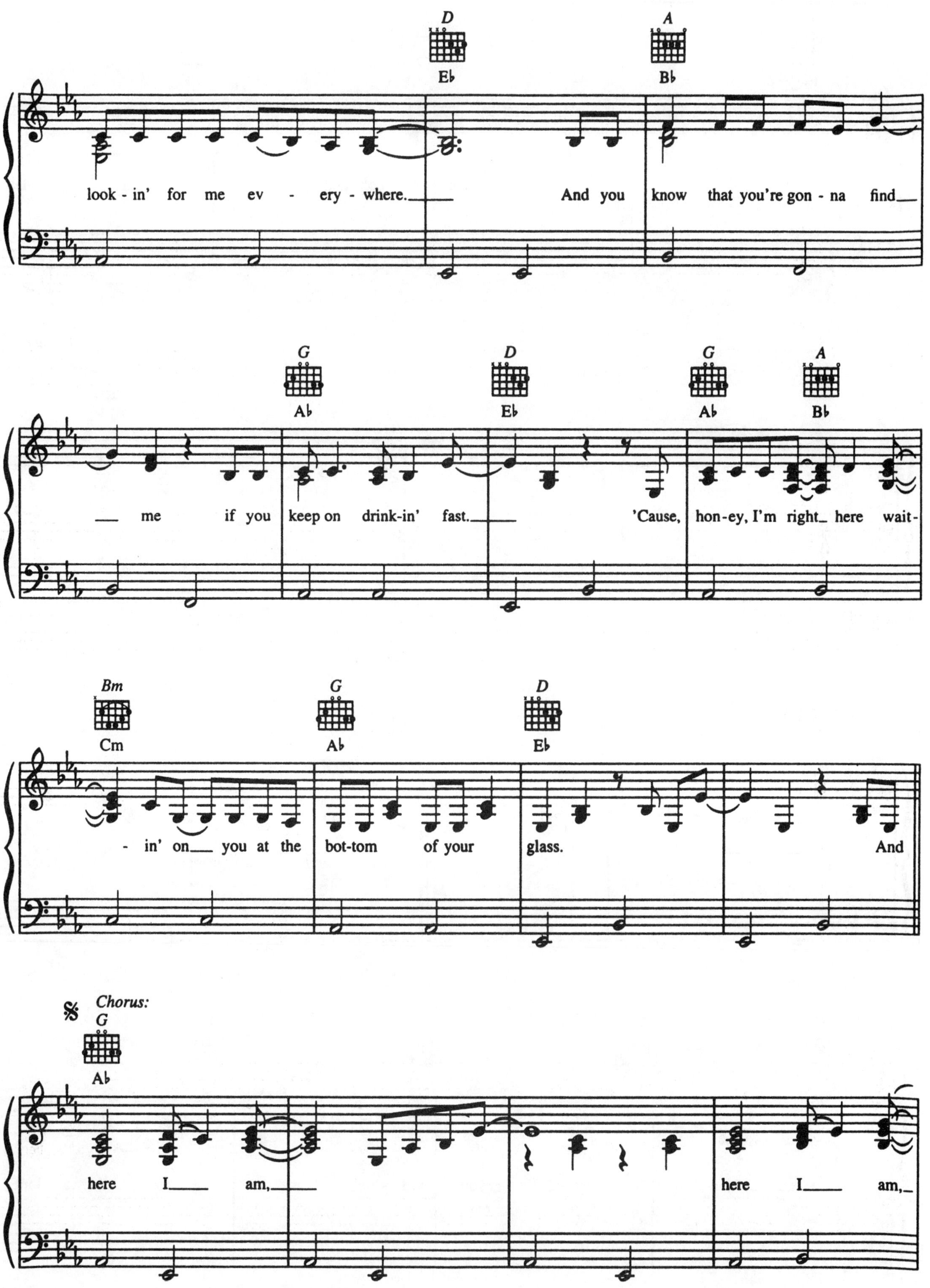
D
E♭
A
B♭
look - in' for me ev - ery - where.
And you
know that you're gon - na find
me if you
G
A♭
keep on drink-in' fast.
'Cause,
hon - ey, I'm right here wait -
Bm
Cm
in' on you at the
bot - tom of your
glass.
And
Chorus:
here I am,
here I am,

D
G
D
E♭
A♭
E♭
in the bour - bon and the wat - er that
To Coda
A
G
A
B♭
A♭
B♭
burn you just like a brand,
here I am.
1.
2.
D
D
E♭
E♭
And hon - ey,
Bridge:
Em7
D/F♯
G
A
Fm7
E♭/G
A♭
B♭
I got o - ver you pass - in' me o - ver a long

Bm7
D/F♯
G
Cm7
E♭/G
A♭
time a - go.
And my pride
Em7
D/F♯
G
A
F♯7/A♯
Fm7
E♭/G
A♭
B♭
G7/B
was strong - er when I was young - er now I'd
D.S. 𝄋 al Coda
Bm
Bm/A
G
G(9)
Cm
Cm/B♭
A♭
A♭(9)
rath - er have you to know,
that
⊕ Coda
D
G
E♭
A♭
Mm, mm.

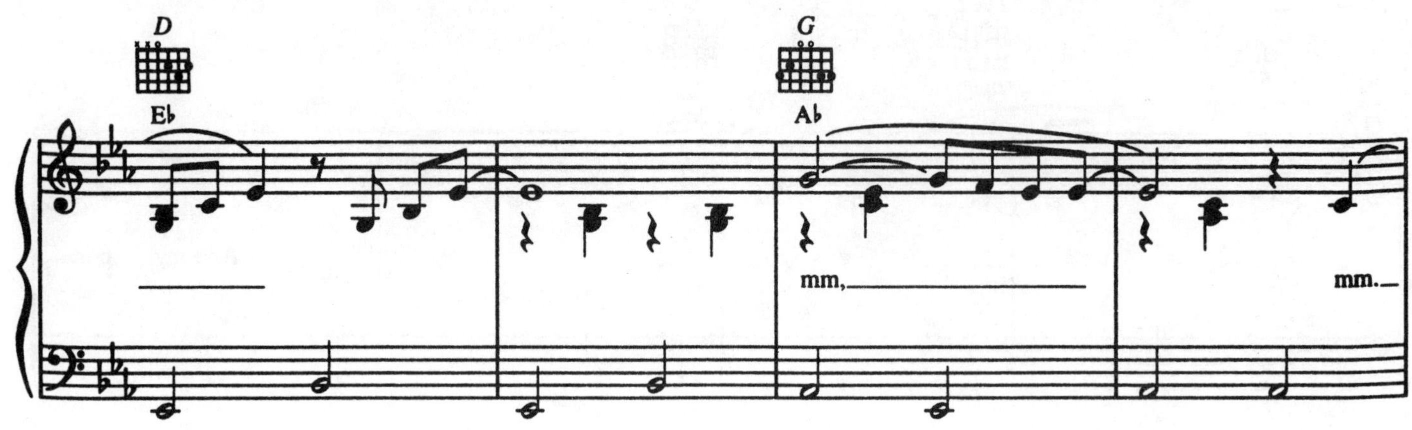

Verse 2:
It ain't workin' darlin', hard as you may try.
You keep hearin' the words you told me in everyone's goodbyes.
And you know that you're just one step from another one being gone.
I know I've seen 'em all unravel,
I've been watchin' it all along.

Chorus 2:
Here I am, here I am,
In every lie you're hearin'
That burn you just like a brand,
Here I am.
(To Bridge:)

Chorus 3:
Here I am, here I am,
I still carry a flame for you
Burnin' me like a brand,
Here I am.

I CAN LOVE YOU BETTER

Words and Music by
PAMELA BROWN HAYES and KOSTAS

E D A E D
tied a-round her lit-tle fin-ger. She's got you think-in' you can
You're gon-na wake up to find I'm your de-sire, my in-
A E D A
nev-er es-cape. Don't you know your heart's in dan-ger?
ten-tions are true. Hey, babe, I know in time
B C♯m D
4fr
There's a dev-il in that an-gel face. If you could on-ly see the love
you're gon-na see what you mean to me. So, o-pen up your eyes 'cause see-
A E D A
that you're wast-ing.
-in' is be-liev-in'.
I can love you bet-ter than that.

E
D
A
E
D
I know how to make you for - get her.
All I'm ask - in' is for
A
E
D
A
one lit - tle chance 'cause, ba - by, I can love you, ba - by, I can love you bet -
E
1
- ter.
2
C♯m
4fr
B
C♯m
4fr
E
Whoa,
whoa.

C♯m
B
C♯m
Yeah,
D
A7
E
D
oh,
yeah.
I can love you bet -
A
E
D
A
- ter than that.
I know how to make you for - get
E
D
A
her.
All I'm ask - in' is for one lit - tle chance 'cause,

E
D
A
E
D
ba - by, I can love you, ba - by, I can love you. I can love you bet -
A
E
D
A
- ter than that. I know how to make you for - get her.
E
D
A
E
D
All I'm ask - in' is for one lit - tle chance 'cause, ba - by, I can love you, ba -
Repeat and Fade
A
- by, I can love you.
Optional Ending
A
E
- by, I can love you bet - ter.

I BREATHE IN, I BREATHE OUT

Words and Music by
CHRIS CAGLE and JON ROBBIN

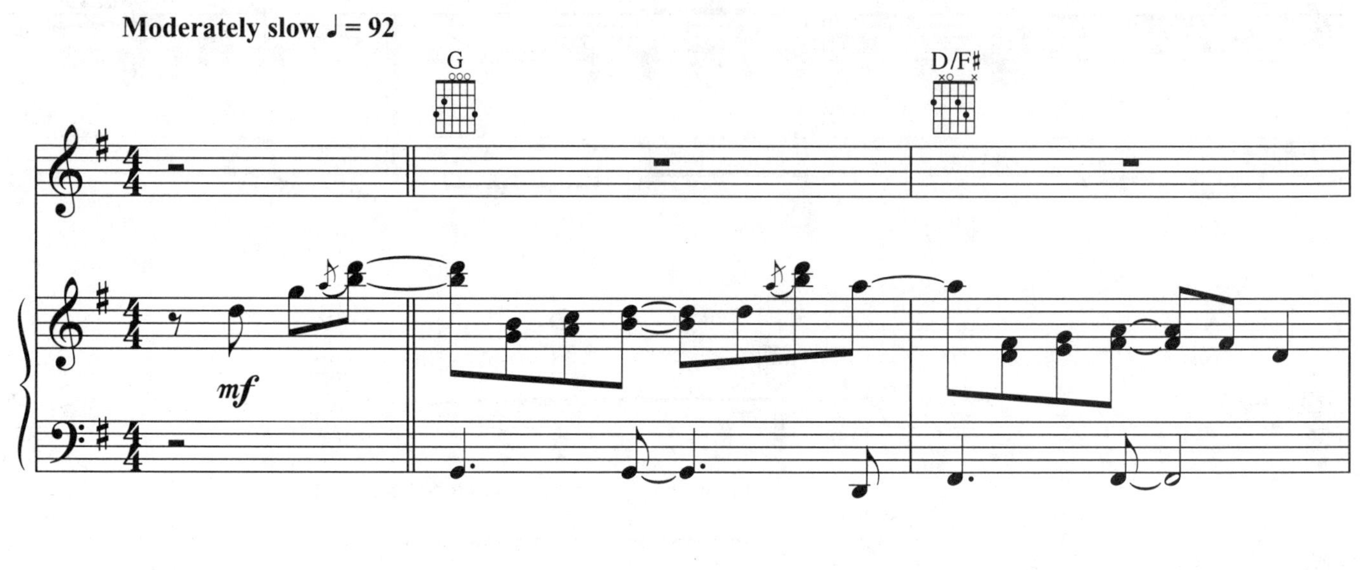

D/F♯
C
some-where in the small talk, some-one al-ways asks where you've been.
D
G
D/F♯
So I tell them what you've told me and they
C
Cm6
G
D/F♯
can't be-lieve we're through.
They ask me what I'm do-
Em7
C
D
Dsus
in' now, and in case you're won-der-ing too...

Chorus:
D
G
D/F♯
I breathe in,
I breathe out,
put one
C
D
G
foot in front of the oth - er, take one day at a time
till you find
D/F♯
C
D
I'm that
some - one
you can't live with - out.
But un - til
C
1.
D
G
then,
I'll breathe in
and breathe out.

D/F♯
C(9)
2. Now,
2.
D
G
and breathe out.
Yes,
Bridge:
Am7
G
C
we were meant to be, girl, there's no doubt.
Am7
G
And if it takes the rest of my life for

C(9)
D
you to fig - ure it out...
I breathe in
Chorus:
A
E/G♯
D
and breathe out,
put one foot in front of the oth -
E
A
E/G♯
er, take one day at a time
till you find
I'm that
D
E
D
some - one you can't live with-out.
But un - til
then,

Verse 2:
Now, I've got every reason to find someone new.
'Cause you swore up and down to me that I've seen the last of you.
But the way you loved me, girl, you left me hopin' and holdin' on.
So until this world stops turning 'round and my heart believes you're gone...
(To Chorus:)

I CROSS MY HEART

Words and Music by
STEVE DORFF and ERIC KAZ

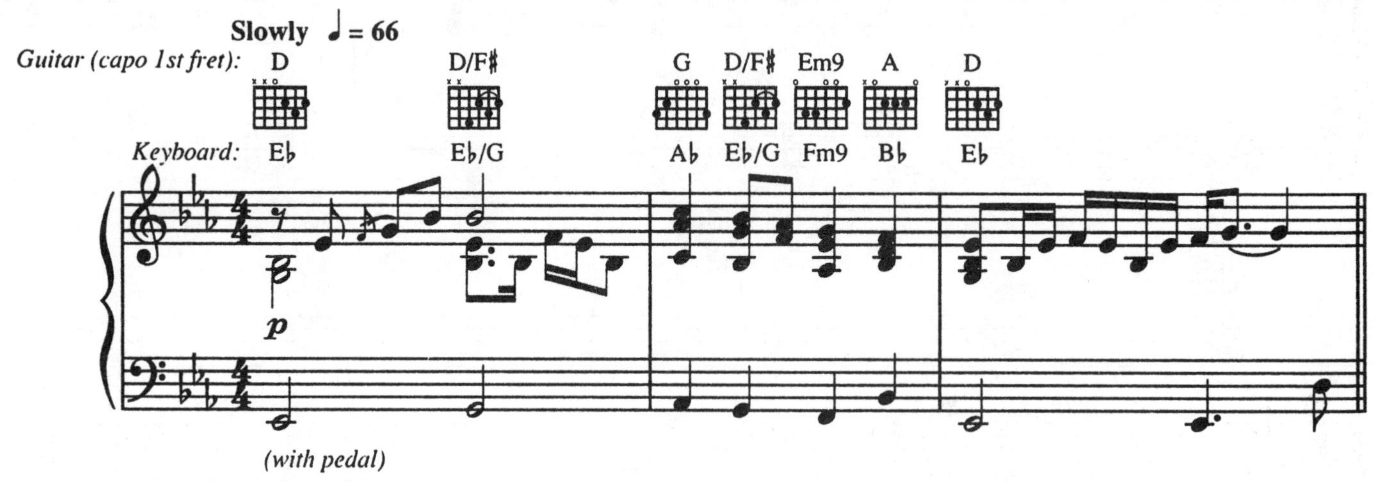

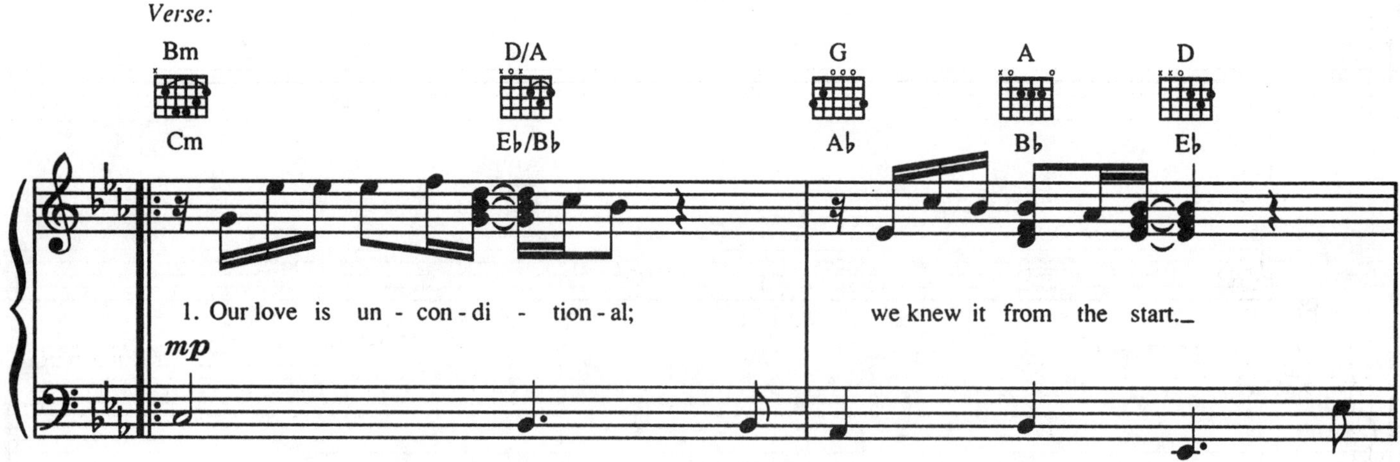

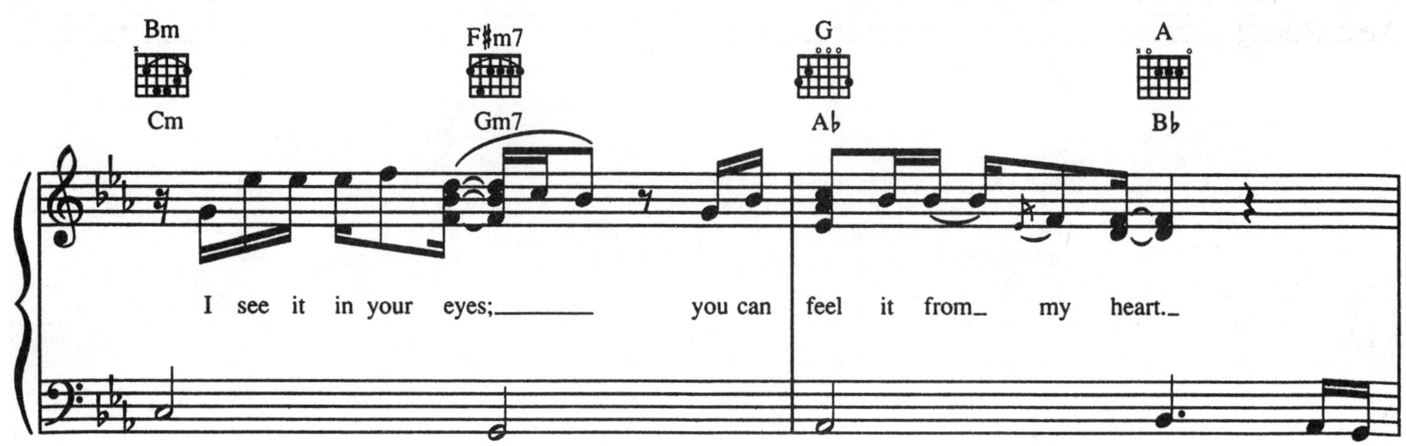

Em7
D/F#
G
Asus
A
Fm7
E♭/G
A♭
B♭sus
B♭
From here on after, let's stay the way we are right now, and share
Em7
D/F#
C
Em7/A
A
Fm7
E♭/G
D♭
Fm7/B♭
B♭
all the love and laugh-ter that a life-time will al low.
cresc.
Chorus:
D
D/F#
G
A
D
D/F#
G
E♭
E♭/G
A♭
B♭
E♭
E♭/G
A♭
1.2. I cross my heart and prom-ise to give all I've got to give to make all
3. (Instrumental solo ad lib...
mf
G/A
A
D
D/F#
G
A♭/B♭
B♭
E♭
E♭/G
A♭
your dreams come true. In all the world,
... end solo)

To Coda
1.
A
A/G
D/F♯
G
D/F♯
Em9
A
D
B♭
B♭/A♭
E♭/G
A♭
E♭/G
Fm9
B♭
E♭
you'll nev-er find
a love_ as true_____ as
mine._
G
D/F♯
Em7
A
D
A♭
E♭/G
Fm7
B♭
E♭
2.
D
E♭
2. You will
mine._
And if a -
cresc.
Bridge:
G
D/F♯
Em7
A
D
A♭
E♭/G
Fm7
B♭
E♭
long the way,_
we find a day_
it starts_ to storm,_____ you've got the
f
D.S. al Coda
F
C/E
Dm7
F/G
G/A
G♭
D♭/F
E♭m7
G♭/A♭
A♭/B♭
prom-ise of_ my love_____
to
keep_____ you warm._______

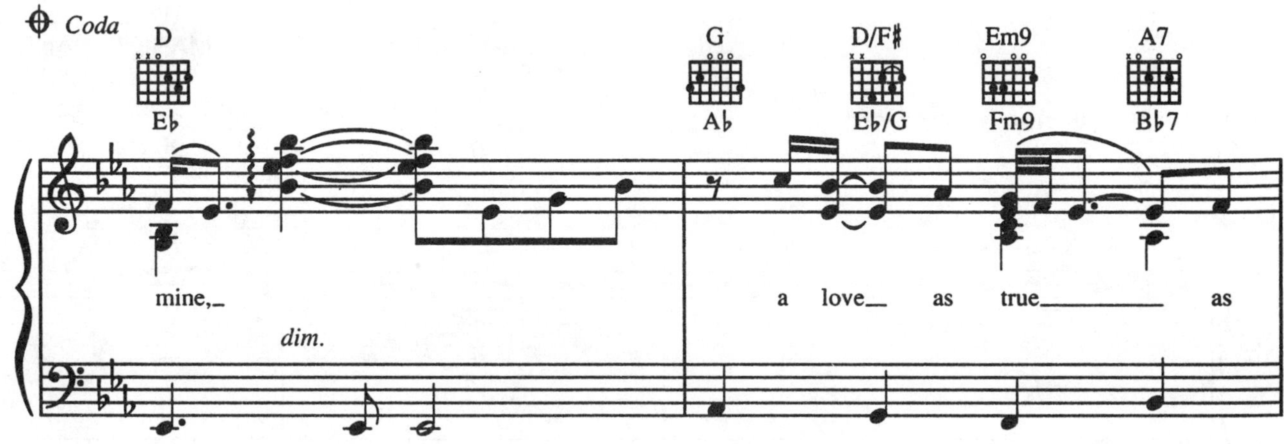

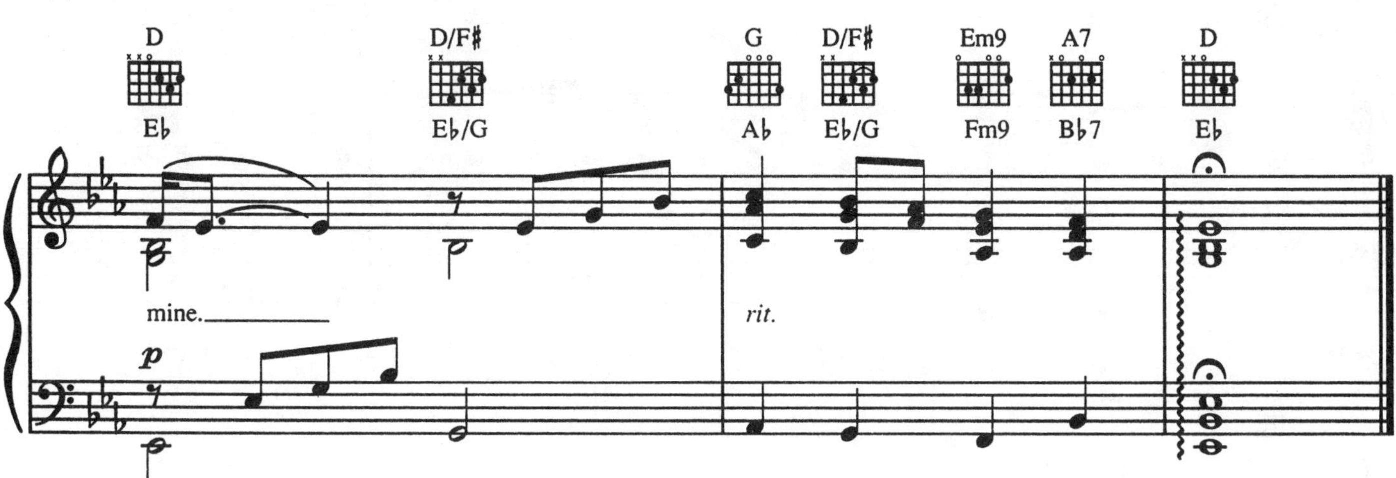

Verse 2:
You will always be the miracle
That makes my life complete;
And as long as there's a breath in me,
I'll make yours just as sweet.
As we look into the future,
It's as far as we can see,
So let's make each tomorrow
Be the best that it can be.
(To Chorus:)

I HOPE YOU DANCE

Words and Music by
MARK D. SANDERS and
TIA SILLERS

F♯m
Gm
to eat, but al - ways keep that hun - ger. May you
D
E♭
nev - er take one sin - gle breath for grant - ed. God for - bid
E
F
love ev - er leave you emp - ty - hand - ed. 1. I hope you still
Chorus:
D
E
A
E♭
F
B♭
(3.) feel small when you stand be - side the o - cean. When - ev - er one
2. See additional lyrics
D
E
A
E♭
F
B♭
door clos - es, I hope one more o - pens. Prom - ise me

Bm7
C♯m7
Dmaj7
Cm7
Dm7
E♭maj7
that you'll give faith a fight - ing chance. And when you
E
To Coda
F
get the choice to sit it out or dance, I hope you dance,
1.
F♯m
D
A
E/G♯
Gm
E♭
B♭
F/A
I hope you
F♯m
D
E
Gm
E♭
F
dance. 2. I hope you
2.
F♯m
D
A
E/G♯
Gm
E♭
B♭
F/A
I hope you dance,
(Time is a wheel in con - stant mo - tion, al - ways roll -

F♯m D E
Gm E♭ F
I hope you dance,
ing us a - long. Tell me
F♯m D A E/G♯
Gm E♭ B♭ F/A
I hope you dance.
who wants to look back on their years and won - der where
F♯m D E
Gm E♭ F
D.S. 𝄋 al Coda
3. I hope you still
those years have gone?
𝄌 Coda
F♯m D A E/G♯
Gm E♭ B♭ F/A
I hope you dance,
(Time is a wheel in con - stant mo - tion, al - ways roll -
F♯m D E
Gm E♭ F
I hope you dance,
ing us a - long. Tell me

Verse 2:
I hope you never fear those mountains in the distance,
Never settle for the path of least resistance.
Livin' might mean takin' chances but they're worth takin'.
Lovin' might be a mistake but it's worth makin'.

Chorus 2:
Don't let some hell-bent heart leave you bitter.
When you come close to sellin' out, reconsider.
Give the heavens above more than just a passing glance.
And when you get the choice to sit it out or dance,...
(To Chorus 3:)

I MELT

Words and Music by
NEIL THRASHER, WENDELL LEE MOBLEY
and GARY LEVOX

I Melt - 5 - 1

E
A/E
E
A/E
Well, I just lie there, star - ing,
si - lent - ly pre - par - ing to love on
E
A/E
you.
B
G♯7/B♯
C♯m
Well, I can feel the heat from a - cross the room.

D
B7sus
Ain't it wild what a lit - tle flame can make you wan - na do?
I melt
Chorus:
E
A
ev - 'ry time you look at me that way.
It nev - er fails,
E
B/E
D
B
an - y time, an - y place.
This
E
D
A/C#
burn in me's the cool - est thing
I've ev - er felt.

To Coda
1.
Am/C
E
A
E
A
I melt.
E
A
E
A
2.
E
A
E
A
D
A/C♯
A/E
E
D
A/C♯
Bsus
D.S. al Coda
I melt

Verse 2:
Don't know how you do it.
I love the way I lose it every time.
What's even better
Is knowing that forever you're all mine.
The closer you get, the more my body aches.
One little stare from you is all it takes.
(To Chorus:)

I SWEAR

Words and Music by
GARY BAKER and FRANK MYERS

C
Db
F/A
Gb/Bb
G/B
Ab/C
C
Db
stand be - side you through the years.
You'll on - ly cry
there's sil - ver in your hair,
you won't have to ask
F
Gb
G
Ab
Am
Bbm
C/G
Db/Ab
those hap - py tears.
And though I'll make mis - takes,
if I still care.
'Cause as time turns the page,
cresc.
D7/F#
Eb7/G
G7sus
Ab7sus
G
Ab
Chorus:
C
Db
I'll nev - er break your heart.
my love won't age at all.
I swear by the moon
Am
Bbm
Em7
Fm7
F
Gb
G
Ab
and the stars in the sky,
I'll be there.
I swear

C
Db
Am
Bbm
Em7
Fm7
by the shad - ow that's by your side,
I'll be there.
F
Gb
G
Ab
Dm7
Ebm7
F/G
Gb/Ab
G
Ab
For bet - ter or worse, 'til death do us part, I'll
To Coda
1.
Dm7
Ebm7
F/G
Gb/Ab
G
Ab
C
Db
love you with ev - er - y beat of my heart, I swear.
Am
Bbm
Em7
Fm7
F/G
Gb/Ab
G
Ab
D.S.
dim.
mp

2.
F/G
G
C
Am
Gb/Ab
Ab
Db
Bbm
of my heart, I swear.
(1st time only)
(Instrumental solo . . .
Em7
Fm7
1.
2.
D.S.S. al Coda
... end solo)
I swear
Coda
of my heart, I swear.
F
C2
Gb
Db(2)
I
swear.
mp
rit. e dim.
p

I WANNA DO IT ALL

Words and Music by
GILLES GODARD, RICK GILES
and TIM NICHOLS

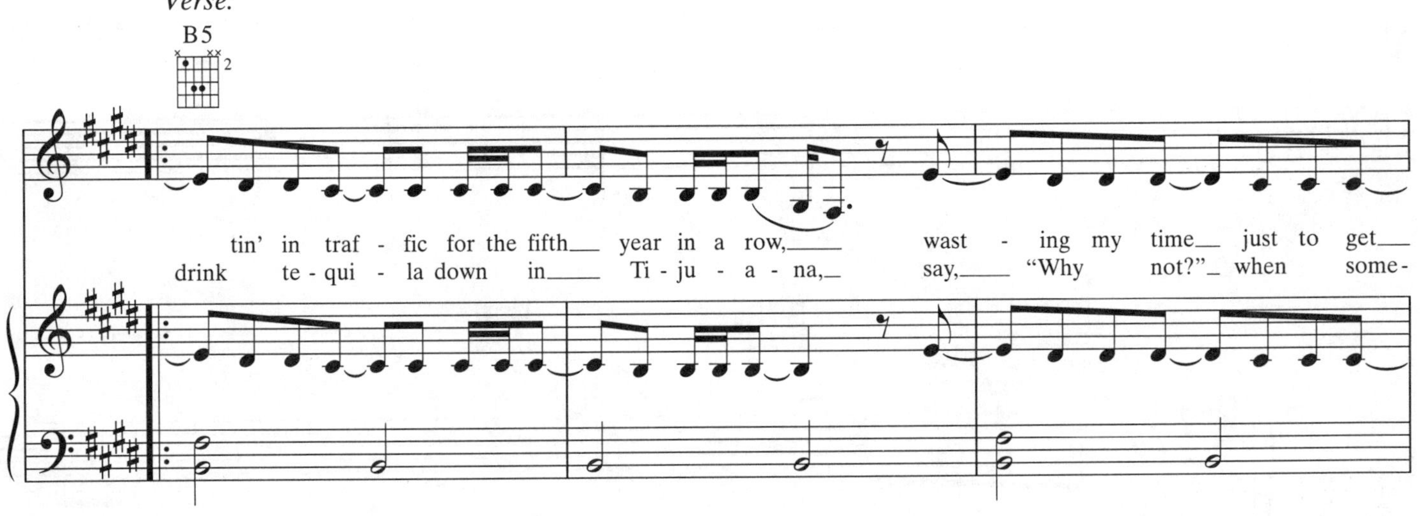

B5
ting things down_ on a Krisp - y Kreme sack._ Ev - ry - thing I'd do___ if I could
___ my heart_ broke once or twice, set-tle down with the love___ of my life,
E
B5
leave this place_ and nev - er look_ back._
rock lit - tle ba - bies to sleep at___ night._
Chorus:
E
C♯m7
I wan - na do it all, vis - it Par - is in the fall,_ watch the Yan -
E
A
kees play ball,_ I wan - na take it all in,___ catch_

B
To Coda
a few beads down at Mar - di Gras, start a tra - di - tion, lay
1.
E
A5
down the law. I wan - na do it all.
2. I wan - na
2.
E
B
E
B
do it all.
Bridge:
E
C♯m
E
I wan - na spend a day ev - 'ry now and

A
B5
A5
B5
then___ just do - in' what I wan - na do when I wan - na do it. (I wan - na do it
A5
B5
D.S. 𝄋 al Coda
all.___) An - y - time I wan - na do it. (I wan - na do it all.___)
Coda
E
___ down the law.___ I wan - na do it all, see Ni -
C♯m7
E
A
a - gra falls,___ fight___ Cit - y Hall,___ feel good___ in my skin,___

B
beat - in' the odds with my back to the wall, try -
E
B
in' to rob Pe - ter with - out pay - ing Paul. I wan - na do it all.
E
B
E
I wan - na do it all. I wan - na
B
E
B
E
do it all.

I WOULD'VE LOVED YOU ANYWAY

*Original recording in F♯ Major: Guitar tuned down 1/2 step.

Em
C
G
D
If I'd - 've read the last page first,
and mem - 'ries with - ered on the vine.
G
D/F♯
if I'd - 've had the strength to walk a - way,
Just to hold you close to me
1.
To Next Strain
Em
C
G
Dsus
D
if I'd - 've known how this would hurt:
for a mo - ment in
2.
G
D
Dsus
D
time.

Chorus:

G C D Em

I would-'ve loved you an - y - way. I'd do it all the same,

G C D Em

not a sec - ond I would change, not a touch that I would trade

G C Cm

To Coda

had I known my heart would

1.

Am7 D G D/F♯

break. I'd - 've loved you an - y - way.

2.
Em
C
G
D
Am7
D
break. I'd-'ve loved you an - y -
G
C
D
Em
G
C
way.
D
Em
Bridge:
Bm
And e - ven if I'd seen it com -
C
Am7
in', you'd still have seen me run - nin' straight in - to your

D
Dsus
D
D.S.𝄋 al Coda
arms.
3
𝄌 Coda
Am7
D
break.
I would have loved you an - y -
G
C
D
Em
G
C
way.
D
G
I would have loved you an - y - way.
rit. e dim.

I WILL ALWAYS LOVE YOU

Words and Music by
DOLLY PARTON

Verse 2:
Bitter sweet memories, that's all I have and all I'm taking with me.
Good-bye, oh please don't cry, 'cause we both know that I'm not what you need, but . . .
(To Chorus:)

Verse 3: (Recite)
And I hope life will treat you kind, and I hope that you have all that you ever dreamed of.
Oh, I do wish you joy, and I wish you happiness, but above all this, I wish you love;
I love you, I will always love you. (To Chorus:)

I WOULDN'T HAVE MISSED IT FOR THE WORLD

Words and Music by
KYE FLEMING, DENNIS MORGAN
and CHARLES QUILLEN

Am7
much sun - shine,
and love was the best it's ev - er been.
D
D/C
Bm7
Bm7/A
G
Chorus
C
I
would - n't have missed it for the world;
Am7
D7
B7/D#
Em7
would - n't have missed lov - in' you, girl.
You made my
D7
Am7
D
G
whole life worth - while with your smile.
I would - n't trade

Verse 2.
They say that all good things must end.
Love comes and goes just like the wind.
You've got your dreams to follow,
But if I had the chance tomorrow,
You know I'd do it all again.
(To Chorus)

I'M ALREADY THERE

Words and Music by
GARY BAKER, FRANK J. MYERS
and RICHIE McDONALD

D
Eb
Asus
Bbsus
A
Bb
G/B
Ab/C
hear her say, "I love you" one more time. And
wor - ry a - bout the kids, they'll be al - right. Wish
A(9)/C#
Bb(9)/D
Gmaj9
Abmaj9
when he heard the sound of the kids laugh - ing in the back - ground, he had to
I was in your arms, ly - in' right there be - side you. But I
wipe a - way a tear from his eye. A lit - tle
know that I'll be in your dreams to - night. And I'll
Bm
Cm
voice came on the phone and said, "Dad - dy, when you com - in' home?" He said the
gen - tly kiss your lips, touch you with my fin - ger - tips. So turn

D Em D/F♯ G Asus A
E♭ Fm E♭/G A♭ B♭sus B♭

first thing that came to his mind. I'm al - read - y there.
out the light and close your eyes." I'm al - read - y there.

𝄋 *Chorus:*

D A/C♯ Bm7 A
E♭ B♭/D Cm7 B♭

1.3. Take a look a - round. I'm the sun - shine in your
2. Don't make a sound. I'm the beat in your

G(9) D Asus A
A♭(9) E♭ B♭sus B♭

hair. I'm the shad - ow on the ground. I'm the whis - per in the wind.
heart. I'm the moon - light shin - ing down. I'm the whis - per in the wind.

D A/C♯ Bm7
E♭ B♭/D Cm7

(1.) I'm your i - mag - i - nar - y friend. And I know
(2.3.) And I'll be there 'til the end. Can you feel

F#m7
G
Asus
A
To Coda
Gm7
A♭
B♭sus
B♭
I'm in your prayers.
the love that we share?
Oh, I'm al - read - y there.
Oh, I'm al - read - y there.
1.
D
Bm7
G
A
E♭
Cm7
A♭
B♭
2. She
2.
Bridge:
D
Em7
D/F#
E♭
Fm7
E♭/G
We may be a thou -
G(9)
F
C/E
A♭(9)
G♭
D♭/F
sand miles a - part.
But I'll be with you wher -

Asus
A
Bbsus
Bb
D.S.𝄋 al Coda
ev - er you are.
I'm al - read - y there.
Coda
Bm
A
G
D/F#
Em7
Asus
Cm
Bb
Ab
Eb/G
Fm7
Bbsus
Oh, I'm al - read - y
N.C.
D
Eb
there.
Bm7
G(9)
C(9)
D
Cm7
Ab(9)
Db(9)
Eb
rit.

I'M GONNA GETCHA GOOD!

Words and Music by
SHANIA TWAIN and
R.J. LANGE

*Original recording in B♭ minor.

N.C.
A5
G5
A5
N.C.
want - cha for a night.
I'm on - ly in - ter - est - ed
C
G
A5
C
G
if I can have you for life.
2. I
Verses 2 & 3:
Am
C
G
Am
know I sound ser - i - ous.
Well, ba - by, I am.
3. See additional lyrics
C
G
Am
C
G
You're a fine piece of real es - tate and I'm gon - na get me some land.

Pre-chorus:

Am C G G6

Oh, yeah. So don't try to run,

Fmaj7 G6 Fmaj7

honey. Love can be fun.

C Dm7 F

There's no need to be alone when you find that

Chorus:

C G

someone. I'm gonna getcha, while I gotcha in sight.

(I'm gonna getcha.) (I'm gonna

Am
F
C
I'm gon - na get - cha if it takes all night.
You can bet - cha by the
get - cha.)
(Yeah, you can bet - cha.)
simile
G
F
time I say go, you'll nev - er say no.
(I'm gon - na get - cha.)
(I'm gon - na
C
G
Am
I'm gon - na get - cha, it's a mat - ter of fact.
I'm gon - na get - cha, don't you
get - cha.)
(I'm gon - na get - cha.)
F
C
G
wor - ry 'bout that.
You can bet - cha bot - tom dol - lar in time, you're gon -
(Yeah, you can bet - cha.)
(I'm gon - na

To Coda
1.
2.
F
G
A5
G5
A5
C5
G5
G
Am
C
G
Am
na be mine.
get - cha,
I'm gon - na get - cha.)
Just like I should,
I'll get - cha good,
yeah.
should,
I'll get - cha good.
I'm gon - na get - cha, ba -
by.
I'm gon - na knock on wood.

Verse 3:
I've already planned it,
Here's how it's gonna be:
I'm gonna love you
And you're gonna fall in love with me, yeah.
(To Pre-chorus:)

I'M IN A HURRY
(And I Don't Know Why)

Words and Music by
ROGER MURRAH and RANDY VAN WARMER

A
E
F♯m
prove. It's not new, but it - 'll do ze - ro to six - ty in five -
D
A
E
A/E
point - two, oh, I'm in a hur - ry to get things done, oh, I
F♯m
D
A
rush and rush un - til life's no fun. All I real - ly got - ta do is
E
A
F♯m
1.
D
live and die, but I'm in a hur - ry and don't know why.
2.
D
A
Asus2
A
know why.

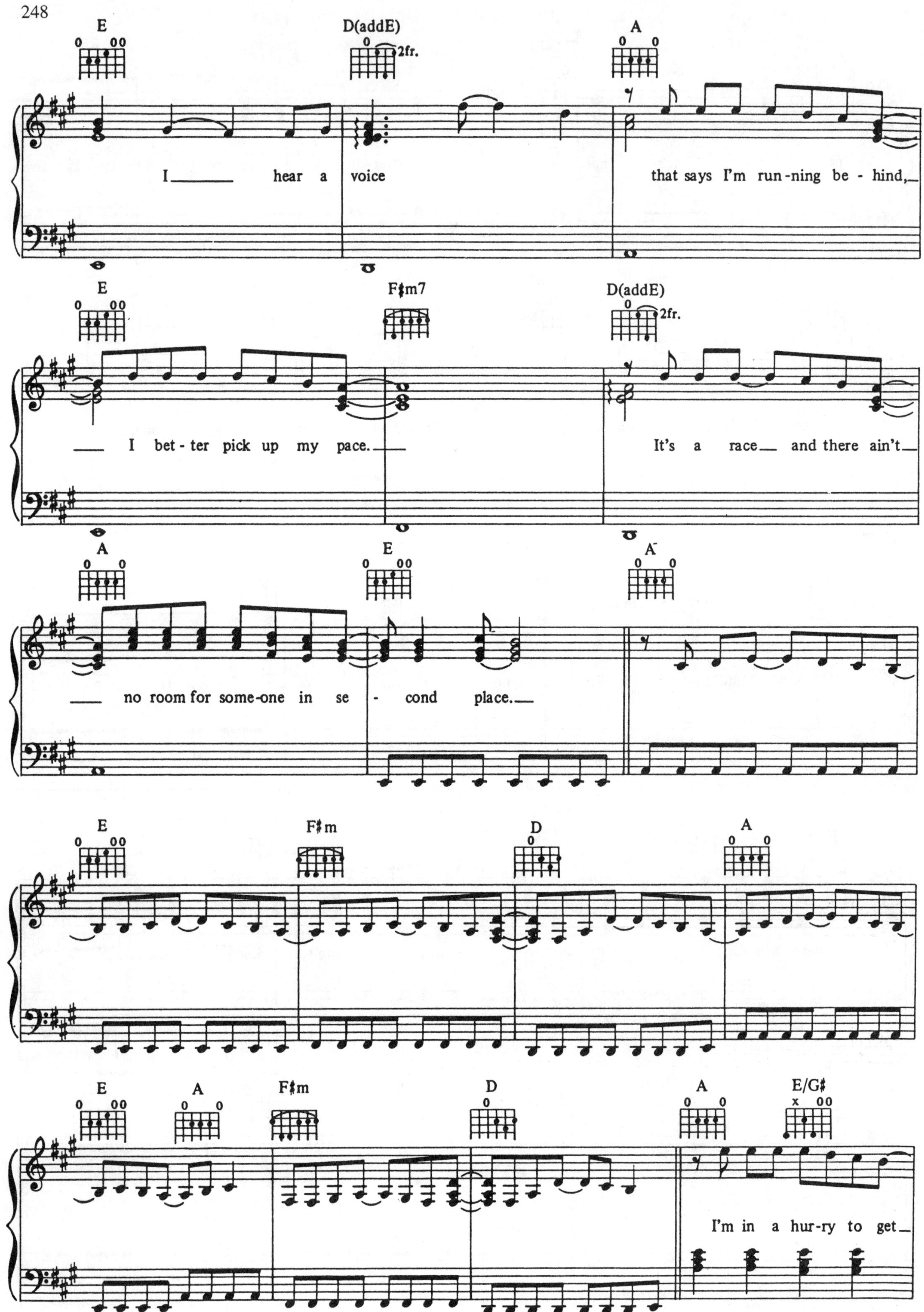
E
D(addE)
2fr.
A
I hear a voice
that says I'm run-ning be - hind,
E
F♯m7
D(addE)
2fr.
I bet-ter pick up my pace.
It's a race and there ain't
A
E
A
no room for some-one in se - cond place.
E
F♯m
D
A
E
A
F♯m
D
A
E/G♯
I'm in a hur-ry to get

D(addE)/F♯ E D(addE) Amaj7/C♯ Bm7(addE) E
2fr. 4fr.
— things done, — I rush and rush un - til life's no fun. All —
A E/G♯ D(addE)/F♯ E D Amaj7/C♯
2fr. 4fr.
— I real - ly got - ta do is — live and die, — but I'm in a hur - ry and don't —
Bm7(addE) E A E A/E
— know why. —— 1.3. I'm in a hur - ry to get — things done, — oh, I
2. Instrumental
F♯m D A
rush and rush un - til life's — no fun. —— All — I real - ly got - ta do is —
1.2.
E A F♯m D
— live and die, — but I'm — in a hur - ry and don't — know why. ——

3. D

N.C.

know why.

I'm in a hur - ry to get things done, oh, I

rush and rush un - til life's no fun. All

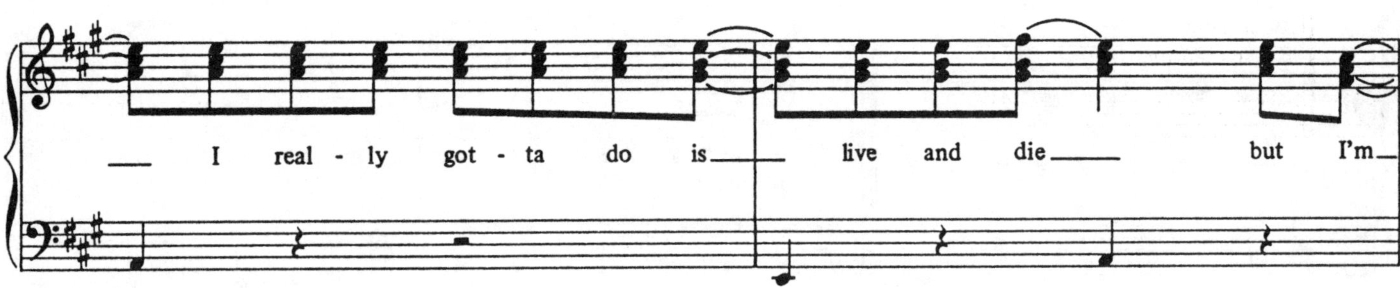

Additional Lyrics

2. Can't be late,
I leave in plenty of time,
Shakin' hands with the clock.
I can't stop,
I'm on a roll and I'm ready to rock.

(To Chorus)

IF YOU EVER HAVE FOREVER IN MIND

Words and Music by
VINCE GILL and TROY SEALS

B♭
Bdim7
F
Dm7
I may be a fool to love by the
Gm7
C7
F
B♭7
F
C7
rules. I want it to last. If you
Chorus:
F
Fmaj7
Cm7
F7
B♭
ev-er (if you ev-er) have for-ev - er in mind,
C7
I'll be here and eas - y to
F
C7
F
Fmaj7
find. If your heart (if your heart) is-n't

Verse 2:
Music has ended, still you wanna dance.
I know that feeling, I can't take the chance.
You live for the moment; no future, no past.
I may be a fool to live by the rules.
I want it to last.
(To Chorus:)

I'M MOVIN' ON

Words and Music by
D. VINCENT WILLIAMS
and PHILLIP WHITE

𝄋 *Verse:*

G G/F♯ Em G/D

dealt with my ghosts and I've faced all my de - mons.
lived in this place and I know all the fac - es.
sold what I could and packed what I could - n't.

C G/B Am D7sus

Fi - n'lly con - tent with a past I re - gret. I've
Each one is dif - f'rent, but they're al - ways the same. They
Stopped to fill up on my way out of town. I've

G G/F♯ Em G/D

found you find strength in your mo - ments of weak - ness. For
mean me no harm, but it's time that I face it. They'll
loved like I should, but lived like I should - n't.

C G/B Am7

once I'm at peace with my - self. I've been
nev - er al - low me to change. But
I had to lose ev - 'ry - thing to find out.

Em
Asus
A
bur - doned with blame, trapped in the past for too
I nev - er dreamed home would end up where I don't be -
May - be for - give - ness will find me some - where down this
C
To Coda
C2
G
1.
long.
long.
road.
I'm mov - in' on.
C/G
G
D7sus
D7
2. I've
2.
C/G
G
C
Dm
C/E
Chorus:
F
I'm mov - in' on. At
cresc.
mf

Dm Bb Bb/C

last I can see___ life has been__ pa - tient - ly wait - ing for

C F Dm

me. And I know there's no guar - an - tees, but I'm___

Bb Csus C F

not___ a - lone.___ There comes a time___

Dm Bb

___ in ev - 'ry - one's_ life when all you can see___ are the years_

B♭/C
C
F
Dm
passing by.
And I have made up my
mind that those days are gone.
B♭
F/C
C
Dsus
D
G
G/F♯
Em
dim.
mp
G/D
C
Dsus
D.S. 𝄋 al Coda
3. I
8va

Coda
D7sus
G
I'm mov - in' on.
C/G
G
I'm mov - in' on.
Dsus
G
G/F♯
I'm mov - in' on.
p
Em
G/D
C
G
8va
rit.
Freely

IF YOU SEE HIM, IF YOU SEE HER

Words and Music by
TERRY McBRIDE, JENNIFER KIMBALL
and TOMMY LEE JAMES

Slowly ♩ = 88

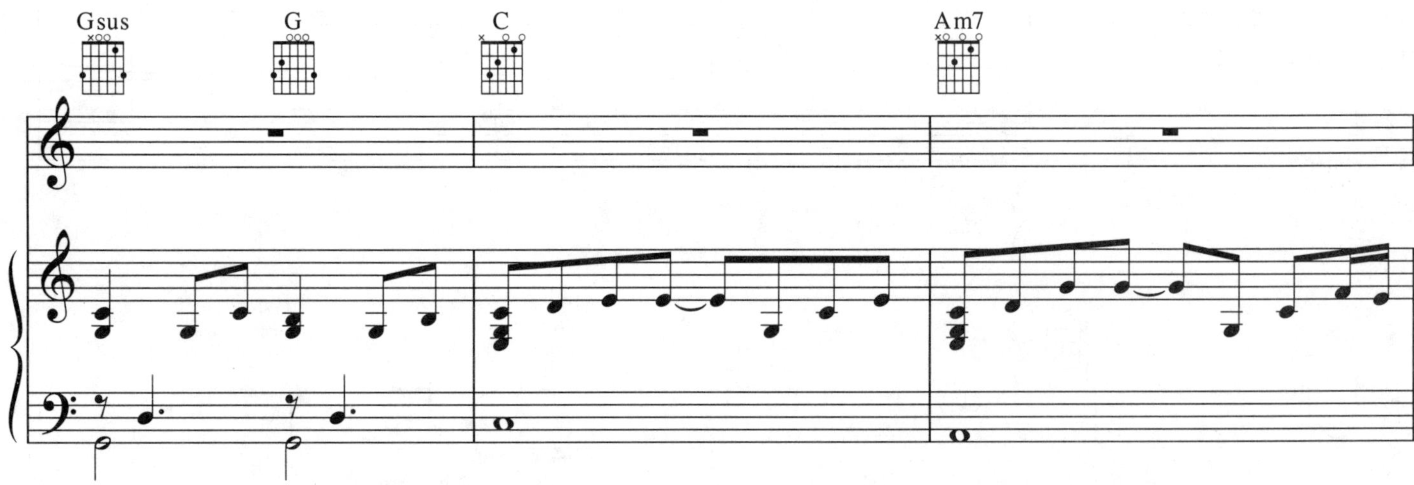

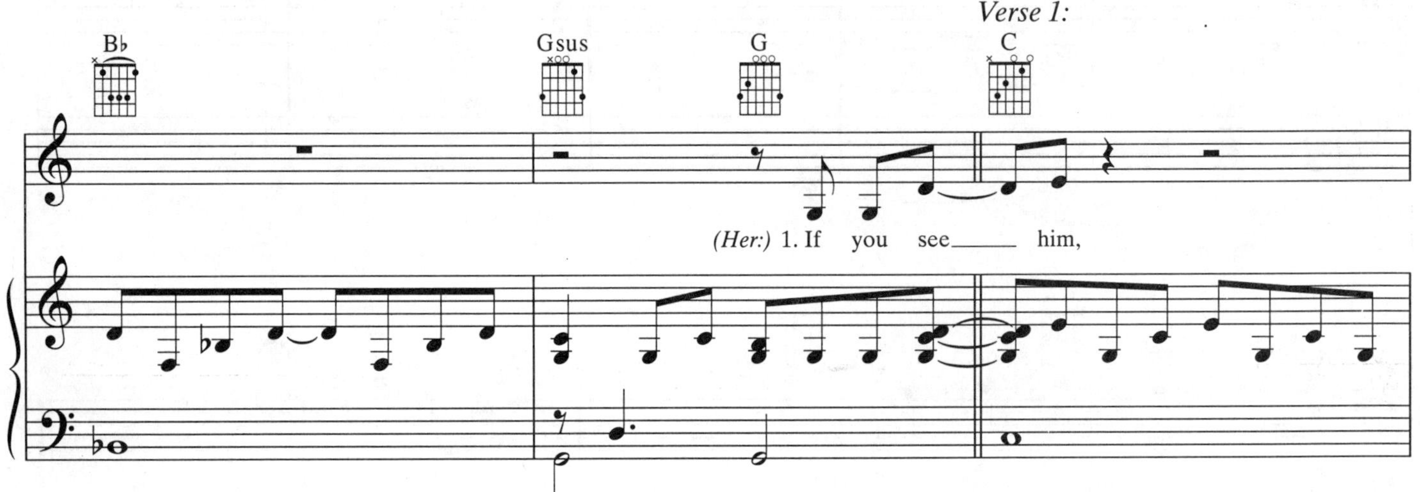

Am7
B♭
Gsus
G
tell him I wish him well.
How am I do-
C
Am7
B♭
ing? Well, some-times it's hard to tell.
Gsus
G
F(9)
G
I still miss him more than ev - er, but
C
F
C/E
Dm
please don't say a word if you see him,

G
C
Dsus
D
if you see him.
(Him:) 2. If you
Verses 2 & 3:
G
Em7
F
see her, tell her I'm do - in' fine.
3. See additional lyrics
Dsus
D
G
Em7
And if you want to, say that I think of her
F
Dsus
D
C(9)
from time to time.
Ask her if she ev -

D G C G/B

er won - ders where we both went wrong if you

To Coda

Am7 D G

see her, if you see her.

Bridge:

D/F♯ Em7 C

(Him:) Whoa, I, I still want her. *(Her:)* And

D C G D D/F♯

I still need him so. *(Both:)* Whoa, I don't

Em7
C
Am7
C
D
G
know why we let each oth - er go.
D/F♯
Em7
C
D
C
D/F♯
D
Em7
C
Am7
C
D
D.S. 𝄋 al Coda
(Him:) 3. If you

Verse 3:
(Him:) If you see her, tell her the light's still on for her.
(Her:) Nothing's changed, deep down the fire still burns for him.
(Both:) And even if it takes forever, say I'll still be here.
(Her:) If you see him.
(Him:) If you see her.

ISLANDS IN THE STREAM

Words and Music by
BARRY GIBB, MAURICE GIBB
and ROBIN GIBB

C
real thing.
You do some - thing to me that I
But that won't hap - pen to us and we
can't ex - plain;
got no doubt;
hold me clos - er and I feel no pain. Ev - 'ry
too deep in love, and we got no way out. And the
Fsus2
C
beat of my heart, we got some - thing go - ing on.
mes - sage is clear; this could be the year of the real thing.
Fsus2
Ten - der love is blind; it re - quires a ded - i - ca - tion. All
No more will you cry; ba - by, I will hurt you nev - er. We

1
C
Dm7
Dm7/G
ly on each oth - er, uh - huh, from one lov - er to an - oth - er, uh -
ly on each oth - er, uh - huh, from one lov -
C
Em
Fsus2
Gsus
3fr
D.S.
huh.
2
Dm7
Dm7/G
C
Em
- er to an - oth - er, uh - huh.
Fsus2
Gsus
3fr
C
Em
I'll be al -

Fm6/A♭
6fr
C
this love we feel needs no con - ver - sa - tion. We ride it to - geth - er, uh -
start and end as one, in love for - ev - er. We can ride it to - geth - er, uh -
huh, from one love to an - oth - er, uh - huh. (1.,2.) Is - lands in
huh, from one love to an - oth - er, uh - huh.
C
F
Dm7
the stream, that is what we are. No one in be - tween; how can we
(3.) per - star; that is what you are, com - ing from a - far, reach - ing for
C
F
be wrong? Get a - way with me to an - oth - er world, and we re -
the stars. Far a - way with me to an - oth - er place, and we re -

Fsus2
Gsus
3fr
3
Dm7
Dm7/G
- right, oh. Get 'em, su - er to an - oth - er, uh -
C
Em
Fsus2
huh. I'll be al - right. Good - bye, to - night.
Gsus
3fr
C
Em
Good - night for now. Good - bye, to - night.
Fsus2
C/G
Gsus
3fr
C
Al - right, for now good - bye.

IT WAS

Words and Music by
GARY BURR and MARK WRIGHT

B♭
A♭
B♭
E♭/B♭
was un - mis - tak - a - ble when I fell for you.
was un - be - liev - a - ble, but I be - lieve it's true.
It was real,
Chorus:
E♭
Cm
Fm
it was mag - ic. It was calm, it was sav -
A♭
E♭
Cm
age. It was cool as a breeze. It was warm to the touch. It was nev -
Fm
A♭
Cm
B♭/D
er e - nough. It was al - ways too much. It did all the things love does.
To Coda
1.
A♭
Cm
B♭
E♭
That's how I knew it was.

2. Bridge:

E♭ A♭/B♭ B♭ A♭/B♭ B♭ A♭/B♭ B♭ A♭/B♭ B♭ A♭/B♭

You ask what I felt___ when you walked___ through the door. Was it fear?___

B♭ A♭/B♭ B♭ E♭/B♭ *D.S.* 𝄋 *al Coda*

___ Was it clear? It was all___ that and more. It was real,___

𝄌 *Coda*

E♭ A♭ Cm B♭

That's how I knew___ it was.___

Cm E♭ Cm E♭

Cm E♭ Cm A♭ E♭

IT'S FIVE O'CLOCK SOMEWHERE

Words and Music by
DONALD ROLLINS
and JIM BROWN

A
D
A
am I. The work-day pass - es like mo - las-ses in win -
the night. To - mor-row morn - ing I know there'll be hell
Bm
A
D
G
ter-time, but it's Ju - ly. Get-tin' paid by the hour and
to pay, hey, but that's all right. I ain't had a day off now in
D
A
D
old-er by the min-ute. My boss just pushed me o - ver the lim - it. I'd like to
o-ver a year. My Ja - mai - can va - ca - tion's gon-na start right here. If the
G
D
A
call him some-thing. I think I'll just call it a day.
phone's for me, you can tell them I just sailed a - way.

Chorus:
D
G
A
Pour me some-thing tall and strong. Make it a Hur-ri-cane be-fore I
D
G
A
go in-sane. It's on-ly half past twelve, but I don't care,
N.C.
D
G
A
it's five o'-clock some-where.
1.
D
2.
D
2. Well,

G
A
D
I could
Bridge:
Bm
G
Em7
A
pay off my tab, pour my - self in a cab and be back to work__ be - fore
D
Bm
G
two.____ At a mo - ment like this, I can't help but won - der:
Em
A
What would Jim - my Buf - fett do? (Spoken:) Funny you should ask, Alan. I'd say:

Chorus:
D
G
A
Pour me some-thing tall and strong. Make it a Hur-ri-cane be-fore I
D
G
go in-sane. It's on-ly half past twelve, but I don't care.
A
D
G
Pour me some-thing tall and strong. Make it a
A
D
Hur-ri-cane be-fore I go in-sane. It's on-ly half past twelve,

Dialogue:
Jimmy: What time zone am I on? What country am I in?
Alan: It doesn't matter. It's five o'clock somewhere.
Jimmy: It's always on five in Margaritaville, come to think of it.
Alan: I heard that.
Jimmy: You've been there, haven't you?
Alan: Yes, sir.
Jimmy: I've seen your boat there.
Alan: I've been to Margaritaville a few times.
Jimmy: All right. That's good.
Alan: Stumbled my way back.
Jimmy: OK. Just want to make sure you can keep it between the navigational beacons.
Alan: Between the bouys. I got it.
Jimmy: All right. It's five o'clock. Let's go somewhere.
Alan: I'm ready. Crank it up.
Jimmy: Let's get out of here.
Alan: I'm gone.

JAMBALAYA
(On the Bayou)

Words and Music by
HANK WILLIAMS

Verse 3:
Settle down far from town,get me a pirogue
And I'll catch all the fish in the bayou
Swap my mon to buy Yvonne what she need-o
Son of a gun, we'll have big fun on the bayou

JOLENE

Words and Music by
DOLLY PARTON

B♭
Cm
B♭
lene, Jo - lene,
please don't take him just be - cause you
Cm
can.
To Coda I
To Coda II
1. Your
Verse:
E♭
B♭/D
Cm
beau - ty is be - yond com - pare, with flow-ing locks of au - burn hair,
2.3. See additional lyrics
B♭
Cm
i - 'vry skin and eyes of em - 'rald green.
E♭
Your smile is like a breath of spring, your voice

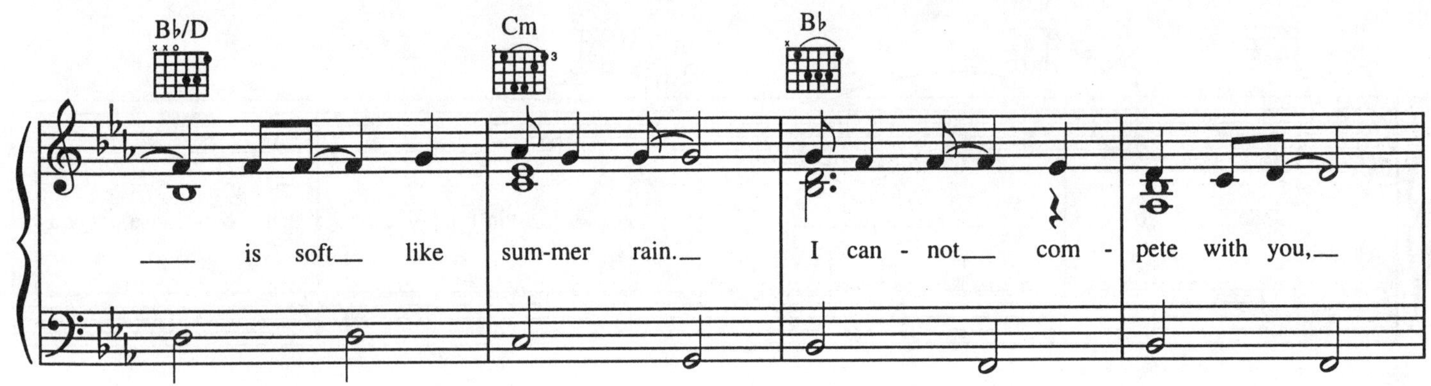
B♭/D
Cm
B♭
is soft like sum-mer rain. I can - not com - pete with you,

Cm
1.
Jo - lene.
2. He

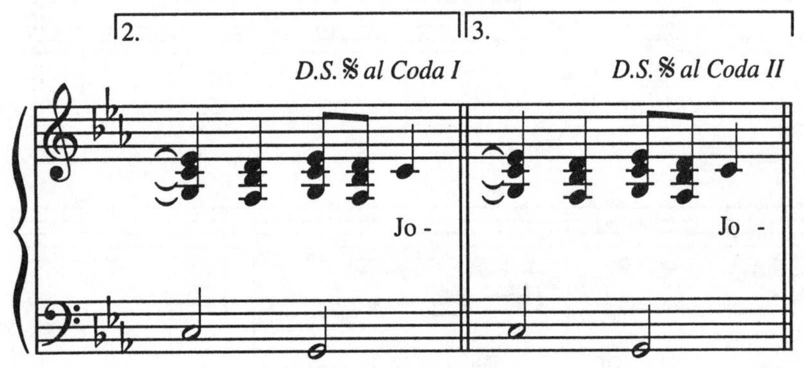
2.
3.
D.S. 𝄋 al Coda I
D.S. 𝄋 al Coda II
Jo -
Jo -

Coda I

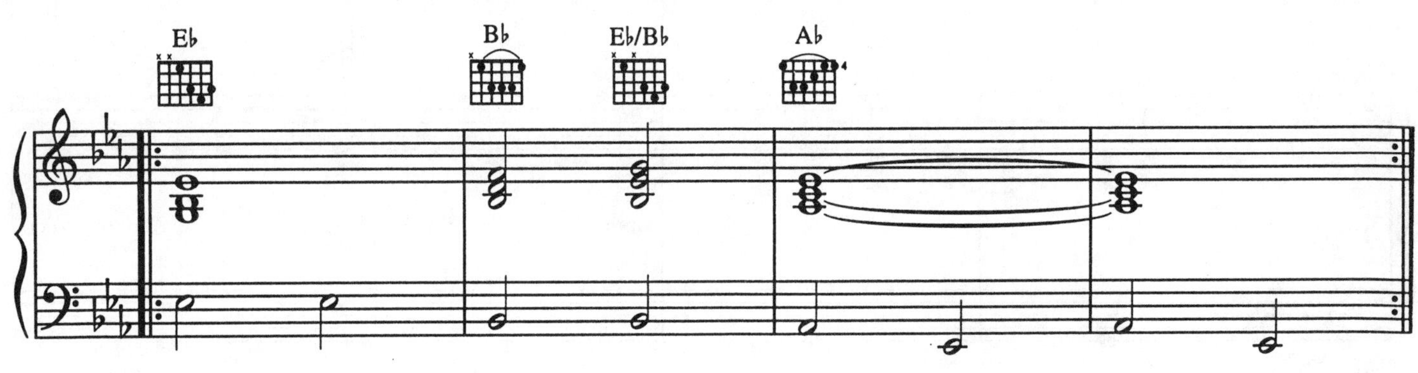
E♭
B♭
E♭/B♭
A♭

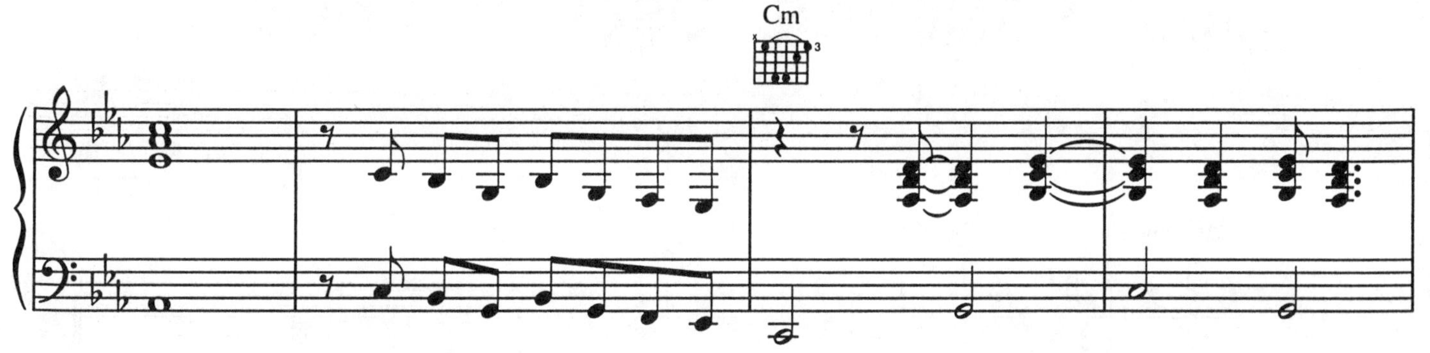

Verse 2:
He talks about you in his sleep.
There's nothing I can do to keep
From cryin' when he calls your name, Jolene.
But I can easily understand
How you could easily take my man.
But you don't know what he means to me, Jolene.
(To Chorus:)

Verse 3:
As you could have your choice of men,
I could never love again.
He's the only one for me, Jolene.
I had to have this talk with you,
My happiness depends on you
And whatever you decide to do, Jolene.
(To Chorus:)

JUST SOMEONE I USED TO KNOW

Words and Music by
JACK CLEMENT

F
F7
B♭
know." Just some - one I used to spend some
time with; Just a flame that's lost it's glow.
C7
I don't tell them of the nights I cry with - out you,
I say, "Just some- one I used to know." "Just some-

Bb
F
Bb
F
one I used to run a-round with; Just a friend
F7
of long a-go." I don't tell them how lost I am with-
Bb
F
C7
F
out you, I say "Just some-one I used to know."
Bb
F
C7
Bb
F
F7
Bb
F
I say, "Just some-one I used to know."

JUST TO HEAR YOU SAY THAT YOU LOVE ME

Words and Music by
DIANE WARREN

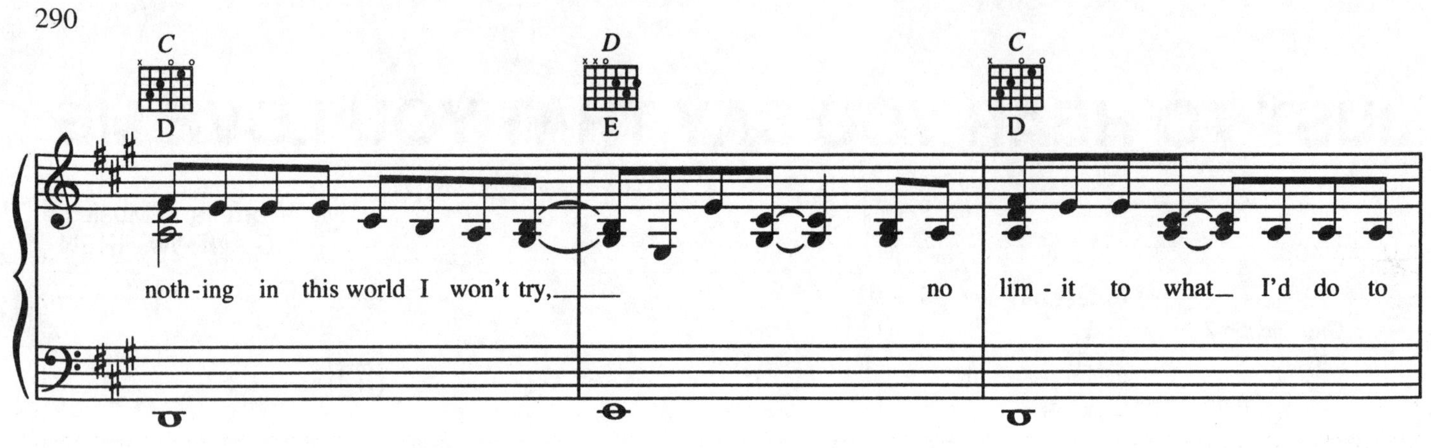
C
D
D
E
C
D
noth-ing in this world I won't try,
no
lim - it to what I'd do to

Chorus:
B7sus
C♯7sus
E
F♯
F♯m/E
G♯m/F♯
make you mine.
1.2. I'd climb right
(3.) you. (Instrumental solo...
up to the sky,

A
B
E/G♯
F♯/A♯
F♯m7
G♯m7
E
F♯
take down the stars just to
be in your arms, ba - by.
I'd go and

F♯m/E
G♯m/F♯
A
B
B7
C♯7
cap-ture the moon, that's what
I would do
just to hear you say that you love

1.
E
To Coda
B7
E
Am7/D
F#
C#7
F#
Bm7/E
me.
Just to hear you say that you love me.
2.
Bridge:
B7
C#m7
B
C#7
D#m7
C#
Just to hear you say that you love me for the rest of my life.
Ba-by,
C#m7
G#m7
E♭m7
D#m7
A#m7
Fm7
love me for the rest of all time.
Just say the word and I'll
F#m7/B
D.S. al Coda
G#m7/C#
give you my world.
There's noth-ing I won't do,
ba - by, just to be with

Coda
B
C♯
...end solo)
Chorus:
F♯
A♭
I'd climb right
G♯m/F♯
B♭m/A♭
up to the sky,
B
D♭
take down the stars
F♯/A♯
A♭/C
just to
G♯m7
B♭m7
be in your arms, ba - by.
F♯
A♭
I'd go and
G♯m/F♯
B♭m/A♭
cap - ture the moon, that's what
B
C♯
I would do
C♯7
E♭7
just to hear you say that you love

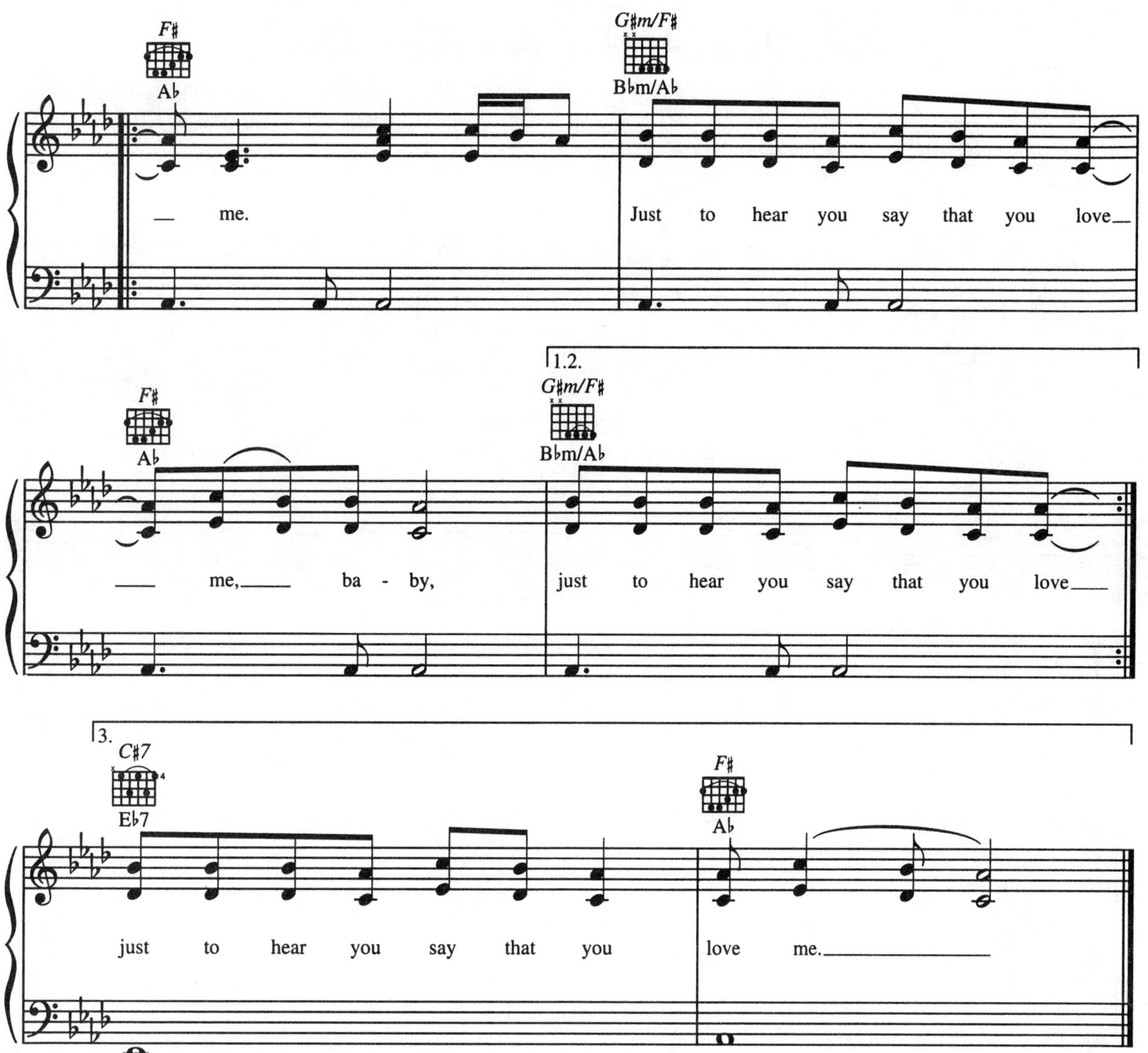

Verse 2:
If I could taste your kiss,
There'd be no sweeter gift heaven could offer, baby.
I want to be the one
Living to give you love.
I'd walk across this world just to be
Close to you, 'cos I want you close to me.
(To Chorus:)

KATIE WANTS A FAST ONE

Words and Music by
RICK CARNES and STEVE WARINER

bang - in' on the wheel, punch - in' ev - 'ry but - ton on the ra - di - o, but
N.C.
Chorus:
G
ev - 'ry - thing's too slow. 1.2.4. Ka - tie wants a fast one,
(Bkgrd.) (Ka - tie wants a fast
3.5.6. etc. Inst. solo ad lib....
D
quick - er than the last one. On - ly two
one, quick - er than the last one.)
G
A
times she gets that rush is mak - in' tracks and kick - in' up

G
dust. Ka - tie wants a fast one. You know_ she's got - ta
(Ka - tie wants_ a fast___ one.

D
G
have one, 'cause that's what makes___ her mo - tor run.
You know_ she's got___ to have_ one.)

1.
A
N.C.
D7
Ka - tie wants a fast one.
3

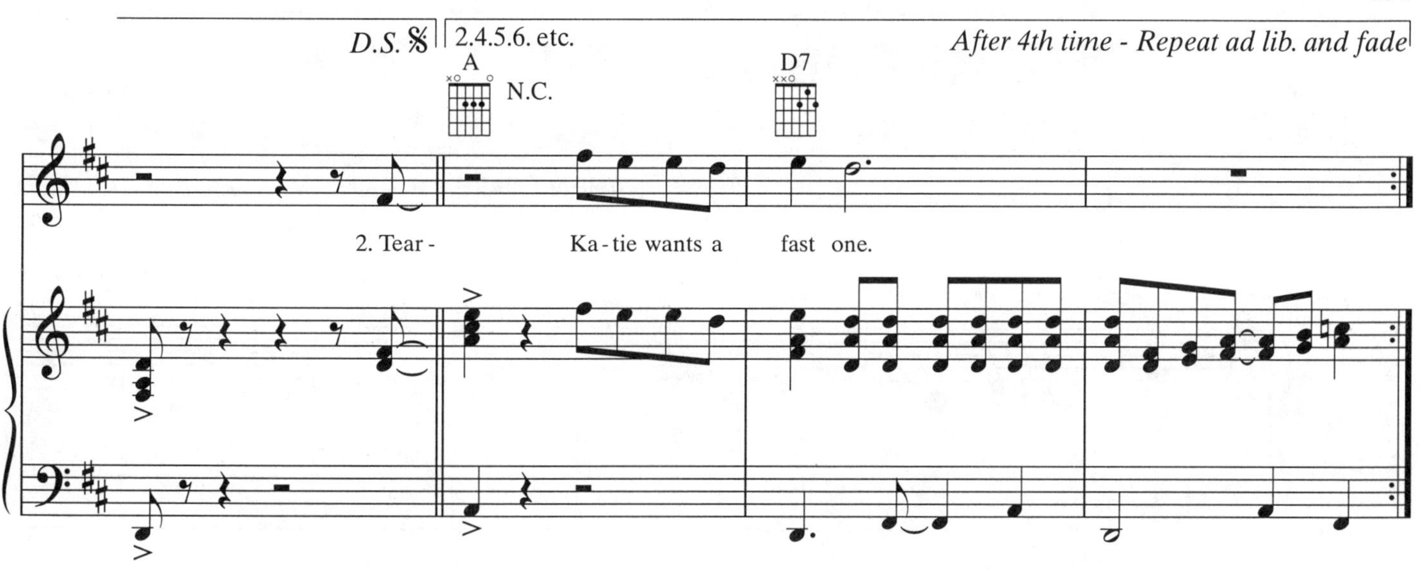

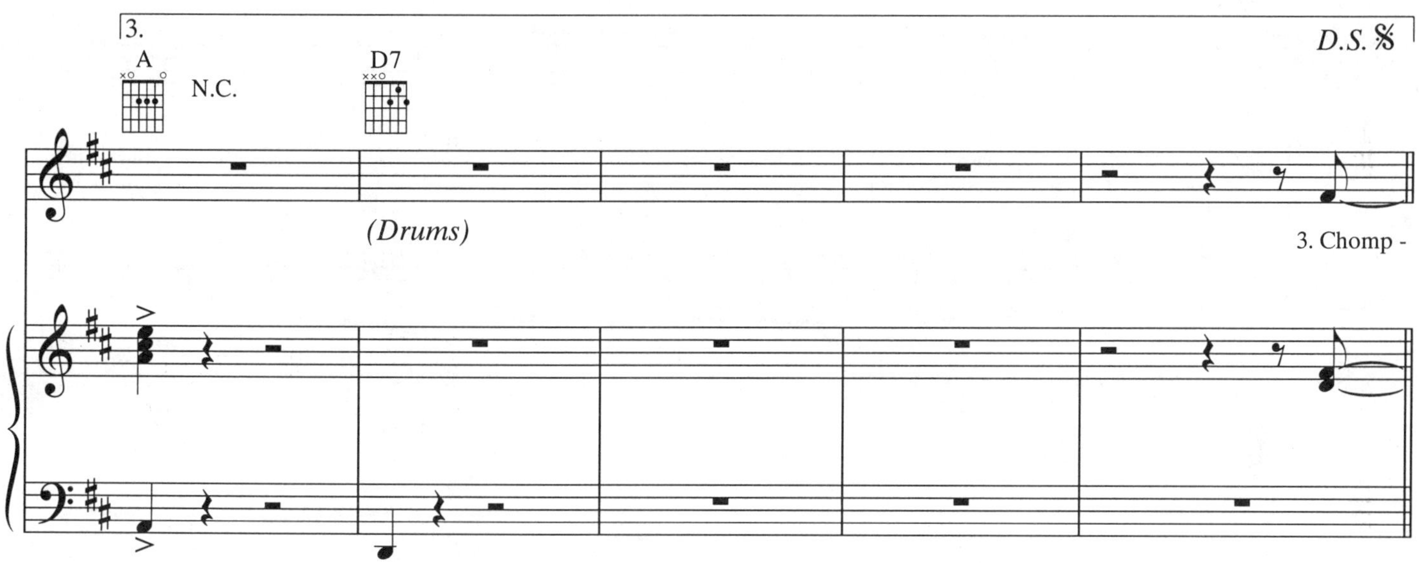

Verse 2:
Tearin' up the yard on her ridin' mower.
A neighbor yells, "Katie, better go a little slower."
Takin' every corner up on two wheels
Is how she gets her thrills.
(To Chorus:)

Verse 3:
Chompin' at the bit in the checkout line,
Katie's got a thing about wastin' time.
If she pulls up behind you in the car pool lane,
Just get out of her way.
(To Chorus:)

THE KEEPER OF THE STARS

Words and Music by
KAREN STALEY, DANNY MAYO and DICKEY LEE

D
A/C♯
Bm
Now, I just can't be - lieve you're in my
I know I don't de - serve a trea - sure like
G
D/F♯
life. Heav-en's smil-in' down on me
you. There real - ly are no words
Em
A7sus
A
N.C.
D/F♯
as I look at you to - night.
to show my grat - i - tude.
I tip my
mf
Chorus:
G
A
F♯m
hat to the keep - er of the stars.

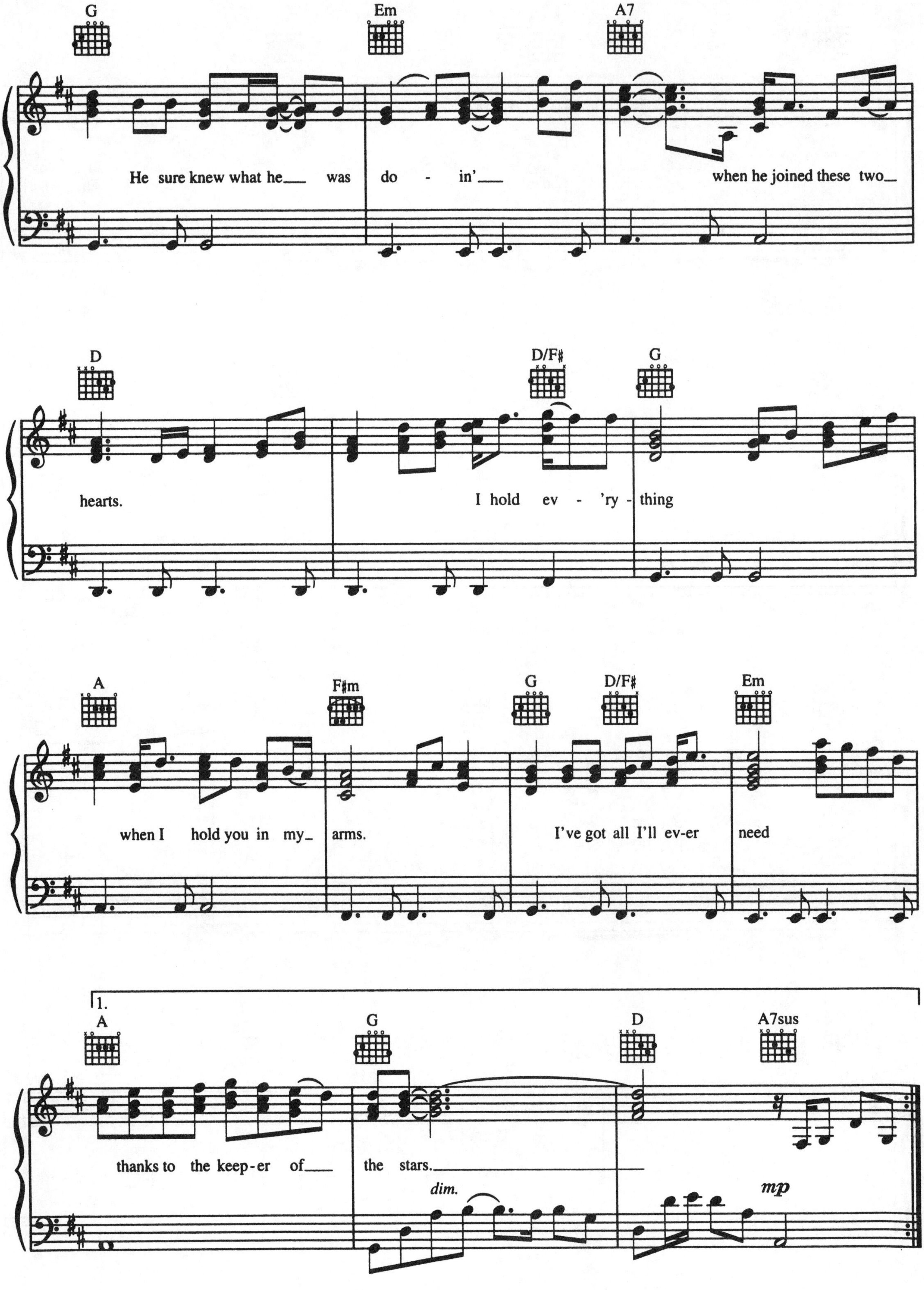

G Em A7

He sure knew what he___ was do - in'___ when he joined these two___

D D/F♯ G

hearts. I hold ev - 'ry - thing

A F♯m G D/F♯ Em

when I hold you in my_ arms. I've got all I'll ev-er need

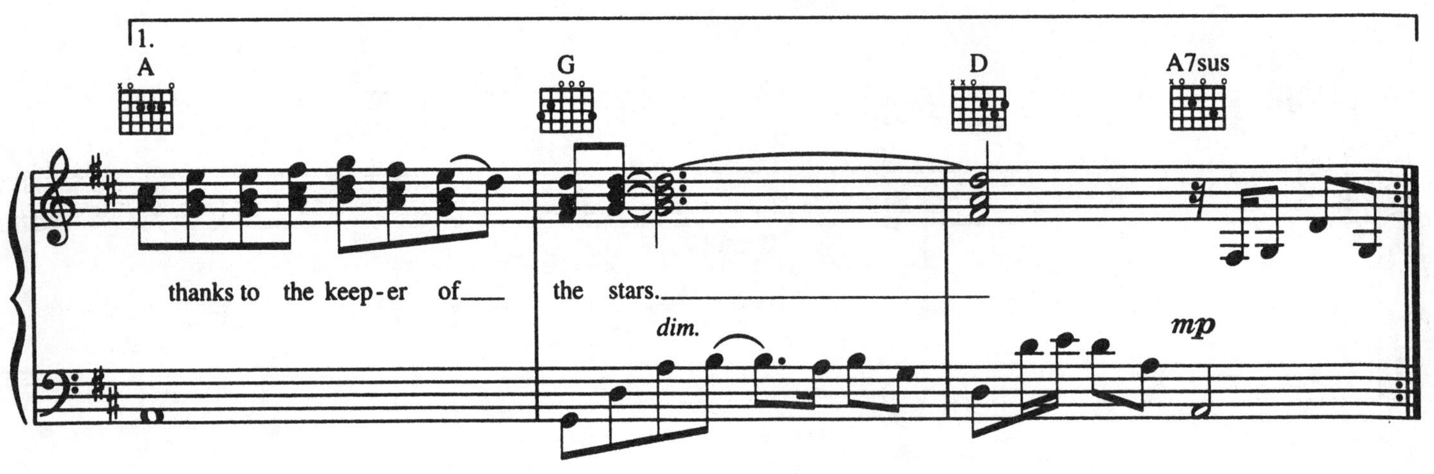

2.
A
D
thanks to the keep - er of___ the stars.__
dim.
A/C♯
Bm
mp
It was_ no ac - ci - dent,_ me find - ing
G
D/F♯
you.
Some-one had a hand_ in it___
Em
A7sus
D
A7sus
D
long be - fore_ we__ ev - er knew.
a tempo
dim. e rit.
p

KILLIN' TIME

Words and Music by
CLINT BLACK and HAYDEN NICHOLAS

G
did the things I ought-a you still would not be
end to all my sor - row, this is the on - ly price I'll
C
G
mine, so I keep a tight grip on the bot - tle get - tin'
pay. I'll be a hap - py man when I go, and I can't
Chorus:
D
G
G7
C
loose and kill - in' time.
wait an - oth - er day.
This kill - in' time
G
D
is kill - in' me. Drink-in' my - self blind
G
G7
C
think-in' I won't see that if I cross that line

G
F
— and they bur - y
me,
well, I just might
find I'll be kill - in'
C
G
1.
time for e - ter - ni - ty.
F
C
G
D.S.
2. I don't know
2.
F
C
G
— Yes, I just might
find I'll be kill - in'
time for e - ter - ni - ty.
F
C
G
—
rit.

KISS THIS

Words and Music by
PHILIP DOUGLAS, AARON TIPPIN
and THEA TIPPIN

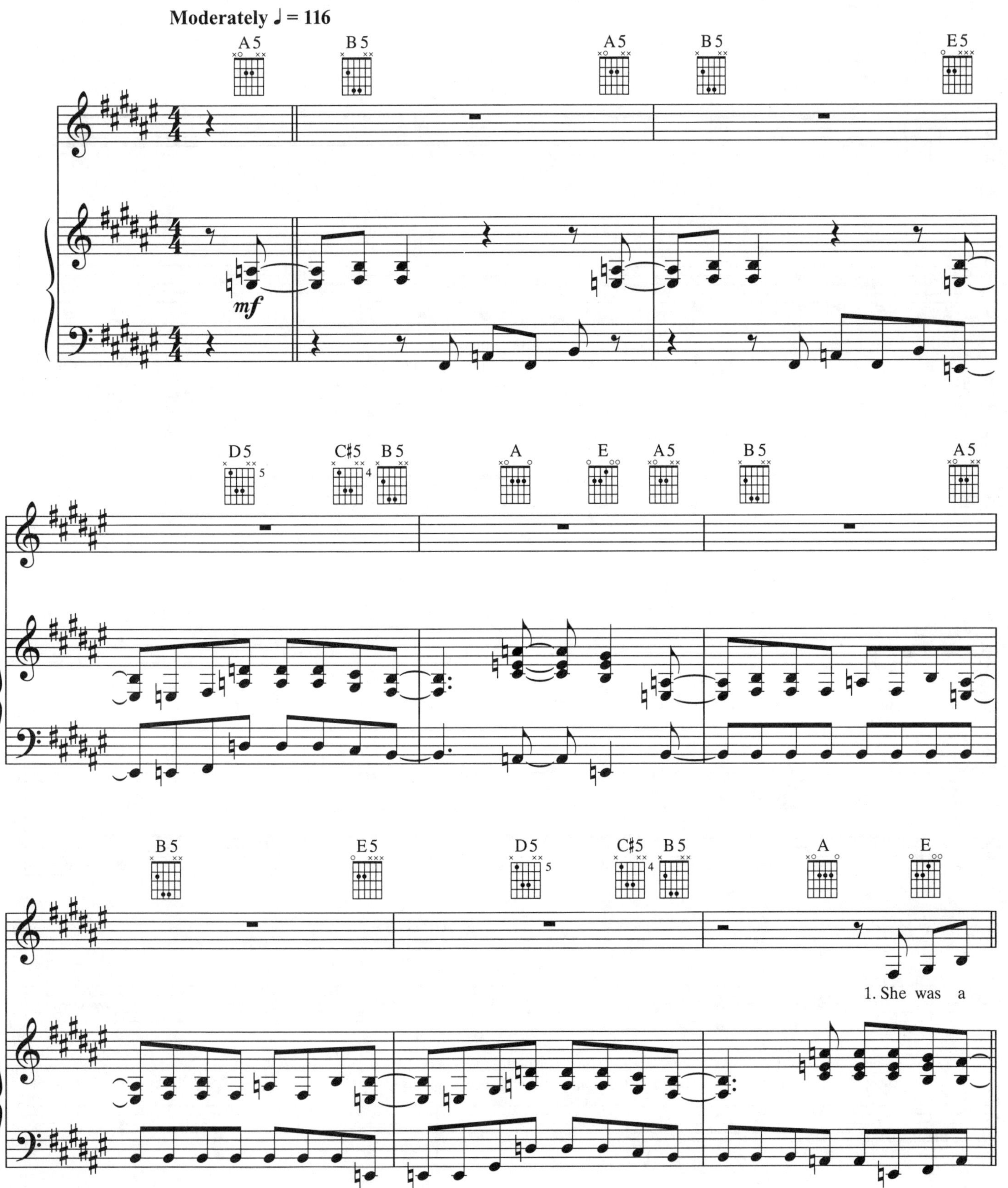

Verse:
B5
wom - an on a mis - sion, tried to drown him and for - get him, so I
next thing I re - call, she had him back a - gainst the wall,
F♯m
B5
set her up a - gain to wash him down. She had
chewed him like a bull - dog on a bone. She was
just a - bout suc - ceed - ed, when that low - down, no good, cheat - in'
put - ting him in his place, and I mean right up in his face,
F♯m
B5
good - for - noth - in' came strut - ting through the crowd. Oh, he was
drag - gin' him down the list of done - me - wrongs. But it was

G♯m
lay - in' it on so thick, he nev - er missed a lick, pro -
just a - bout now that the crowd gath - ered 'round. They'd come to
E7
fess - ing his nev - er - end - ing love.
watch him pay for his ev - 'ry sin.
Oh, but I
She called him
B5
F♯5
nev - er will for - get, when she stood up and said, "So,
ev - 'ry-thing un-der the sun. And when we thought that she was done, she
E
I guess you think we're just gon - na kiss and make up, don't - cha?" And
reared back, and she let him have it a - gain, man. She said,

Chorus:
A
B5
E/B
that's when she said,
she said,
"Why don't you kiss,
kiss
B5
E7
B5
E/B
this.
And I don't mean on my ros - y red lips.
Me and
B5
E7
you,
we're through,
and there's on - ly one thing left for you to
B5
F♯5
E
A/E
do.
You just come on o-ver here one last time, puck-er up and close your eyes

1.
E
N.C.
and kiss this good - bye."
E5
D5
C♯5
B5
A
E
2. Well, the
2.
D.S. 𝄋
3.
and kiss,
and kiss this good -
bye. Kiss this good - bye."

LAREDO

Words and Music by
CHRIS CAGLE

* *Original recording in D♭ major.*

C
B♭
F
B♭
'Cause now you know she's leav-ing me, and I need your help to make her see.
C
B♭
F
So, turn on your charm and let it shine.
G
Am7
'Cause you've al-ways been the one who could make her stay a-round.
F
G
A
So, when she gets to the cit-y lim-it sign, don't let me down.

Chorus:
D
A
G
A
Oh, La - re - do, don't let her go.
Just take her by the heart and let the wheels turn slow.
Oh, La - re - do, you're my on - ly hope.
1.
Em7
So, get her back to the day we met, 'cause that's as far as she needs to get.

Bm7
A
G
A
But, oh no, please, don't let her go, oh, La - re -
C
B♭
F
B♭
do.
C
B♭
F
B♭
2.
Em7
A
Em7
A
So, get her back to the day we met, 'cause that's as far as she needs to get.

Bm7
A
G
A
Oh, but please, don't let her go, oh, La - re -
C
B♭
F
B♭
do.
Dm7
G
A
D.S.𝄋
3.
Em7
A
Em7
A
So, get her back to the day we met, 'cause that's as far as she needs to get.

Bm7 A G A

But, oh no, please, don't let her go, oh, La - re -

D A G A

do. *(Lead vocal ad lib.)*

(Bkgrd.) Oh, La - re - do.

D A G A *Repeat ad lib. and fade*

Oh, La - re - do.

Verse 2:
Make her think about the moonlit walks
And the long, long talks by the water's edge,
With her feet hangin' off the Cane Creek Bridge.
And bring to mind the first kiss we shared
At the old town square when she drives down there,
'Cause that's a day she said she could never forget.
Keep the nights by the candlelight as an ace in the hole,
'Cause those are nights of passion that I know will bring her home.
(To Chorus:)

LET ME LET GO

Words and Music by
DENNIS MORGAN and
STEVE DIAMOND

C
Dsus
C(9)
go - in' through my mind.
In fact, not a sin -

Bm7
C
G
- gle min - ute
pass - es with - out you in it.

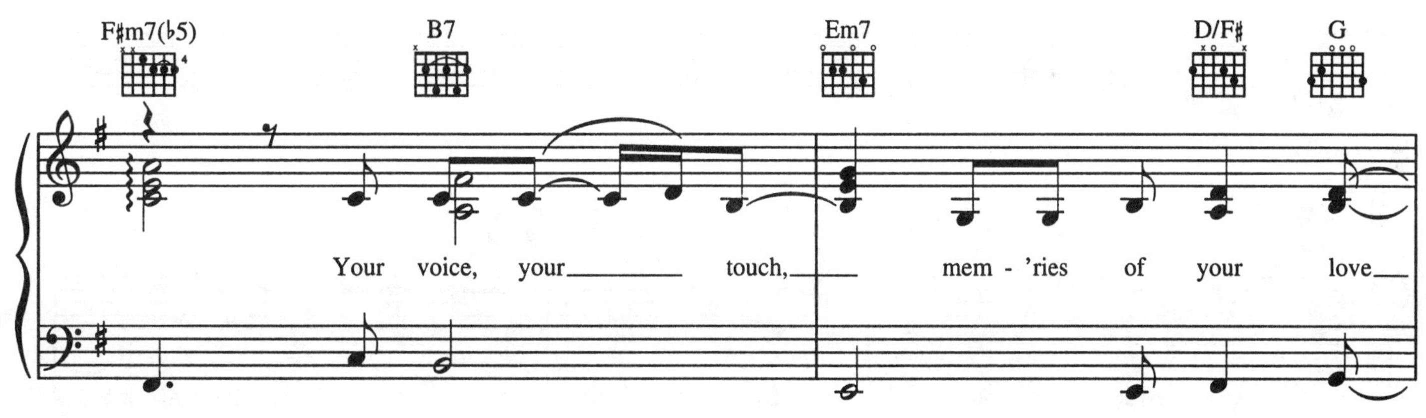
F♯m7(♭5)
B7
Em7
D/F♯
G
Your voice, your touch, mem - 'ries of your love

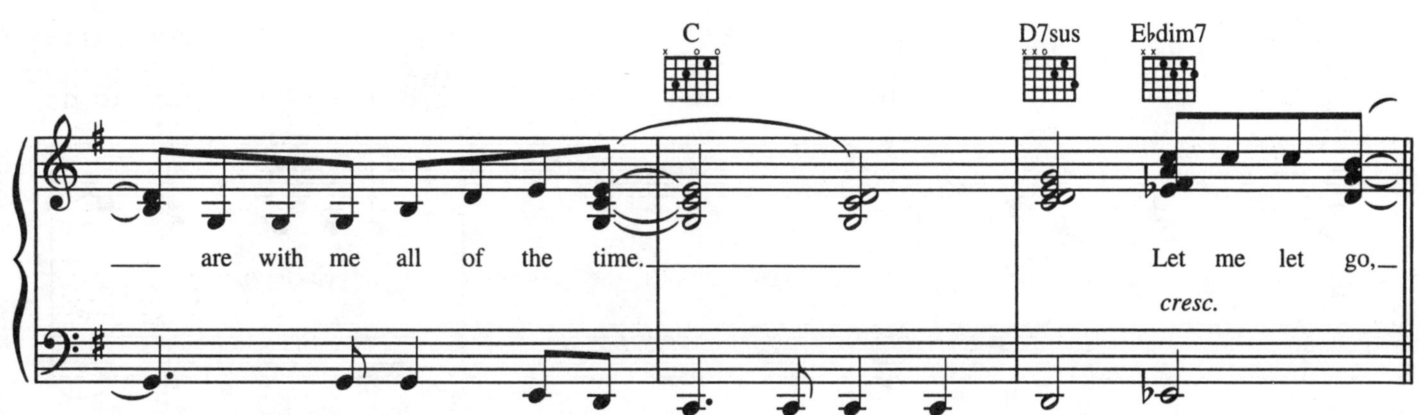
C
D7sus
E♭dim7
are with me all of the time.
Let me let go,
cresc.

Chorus:
Em7
Bm7
Am7
E♭dim7
Em7
D
ba - by.
Let me let go.
mf
C
Am7/D
G
B7sus
B7
Em7
Dm7
If this is for the best, why are you still in my heart, are you still in my
C
Cm
G
Cm/G
soul?
Let me let go.
dim.
Verse 2:
G
Bm7
C
2. I talked to you the oth - er day.
Looks like you made
mp
G
F♯m7(♭5)
B7
Em7
D/F♯
G
your es - cape.
You put us be - hind; no mat - ter how I try,

C
D7sus
E♭dim7
I can't do the same.
Let me let go,
cresc.
Chorus:
Em7
Bm7
Am7
E♭dim7
Em7
D
ba - by.
Let me let go.
mf
C
Am7/D
G
B7sus
B7
Em7
Dm7
It just is - n't right;
I've been two thou-sand miles
down a dead-end road.
C
Am7/D
E♭dim7
Em7
Bm7
Let me let go,
dar - lin', won't
Am7
E♭dim7
Em7
D
C
Am7/D
you? I just got - ta know,
yeah.
If this is for the best,

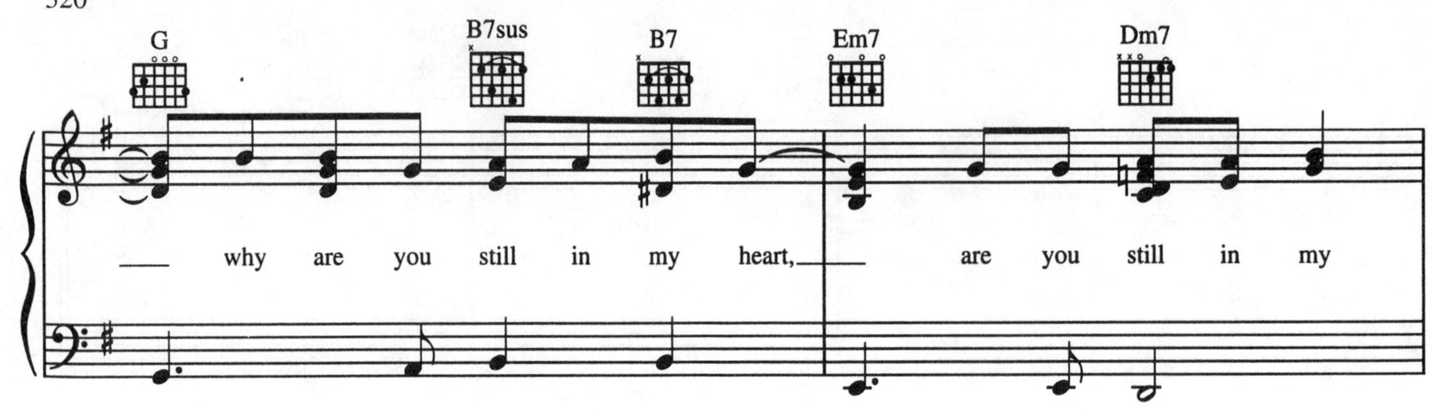
G
B7sus
B7
Em7
Dm7
why are you still in my heart,
are you still in my

To Coda
C
Cm
G
soul?
Let me let go.

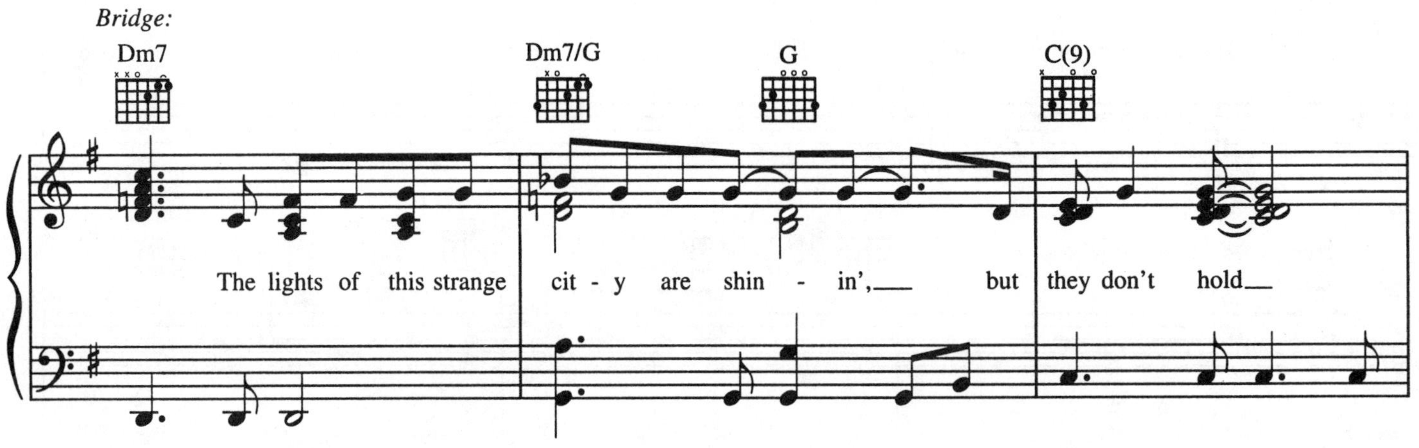
Bridge:
Dm7
Dm7/G
G
C(9)
The lights of this strange city are shinin', but they don't hold

Cm
Bm7
Bm7/E
Em7
no fas - ci - na - tion for me. I try to find the bright side, ba - by, but

Am7
G/B
C
ev - 'ry - where I look, ev - 'ry - where I turn, you're all I see.
Am7/D
E♭dim7
D.S. 𝄋 al Coda
Let me, let me let go,
Coda
G
Cm/G
Let me let go.
G
Cm/G
G(9)
Let me let go.
poco rit.

LET'S MAKE SURE WE KISS GOODBYE

Words and Music by
VINCE GILL

D
G
A
D/A
A
E♭
A♭
B♭
E♭/B♭
B♭
Hold me like we'll never make sweet love again.
G
Asus
A
D
A♭
B♭sus
B♭
E♭
Please make me feel like a man. Well, let's
cresc.
Chorus:
Gmaj7
A
Gmaj7
A
A♭maj7
B♭
A♭maj7
B♭
send up a prayer for this love that we share, 'cause it could
f
Gmaj7
A
Bm7
D/A
Gmaj7
A
A♭maj7
B♭
Cm7
E♭/B♭
A♭maj7
B♭
change in the blink of an eye. No, you just never know how to -

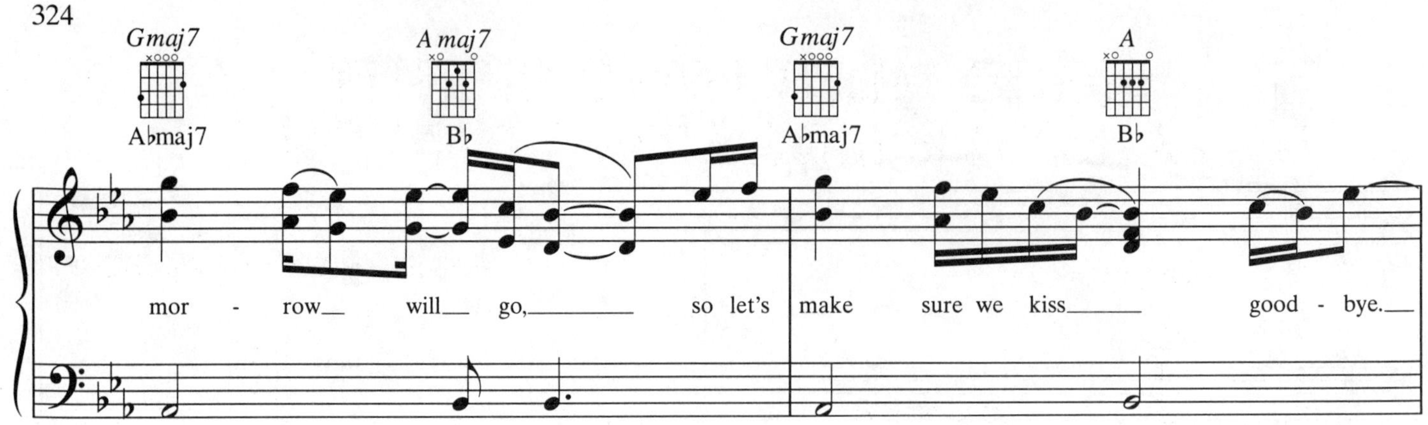

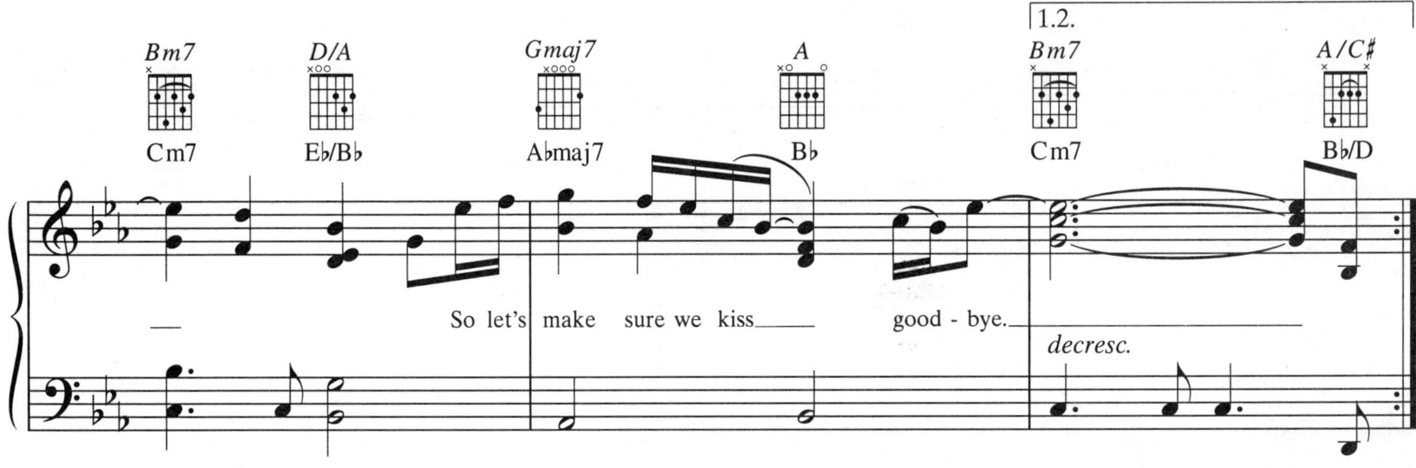

Verse 2:
Look at me just like the day we fell in love
And found the missing pieces to our soul.
You and me have always been just like the birds:
Wherever you are feels like home.
(To Chorus:)

Verse 3:
(Instrumental solo ad lib.)
(To Chorus:)

(GOD MUST HAVE SPENT) A LITTLE MORE TIME ON YOU

Words and Music by
CARL STURKEN and EVAN ROGERS

F
Dm7
E♭
life was com - plete.
I thought it was whole.
Why do I feel like I'm los -
B♭
E♭
B♭
ing con - trol?
1.3. Nev - er thought that love could feel like this.
And you
E♭
B♭
E♭
changed my world with just one kiss.
How can it be that right
D
E♭
Fsus
F
here with me there's an an - gel?
It's a mir - a - cle.
Your
cresc.

Chorus:
B♭
E♭
F
Gm7
love is like a riv - er, peace - ful and deep. Your
mf
B♭
E♭
F
B♭
soul is like a se - cret that I could nev - er keep.
B♭
E♭
F
Gm7
When I look in - to your eyes I know that it's true,
A♭
Gm7
B♭/D
F
To Coda
1.
B♭
E♭
God must have spent a lit - tle more time on you.

F
Gm7
B♭
E♭
2.
On you, on you, on you,
you.
you.
3. Nev - er
D.S. % al Coda

Verse 2:
In all of creation,
All things great and small,
You are the one that surpasses them all.
More precious than
Any diamond or pearl;
They broke the mold
When you came in this world.
And I'm trying hard to figure it out,
Just how I ever did without
The warmth of your smile.
The heart of a child
That's deep inside,
Leaves me purified.
(To Chorus:)

THE LOVE SONG

Words and Music by
JEFFREY BATES, CASEY BEATHARD
and KENNY BEARD

Am7
B♭m7
C
D♭
D
E♭
scared, had a night - mare, Ma - ma was there for me to hold.
G
A♭
Bm7
Cm7
C
D♭
G/B
A♭/C
Dad - dy, he was dif - f'rent, he nev - er said it much. But I
Am7
B♭m7
C
D♭
D
E♭
heard him loud and clear when he brought home that ball and glove.
Em
Fm
Em/D
Fm/E♭
C(9)
D♭(9)
D
E♭
Then it took on a brand new mean - ing.

Em
Em/D
C(9)
G/B
Fm
Fm/E♭
D♭(9)
A♭/C
I was-n't just a boy no more, when she moved in next
Chorus:
B♭6
D
G
G/F♯
C♭6
E♭
A♭
A♭/G
door.
1. Where you from? What's your name? Wan-na go to my
2. See additional lyrics
Em7
C
D
G
G/F♯
Fm7
D♭
E♭
A♭
A♭/G
game? Got the keys to my dad's old truck.
Turned the ra-di-o on, still re-mem-ber the
1.
Em7
D
C(9)
G/D
Fm7
E♭
D♭(9)
A♭/E♭
song. We held hands and there it was: love.

G
Ab
G/F#
Ab/G
Em7
Fm7
C(9)
Db(9)
D
Eb
2.
C(9)
Db(9)
G/D
Ab/Eb
G
Ab
G/F#
Ab/G
was
love.
(Instrumental solo...
Em7
Fm7
C
Db
D
Eb
G
Ab
G/F#
Ab/G
Em7
Fm7
C
Db
D
Eb
Em
Fm
Em/D
Fm/Eb
...end solo)
Then it took on a brand new

C(9)
D
Em
Em/D
D♭(9)
E♭
Fm
Fm/E♭
mean - ing
when the doc - tor said it's
C(9)
G/B
B♭6
D
D♭(9)
A♭/C
C♭6
E♭
time to watch your mir - a - cle ar - rive.
Chorus:
A
A/G#
F#m7
A/E
B♭
B♭/A
Gm7
B♭/F
Thank the Lord. Cut the cord. Take her home. Help her grow, and com - plete the cir - cle
D
A/E
E♭
B♭/F
of
love.

A A/G# F#m7 D E

B♭ B♭/A Gm7 E♭ F

Love.

Repeat ad lib. and fade

A A/G# F#m7 D E

B♭ B♭/A Gm7 E♭ F

That's the cir - cle of love.

Verse 2:
Pages kept on turnin', there I was with someone else.
First time in my lifetime, I wasn't livin' for myself.
I knew I wasn't fallin' anywhere I'd fell before.
This place was different, it was deeper, it was more.
Then it took on a brand new meaning,
Yeah, it was strong and it was true.
Knew what I had to do.

Chorus 2:
Found a ring, hit my knees,
Couldn't talk, couldn't breathe.
My heart had me all choked up.
Said, "I do," as we cried.
Wedding bells, waved goodbye.
The whole church knew it was love.
(To Inst.)

LUCKENBACH, TEXAS

(Back to the Basics of Love)

Words and Music by
BOBBY EMMONS and
CHIPS MOMAN

D7
G
(in tempo)
G
back to the ba - sics of love.
Let's go to Luck - en - bach, Tex - as, with
C
Way - lon and Wil - lie and the boys.
This suc -
D7
G
ces - ful life we're liv - in' got us feud - in' like the Hat - fields and Mc - Coys.
G
Be - tween Hank Wil - liam's pain songs and New - ber - ry's train songs and

C
Am
D7
Am
"Blue Eyes Cry - in' in the Rain," out in Luck - en - bach, Tex - as,
D7
G
ain't no - bod - y feel - in' no pain.
Am
D7
G
So, ba - by, let's sell your dia - mond ring,
Am
D7
G
buy some boots and fad - ed jeans and go a - way.
This

Am
D7
G
coat and tie is cho - kin' me; In your high so - ci - e - ty you cry all day.
G7
We've been so bus - y keep - in' up with the Jones'
C
A
C
G
four car ga - rage, and we're still build - in' on, may - be it's time we got
D7
G
D.S. and Fade
back to the ba - sics of love. Let's go to

MAN! I FEEL LIKE A WOMAN!

Words and Music by
SHANIA TWAIN and R.J. LANGE

ly raise my voice. Yeah, I wan - na scream and shout.
D5
E♭5
A5
B♭5
N.C.
Ah! 2. No
Verses 2 & 3:
A5
B♭5
in - hi - bi - tions, make no con - di - tions. Get
3. See additional lyrics
D5
E♭5
A5
B♭5
a lit - tle out - ta line. I
ain't gon - na act po - lit - i - c'lly cor - rect. I on -

D5
A5
E♭5
B♭5
ly wan - na have a good time.
G
A♭
The best thing a - bout be - ing a wom - an
A
B♭
is the pre - rog - a - tive to have a lit - tle fun and...
Chorus:
E
F
Oh, oh, oh, go to - tal - ly cra - zy,
for - get I'm a la - dy,
men's shirts, short

A
B♭
skirts, oh, oh, oh, real-ly go wild, yeah, do - in' it in
E
F
style. Oh, oh, oh, get in the ac - tion, feel the at-trac - tion.
C♯m7
Dm7
Col-or my hair, do what I dare. Oh, oh, oh, I wan-na be free, yeah, to
A
B♭
To Coda
F♯m7
Gm7
1.
N.C.
feel the way I feel. Man! I feel like a
A5
B♭5
wom - an.

D5
E♭5
2.
N.C.
3. The girls_
Man! I feel__ like a
A5
B♭5
D5
E♭5
wom - an.
(Instrumental solo ad lib....
A5
B♭5
G5
A♭5
D5
E♭5
A5
B♭5
D.S. 𝄋 al Coda
...end solo)
Coda
A
B♭
feel._____
(Do the way I
feel._______)
Man! I feel like a
wom - an.

A G
B♭ A♭

1.2. D A 3. G
E♭ B♭ A♭

D A5
E♭ B♭5

I feel like a wom - an.

Verse 3:
The girls need a break.
Tonight we're gonna take
The chance to get out on the town.
We don't need romance.
We only wanna dance.
We're gonna let our hair hang down.
The best thing about being a woman
Is the prerogative to have a little fun and...
(To Chorus:)

MENDOCINO COUNTY LINE

Words and Music by
BERNIE TAUPIN and MATT SERLETIC

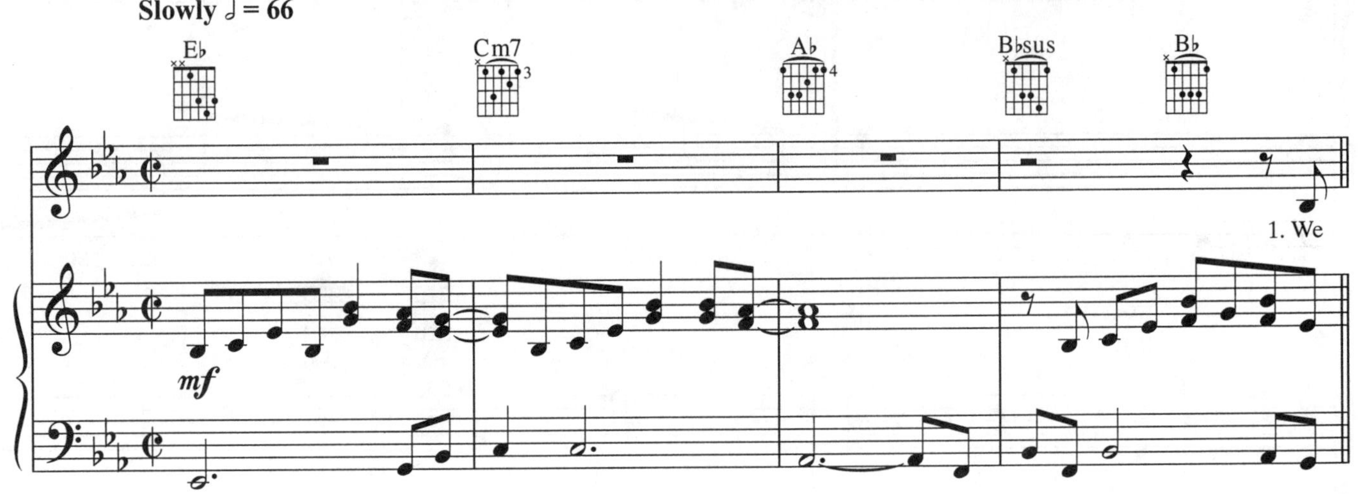

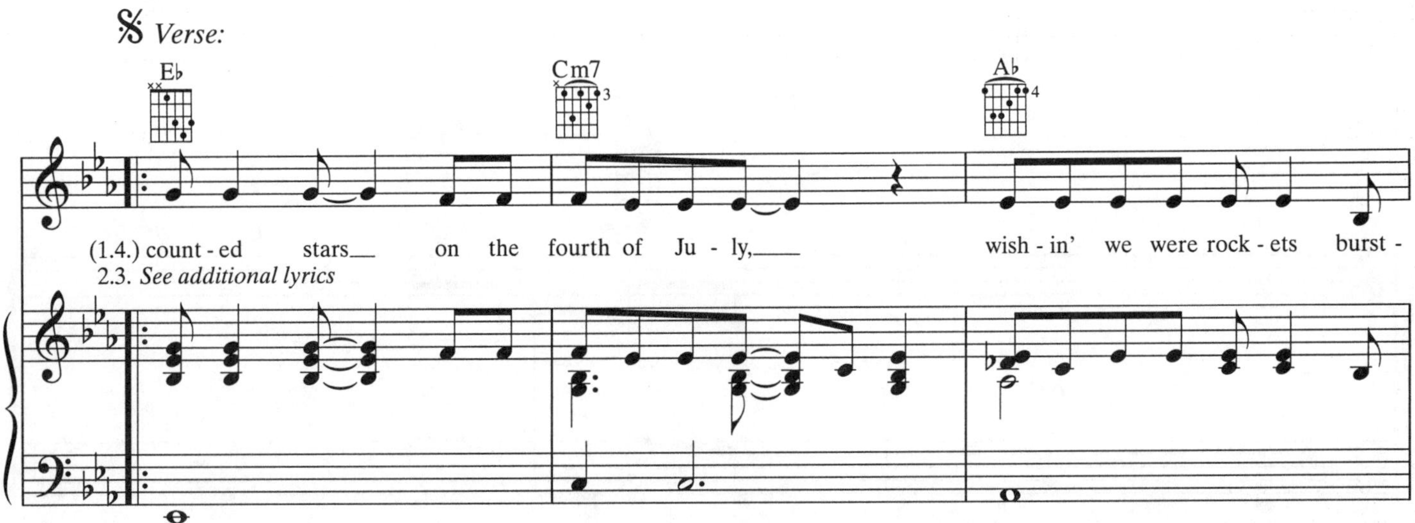

1.
A♭
B♭sus
as the sun sank west of the Men - do - ci - no___ coun - ty line.___
E♭
Cm7
A♭
B♭sus
B♭
2. 3.
A♭
B♭sus
as the sun sinks west of the Men - do - ci - no___ coun - ty
E♭
To Next Strain
4.
Chorus:
A♭2
line.
I have these pic-tures, and

B♭sus
B♭
B♭sus
B♭
I keep these pho - to - graphs___ to re - mind me of a time.___
A♭2
B♭sus
B♭
These pic - tures and___ these___ pho - to - graphs let me know___
B♭sus
B♭
A♭2
Gm
___ I'm___ do - in' fine. I used to make you hap - py___
Fm9
A♭
To Coda
once up - on a time, but the sun sank west of the

1.
B♭sus
E♭
Cm7
A♭
Men - do - ci - no coun - ty line.
D.S. 𝄋
B♭sus
B♭
2.
B♭sus
E♭
3. The Men - do - ci - no coun - ty line.
Bridge:
D♭
I don't talk to you too much these
A♭
days.
D♭
I just thank the Lord

E♭
pic - tures don't fade.
D♭
I spent time with an an - gel
A♭
just pass - ing through.
B♭
Now all that's
Gm
left is this im - age of you.
3

Solo:

A♭ B♭

A♭ B♭

Cm B♭ A♭ *D.S. 𝄋 al Coda*

4. We

𝄌 *Coda*

B♭sus E♭ Cm7

Men - do - ci - no___ coun - ty line.___ But, the

A♭ B♭sus E♭

sun sank west of the Men - do - ci - no coun - ty line.

Cm7 A♭ B♭sus

Men - do - ci - no coun - ty

E♭ Cm7 A♭ B♭sus

Repeat ad lib. and fade

line. Men - do - ci - no coun - ty

Verse 2:
As fierce as Monday mornin', feelin' washed away,
I orchestrated paradise but couldn't make you stay.
You dance with the horses through the sands of time
As the sun sinks west of the Mendocino county line.
(To Chorus:)

Verse 3:
The two of us together felt nothin' but right.
Feelin' near immortal ev'ry Friday night,
Lost in our convictions, lips stained with wine,
As the sun sank west of the Mendocino county line.
(To Chorus:)

MY HEROES HAVE ALWAYS BEEN COWBOYS

Words and Music by
SHARON VAUGHN

F
I learned all the rules of a mod-ern day drift-er, don't you
Pick-in' up hook-ers in-stead of my pen I let the
Bb
F
Bb
hold on to noth-in' too long. Just take what you
words of my youth fade a-way. Old worn out
F
Bb
F/C
C7
need from the la-dies then leave them with the words of a sad coun-try
sad-dles and old worn out mem-'ries with no one and no place to
F
Bb
F
song.
stay.
My he-roes have al-ways been cow-boys,

G7
C7
B♭
and they still are, it seems.
Sad - ly in
F
B♭
F
C7
To Coda
search of and one step in back of them - selves and their slow mov - in'
1. F
2. F
D.S. al Coda
dreams.
dreams.
CODA
B♭
F
B♭
F
dreams.

MY MARIA

Words and Music by
DANIEL J. MOORE and B.W. STEVENSON

Eb
Bb
Ab
3fr
4fr
she takes my blues a - way.
Sweet Ma - ri - a,
my peace of mind.
Gyp - sy la - dy,
the sun-light sure - ly hurts my eyes.
you're a mir - a - cle work for me.
I'm a lone - ly dream - er on a high - way in the skies.
You set my soul free like a ship sail - in' on the sea.
To Coda

Eb
3fr
Bb
Ab
4fr
Ma - ri -
Eb
3fr
Ab
4fr
Bb
Ab
4fr
Eb
3fr
- a, Ma -
Bb
Ab
4fr
Eb
3fr
Ab
4fr
Eb
3fr
ri, Ma - ri - a, I love you.
Bb
Ab
4fr

Eb
Bb
Ab
D.S. al Coda
My Ma-ri -
CODA
Bb
Ab
She is the sun - light when the
N.C.
Eb
Bb
Ab
skies are grey.
Bb
She treats me so
Ab
right. La - dy,
N.C.
Eb
Bb
Ab
take me a - way.

Eb
Bb
Ab
N.C.
3fr
4fr
My Ma - ri -
Eb
Bb
Ab
Eb
Ab
Bb
Ab
Eb
- a, Ma - ri, Ma -
Bb
Ab
Eb
ri - a, I love you.
My Ma - ri -
Ab
Eb
Repeat and Fade

MY ONLY LOVE

Words and Music by
JIMMY FORTUNE

Chorus:
A
Bb
G
Ab
F#m
Gm
mean so much to me. And you're my on - ly
Em
Fm
Dmaj7
Ebmaj7
Bm7
Cm7
G
Ab
love, my on - ly love, and I just thank the Lord a -
A
Bb
Asus
Bbsus
A
Bb
G
Ab
bove for you each day. I can't be - lieve the way I feel,
Em
Fm
Dmaj7
Ebmaj7
Bm
Cm
G
Ab
you're so spe-cial, you're so real. And I know you'll al - ways

Verse 2:
Listen closely to the words I'm sayin',
I know I've never meant them more.
For your love only I've been prayin'.
You and I are what this love is for.

(To Chorus:)

MODERN DAY BONNIE AND CLYDE

Words and Music by
JAMES LeBLANC
and WALT ALDRIDGE

D5
and a pis - tol by my side,
A7
tear - in' down that high - way like a
C
G
D5
mod - ern day Bon - nie and Clyde.
𝄋𝄋 Verse:
D5
1. We met at a truck - stop,
2.3. See additional lyrics

G
D5
Johnson City, Tennessee.
G
I was gassin' up my Firebird,
D5
when I heard her callin' me.
A7
Said "Which way are you headed, boy,

C
G
D5
do you need some com - pan - y?"
1.
2.3.
2. She had me
And it's a
Chorus:
D5
G
long way to Rich - mond, roll - in' north on Nine - ty - five,
Clyde.
(Inst. solo ad lib....
3. See additional lyrics
D5
with a

G
red - head rid - in' shot - gun and a pis - tol by my side,
D
A7
tear - in' down that high - way like a mod - ern day Bon - nie and
1.
C
G
D.S.
2.
C
G
D5

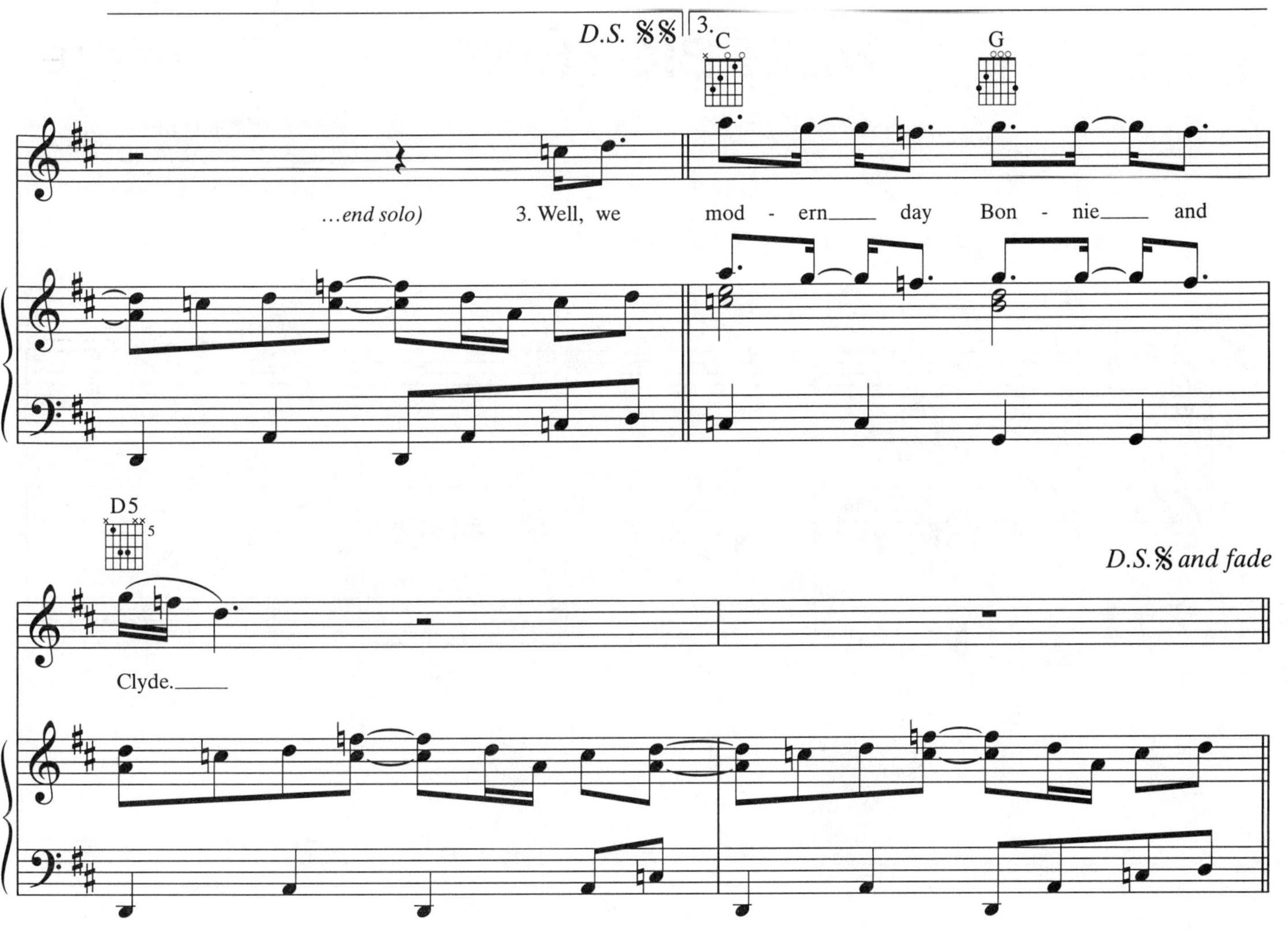

Verse 2:
She had me stoppin' at a quickmart
Before me made it out of town.
Next thing she was runnin' at me
Tellin' me to lay that hammer down.
'Cause there's a man right behind me
Doin' his best to slow me down.
(To Chorus:)

Verse 3:
Well, we pulled up to a motel
In the middle of the night.
We were countin' all the money,
Smokin' stolen Marlboro Lights.
Lord, we never saw 'em comin'
Till they read us both our rights.

Chorus 3:
Well, it's a long way to Richmond
Rollin' north on 95,
With a sheriff right beside me,
A pistol pointed at my side, oh Lord.
Such a disappointing ending
For this modern day Bonnie and Clyde.

NEXT BIG THING

Words and Music by
VINCE GILL, AL ANDERSON
and JOHN HOBBS

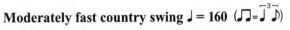

boy and girl. An aw - ful lot of noise on the ra - di - o; it
1.
C
G/B
F
D
real - ly don't rock, it real - ly don't roll.
2. 3.
C
G/B
G
F
2. Well, a Ev - 'ry - bod - y's wait - in' for the next big
D
Chorus:
G
thing. Big ci - gars,

A
D
G
A
D
dia - mond rings,
rid - in' all a - round in a
lim - ou - sine.
When you
A
F
F♯
G
fi - n'ly hit the top, man, you
know what that
means:
D
N.C.
well,
ev - 'ry - bod - y's read - y for the
next big thing.
1.
D
D.S.𝄋
3. For a

2.
D
E7
F6
F♯+
G
(Inst. solo ad lib....
D
...end solo)
I'll get a
Bridge:
G
A
D
G
cow - boy hat,__ some real tight jeans;__ I'll lose a lit - tle weight and get a
A
D
A
F
F♯
bel - ly but - ton__ ring.__ You bet - ter stand back; I'm a lean__ ma - chine,_

G
D
N.C.
yeah.
Well, may-be I'm gon-na be the next big thing.
Chorus:
G
A
D
G
Big ci-gars,
dia-mond rings,
rid-in' all a-round in a
A
D
A
F
F♯
lim-ou-sine.
When you fi-n'ly hit the top, man, you know what that
G
D
N.C.
means:
well, ev-'ry-bod-y's read-y for the

Verse 2:
Well, a kid will come along, make the young girls swoon.
They'll all put his picture in their pink bedrooms.
We'll all hail the brand new king.
Ev'rybody's waitin' for the next big thing.
(To Chorus:)

Verse 3:
For a little while, you can do no wrong.
Well, live it up, son, 'cause it don't last long.
There's always somebody waitin' in the wings,
Thinkin' they're gonna be the next big thing.
(To Chorus:)

99.9% SURE (I'VE NEVER BEEN HERE BEFORE)

Words and Music by
WILLIAM D. AUSTIN and
GREG W. BARNHILL

D G D C D

scen - er - y. And now ev - 'ry - thing is new to me, but it looks just
all be - gan. And I don't e - ven wan - na un - der - stand, 'cause it feels that

G D C D Em

right, yeah, it looks just right. Woah, it's strange, but it's beau -
good, yeah, it feels that good. It's a state that ain't on

C Am Dsus D

ti - ful. Yet, I know where I am, oh.
a map. Yet, I know where I'm at, oh.

Chorus:

G D C D

I've nev - er been here be - fore. I've nev - er been loved like this.

G
D
C
D
Nev-er been tum-bl-in', stum-blin' o-ver the words that get tan-gled in-side of me.
I've nev-er been moved this way. No-bod-y's ev-er made me say,
1.
"I'm nine-ty-nine point nine per-cent sure I've nev-er been here be-fore."

2.
C
D
G
D
C
D
I've nev-er been here be - fore,"
Nine-ty-nine point, nine-ty-nine point, na na na na na na na na na na na na.
G
D
C
D
Nine - ty - nine point, nine - ty - nine point, na na na na na na na na na na na na.
Solo:
Em
C
Am
Dsus
D
Em
C
Am
Dsus
D

Em
C
Am
It's a state___ that's not on a map.
Yet, I know___ where I'm___
Chorus:
Dsus
D
G
D
C
D
___ at,___ oh.
I've nev-er been here be - fore.___
I've nev-er been loved like___ this.
G
D
C
D
Nev-er been tum-bl-in',___ stum-blin' o-ver the words___ that get tan-gled in-side of me.
G
D
C
D
I've nev-er been moved this___ way.___
No-bod-y's ev-er made me___ say,___

G
D
C
D
"Nine - ty - nine point nine per - cent sure I've nev - er been here be - fore."
I've nev - er been here be - fore. I've nev - er been loved like this.
Nev - er been tum - bl - in', stum - blin' o - ver the words that get tan - gled in - side of me.
I've nev - er been moved this way. No - bod - y's ev - er made me say,

G
D
C
D
"Nine - ty - nine point nine per - cent sure I've nev - er been here be - fore."
G
D
C
D
G
D
No, I've nev - er been here be - fore.
C
D
G
D
C
D
I've nev - er been here be - fore. (I've nev - er been moved this way.) I've nev - er been here be - fore.
G
D
C
N.C.
C
G
Nine - ty - nine point nine per - cent sure I've nev - er been here be - fore.

NO MERCY

Words and Music by
DENNIS MORGAN, STEVE DAVIS
and TODD CERNEY

Esus
E
A
D
Fsus
F
B♭
E♭
talk - ing a - bout.
Let's take the hurt and turn it
in - side - out.
Bm
E
Esus
E
Cm
F
Fsus
F
Lay it on me, ba - by, till I can't take an - y - more.
cresc.
Chorus:
A
Esus
F♯m
B♭
Fsus
Gm
f
1.2. No mer - cy, show me no mer - cy.
3. (Inst. solo ad lib....
Love me all night long
D
Bm
A
E
F♯m
D
E♭
Cm
B♭
F
Gm
E♭
and don't hur - ry.
Take it slow and eas - y, no mer - cy to - night.

A E F♯m D A
B♭ F Gm E♭ B♭
(No mer - cy, show me no mer - cy.)
...end solo)
Hold me, ba - by, you know
Esus F♯m D Bm
Fsus Gm E♭ Cm
I've been hurt - in'.
Love this love back to life 'cause it's worth it.
To Coda
1.
A E F♯m D A E F♯m D
B♭ F Gm E♭ B♭ F Gm E♭
Love me strong, ba - by, show me no mer - cy to - night.
A E F♯m D A D A
B♭ F Gm E♭ B♭ E♭ B♭
dim.

2.
Bridge:
A
B♭
E
F
dim.
mf
In the si - lence of the
F♯m
Gm
D
E♭
Bm
Cm
ear - ly hours,
I look at you and I
feel the pow - er.
E
F
F♯m
Gm
We don't need prom - is - es to
make it right,
let's just
D
E♭
E
F
D.S. 𝄋 al Coda
fol - low what we're feel - in' in - side.
cresc.

Verse 2:
Remember when we thought that bein' apart
Would be the best thing for both our hearts?
It's a prison out there when you're livin' alone, for sure.
Now I know how much I really missed you.
No more games, just wanna be with you.
Just give me all your love till you can't give anymore.
(To Chorus:)

NOTHIN' BUT THE TAILLIGHTS

Words and Music by
CLINT BLACK and STEVE WARINER

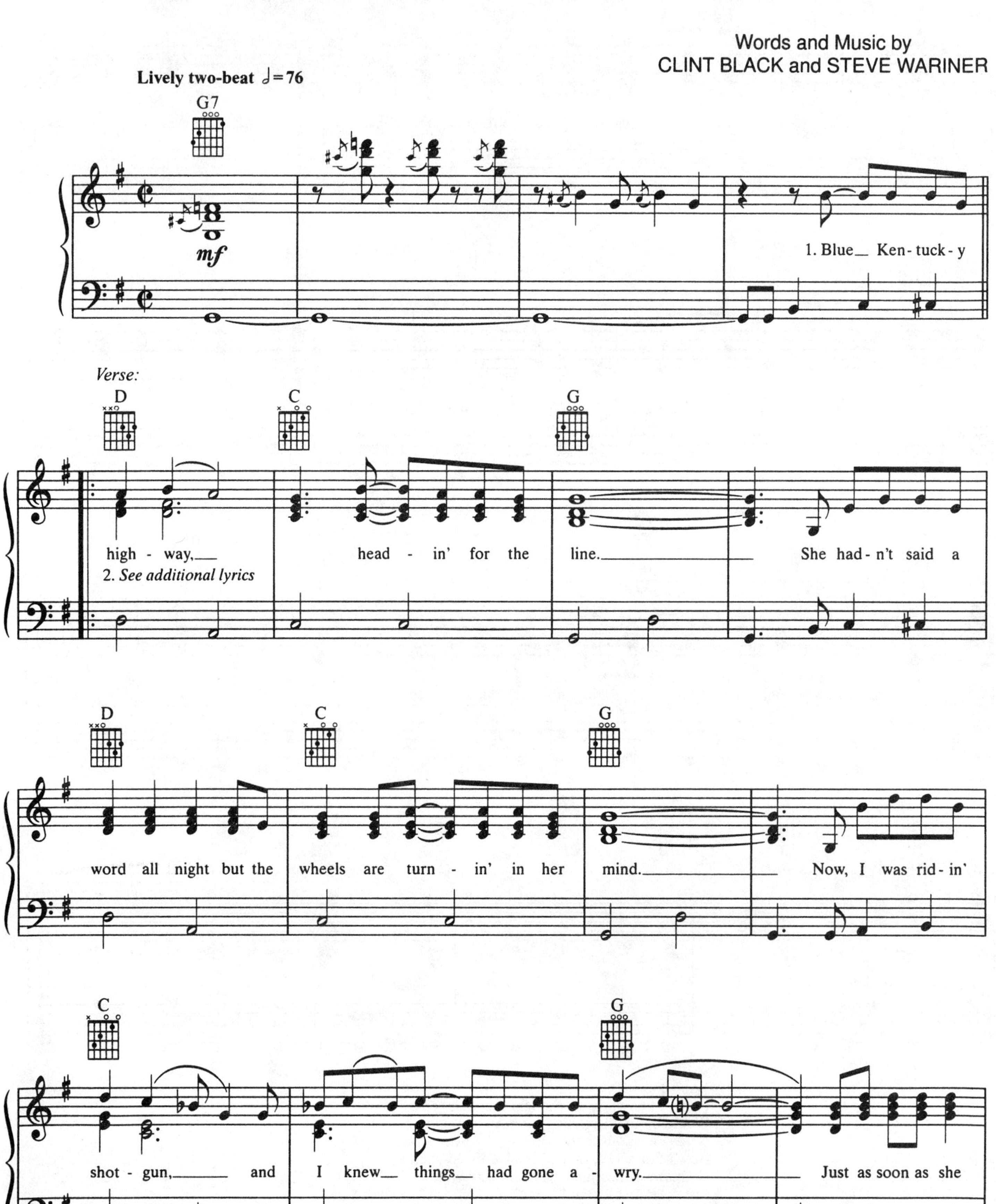

A7
D
dropped me off at the side of the road and she let that grav - el fly.
N.C.
Chorus:
G
Now, I'm walk - in'
Now, I'm talk - in'
in the moon - light, see - in' noth - in' but the
C
G
tail - lights. And that's a pair of tail -
Em
A
D
lights (1.2.) I may nev - er
(3.) she won't ev - er
see a - gain. She hit me with a
G
C
left and right, (1.2.) show - in' me
(3.) and with
noth - in' but the tail - lights.

G
Em
(1.2.) And
(3.) And I know
that's
that's
a - bout as lone - ly as a
A
Am7
high - way's ev - er been,
back here with my thumb
D
To Coda
1.
G7
out in the wind.
2.
G
2. Was it some - thin' that I
Well, I'll
Bridge:
Em
A
Asus
A
bet right now, she's
laugh - in' at how she
brought me to my knees.

Verse 2:
Was it somethin' that I did to her
Or the things I never said?
I wonder if the way we were
Was only in my head?
Now, if I even make it back to town
Before the sun comes up,
I'm gonna hit every parkin' spot around
'Til I find that pickup truck.
(To Chorus:)

ODE TO BILLY JOE

Words and Music by
BOBBIE GENTRY

Ode to Billy Joe - 3 - 1

D7
And at din - ner time we stopped and walked back to the house__ to
A7
eat,___ And Ma - ma hol - lered at the back door, "Y'all re -
Em7
A7
mem - ber to wipe your feet."___ Then she
D7
said, "I got some news this mor - in' from Choc - taw Ridge,___ To - day__

2. Papa said to Mama, as he passed around the black-eyed peas,
"Well, Billy Joe never had a lick o' sense, pass the biscuits please,
There's five more acres in the lower forty I've got to plow,"
And Mama said it was a shame about Billy Joe anyhow.
Seems like nothin' ever comes to no good up on Choctaw Ridge,
And now Billy Joe McAllister's jumped off the Tallahatchee Bridge.

3. Brother said he recollected when he and Tom and Billy Joe,
Put a frog down my back at the Carroll County picture show,
And wasn't I talkin' to him after church last Sunday night,
I'll have another piece of apple pie, you know, it don't seem right.
I saw him at the sawmill yesterday on Choctaw Ridge,
And now you tell me Billy Joe's jumped off the Tallahatchee Bridge.

4. Mama said to me, "Child what's happened to your appetite?
I been cookin' all mornin' and you haven't touched a single bite,
That nice young preacher Brother Taylor dropped by today,
Said he'd be pleased to have dinner on Sunday, Oh, by the way,
He said he saw a girl that looked a lot like you up on Choctaw Ridge
And she an' Billy Joe was throwin' somethin' off the Tallahatchee Bridge."

5. A year has come and gone since we heard the news 'bout Billy Joe,
Brother married Becky Thompson, they bought a store in Tupelo,
There was a virus goin' 'round, Papa caught it and he died last spring,
And now Mama doesn't seem to want to do much of anything.
And me I spend a lot of time pickin' flowers up on Choctaw Ridge,
And drop them into the muddy water off the Tallahatchee Bridge.

OKLAHOMA

Words and Music by
D. VINCENT WILLIAMS and FREDRICK ALLEN

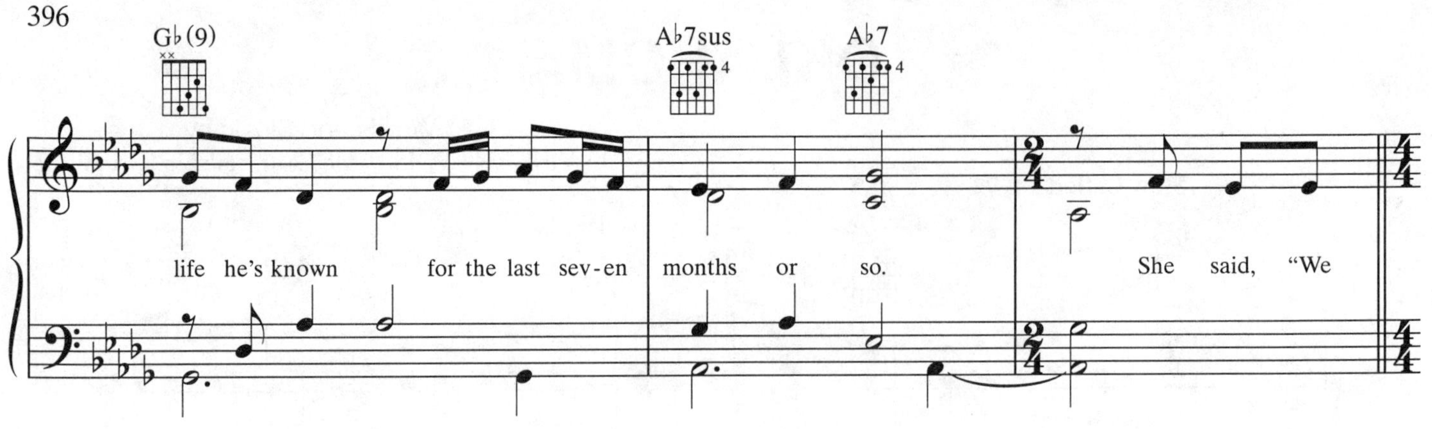
Gb(9)
Ab7sus
Ab7
life he's known for the last sev-en months or so. She said, "We

Chorus:
Gbmaj7
Db/F
found a man who looks like you who cried and said he nev - er knew a -
2.3. See additional lyrics

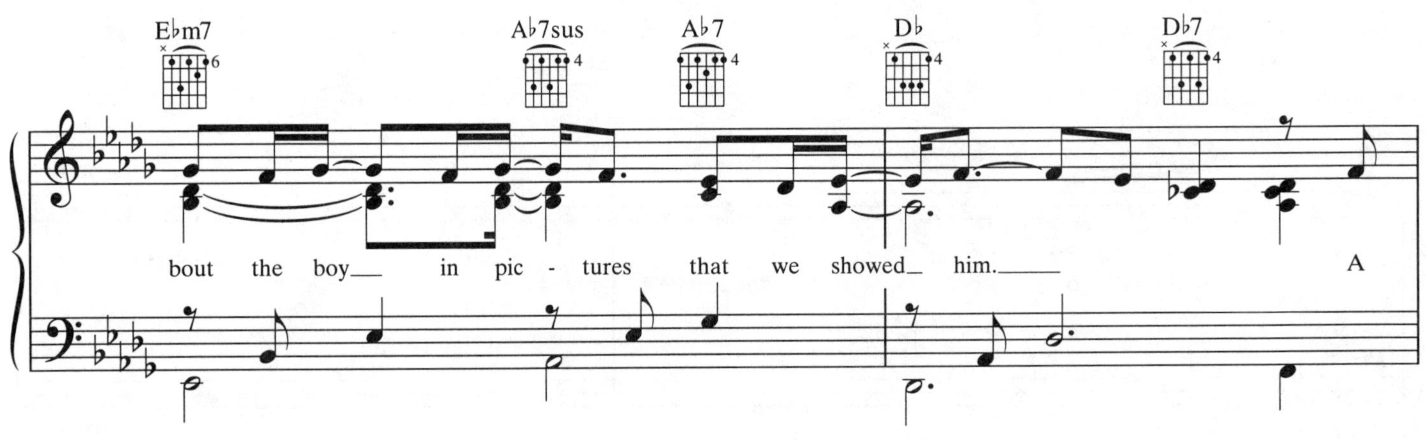
Ebm7
Ab7sus
Ab7
Db
Db7
bout the boy in pic - tures that we showed him. A

Gbmaj7
Fm7
Bbm7
ram - bler in his young - er days, he knew he'd made a few mis - takes, but he

E♭m7
D♭/F
G♭maj7
To Coda
swore he would have been there had he known it. Son, we
1.
E♭m7
D♭/F
G♭
A♭
D♭
A♭
A♭7sus
A♭7
think we found your dad in O - kla - ho - ma."
2.
E♭m7
D♭/F
G♭maj7
said that this was some - thin' that you want - ed. Son, it's time
E♭m7
D♭/F
G♭
A♭
D♭
A♭/C
to meet your dad in O - kla - ho - ma."
cresc.

Bridge:
B♭m7
E♭7sus
E♭7
One last turn, he held his breath till they reached the big house on the left, and
f

G♭
D♭
A♭/C
all at once, the tears came roll - in' in. And

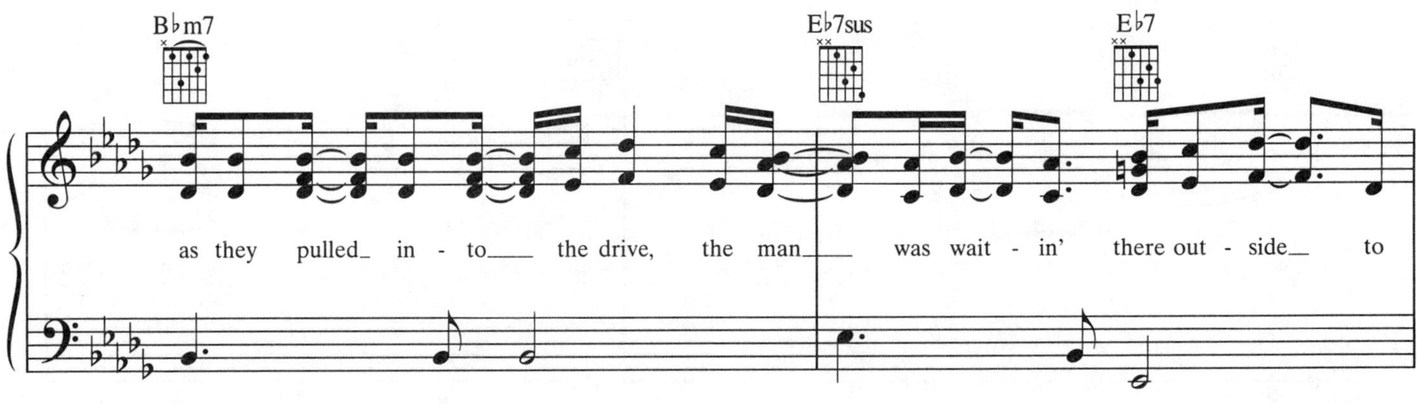
B♭m7
E♭7sus
E♭7
as they pulled in - to the drive, the man was wait - in' there out - side to

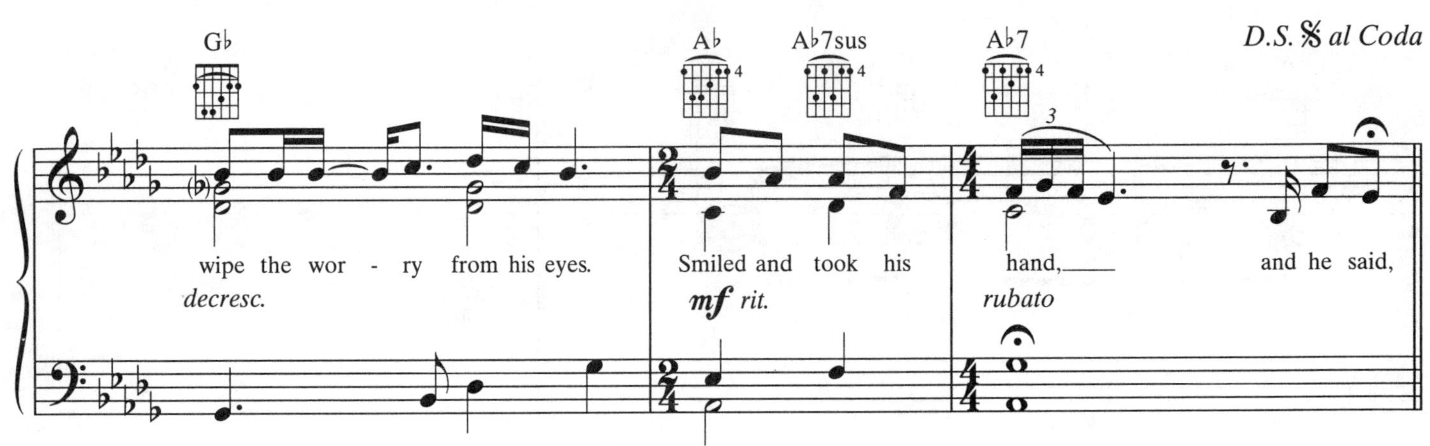
G♭
A♭
A♭7sus
A♭7
D.S. 𝄋 al Coda
wipe the wor - ry from his eyes. Smiled and took his hand, and he said,
decresc.
mf rit.
rubato

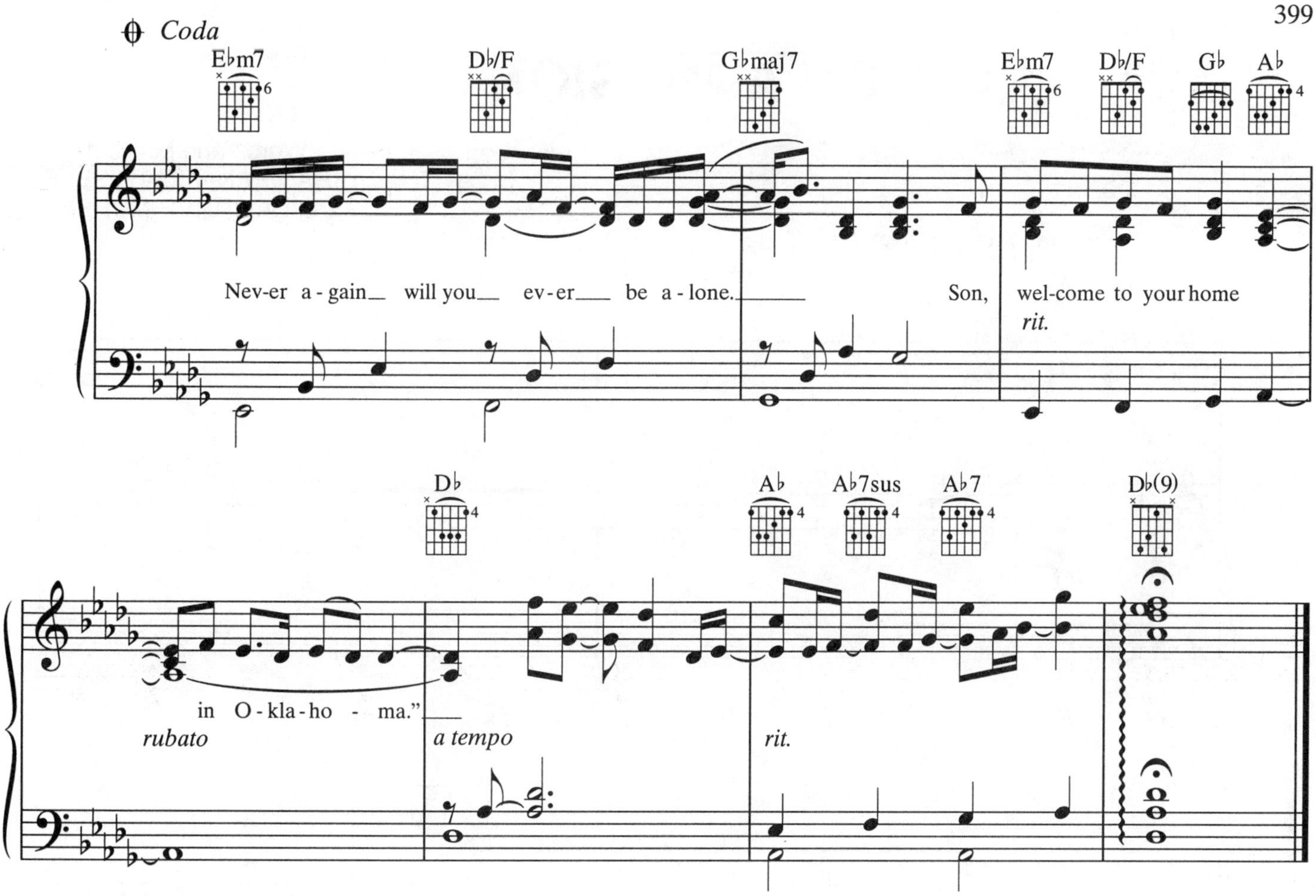

Coda

E♭m7 D♭/F G♭maj7 E♭m7 D♭/F G♭ A♭

Nev-er a-gain will you ev-er be a-lone. Son, wel-come to your home

rit.

D♭ A♭ A♭7sus A♭7 D♭(9)

in O-kla-ho - ma."

rubato *a tempo* *rit.*

Verse 2:
A million thoughts raced through his mind.
What's his name? What's he like?
And will he be anything like the man in his dreams?
She could see the questions in his eyes.
Whispered, "Don't be scared, my child.
I will let you know what we know...

Chorus 2:
About the man we found, he looks like you,
Who cried and said he never knew
About the boy in pictures that we showed him.
A rambler in his younger days, he knew he'd made a few mistakes,
But he swore he would have been there had he known it.
Boy, we said that this was something that you wanted.
Son, it's time to meet your dad in Oklahoma."
(To Bridge:)

Chorus 3:
"I'm the man who looks like you,
Who cried because I never knew
About the boy in pictures that they showed me.
A rambler in my younger days, I knew I made a few mistakes,
But I swear I would have been there had I known it.
Never again will you ever be alone.
Son, welcome to your home in Oklahoma."

ON A MISSION

Words and Music by
IRA DEAN, KIM TRIBBLE
and DAVID LEE MURPHY

Verse:
twelve months is a long, long time for some - one to sud - den-ly change
(2.) See additional lyrics
their mind. He was in and out; now it's just too late.
D♭
A♭/C
E♭
But I won't lose one night
of sleep wor - ry-in' a-bout what was meant to be. His

D♭
A♭/C
B♭
leav - in' is just a rea - son to cel - e - brate.
Chorus:
N.C.
E♭
N.C.
E♭
N.C.
I'm on a mis - sion, I got a cause. I'm gon - na
E♭ N.C.
E♭ N.C.
E♭
A♭
hit ev - 'ry rock - in' lit - tle honk - y - tonk bar. And the way I'm think - in', it
B♭
E♭
B♭
ought - ta be a - gainst the law.
Gon - na see what kind of

E♭
trou - ble I can find. I'm on a head - on col - li - sion with a
A♭
real good time. I'm on a mis - sion, and it's all
B♭
E♭
To Coda
a - bout for - get - tin' to - night.
1.
2.
2. For -
Ain't wor -

Bridge:
G♭
A♭/C
E♭
ried a - bout a five - day, no - sleep, bus - 'ness - week, no - es - cape, work - in' - girl
G♭
A♭/C
blues. Yeah, I'm - a just do - in' what an - y oth - er mod - ern day A -
B♭
N.C.
D.S. 𝄋 al Coda
mer - i - can wom - an might do.
I'm on a
Coda
A♭
Yeah, yeah, I'm on a mis - sion, and it's all

Verse 2:
Forty-hour week and I'm out the door.
Seems like all I'm workin' for
Is that time when I can fin'lly just cut loose.
I got a few good friends and they're waitin' to go.
Just gimme some time to change my clothes.
Till Monday mornin', there ain't nothin' I gotta do.
(To Chorus:)

ONE LAST TIME

Words and Music by
KERRY KURT PHILLIPS
and JASON MATTHEWS

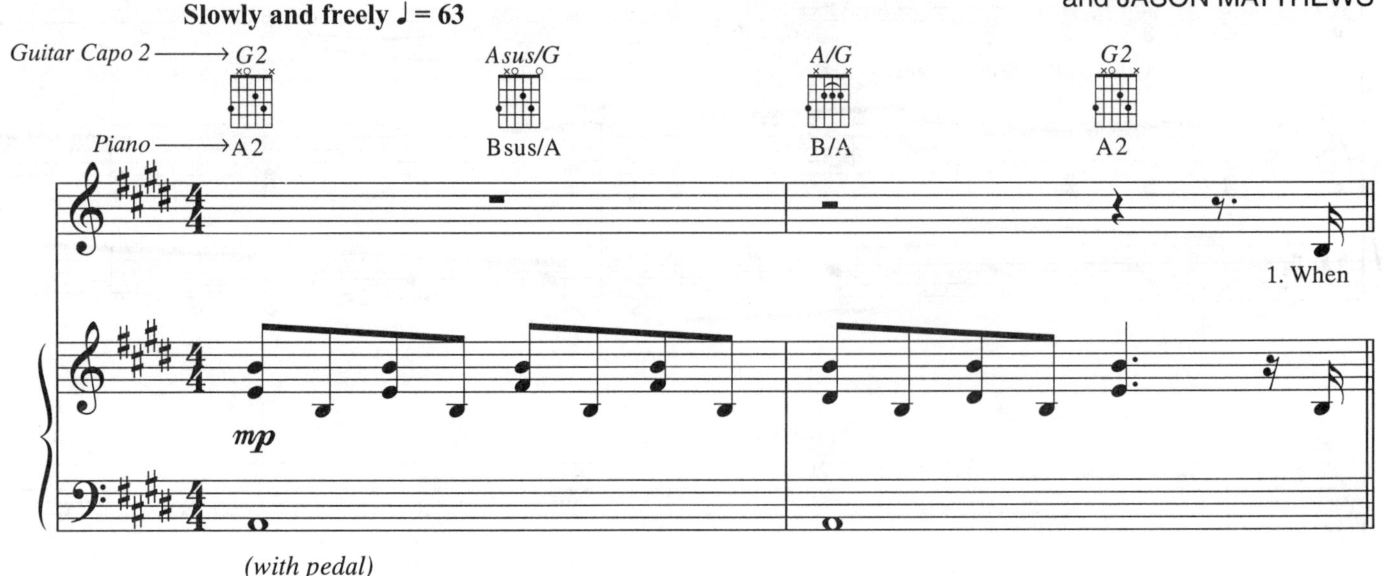

Verse 1:

G2 F♯m7 Bm7
A2 G♯m7 C♯m7

"What am I___ sup - posed_ to do?___ I can't han - dle los - ing you."_ He said, "I

Em11 D(9)/F♯ G(9)
F♯m11 E(9)/G♯ A(9)

just had___ to call___ and say___ good - bye________

Verse 2:

Em9 A D G2 Asus/G
F♯m9 B E A2 Bsus/A

one last time." 2. He said, "There are some_ things in___ this life___ that are

A/G G2 D D2
B/A A2 E E2

out of our___ con - trol,_______ like who we fall___ in love___ with_____ and

A/D
D
G2
Asus/G
B/E
E
A2
Bsus/A
when it's time to go."_ She said, "What a - bout_ the plans_ we had?"_ He said,
F♯m7
Bm7
Em11
D(9)/F♯
G♯m7
C♯m7
F♯m11
E(9)/G♯
"This con - nec - tion's get - ting bad. Now, come on, ba - by, let_ me hear_ you_
G(9)
D/F♯
Em7
A
D
A(9)
E/G♯
F♯m7
B
E
smile_ one last time." She
Bridge:
Gmaj9
D/A
A/C♯
Amaj9
E/B
B/D♯
start - ed to_ a - pol - o - gize_ for all the things that she'd_ done wrong._ She said, "I
mf

Bm7
C♯m7
A
B
D/F♯
E/G♯
G
A
A
B
would - 've loved_ you bet - ter, if on - ly I'd_ known." He
Gmaj9
Amaj9
D/A
E/B
A
B
said, "You were_ the per - fect wife._ Prom-ise me you'll go_ on with your life."_ She
B♭dim7
Cdim7
said, "The boys_ won't un - der - stand." He said, "Tell them Dad - dy loves them and
Bm
C♯m
A
B
be strong."
f

Gmaj7
D
A/C#
Bm7
A
Amaj7
E
B/D#
C#m7
B
G(9)
A(9)
decresc.
Verse 3:
G2
Asus/G
A/G
G2
A2
Bsus/A
B/A
A2
3. He said, "Hon, I've got to go." She said, "Don't you dare hang up. There's so
mp
D
D2
A/D
D
E
E2
B/E
E
man - y things I need to say. I love you so much." It was

G2
A2
Asus/G
Bsus/A
F♯m7
G♯m7
Bm9
C♯m9
al - most like__ she felt__ him leave.__ She cried out, "Can you still__ hear me?" She fell down
Very free
Em11
F♯m11
D(9)/F♯
E(9)/G♯
G(9)
A(9)
on the kit - chen floor when the sig - nal died,__ as the
Em11
F♯m11
D(9)/F♯
E(9)/G♯
G(9)
A(9)
pi - lot tried__ to pull__ out of the dive__
Repeat ad lib. and fade
Em
F♯m
A
B
G2
A2
Asus/G
Bsus/A
A/G
B/A
G2
A2
one last...
a tempo

ONE MORE DAY

Words and Music by
BOBBY TOMBERLIN and
STEVEN DALE JONES

C♯m7
A
E
B/D♯
C♯m7
B
I didn't ask for mon - ey, or a man-sion in Mal - i - bu. I
A
B
E
sim-ply wished for one more day with you. One more day,
Chorus:
Amaj7
B
E
C♯m7
one more time, one more sun -
F♯m7
B
E
E/G♯
set, may - be I'd be sat - is - fied. But, then a - gain,

Amaj7
B
E
B/D♯
C♯m7
B
I know what it would do: leave me
1.
A
B
E
wish - ing still for one more day with you.
C♯m7
A
B
E
One more day.
C♯m7
A
B
2. First

2.
D.S.𝄋
B
E
one more day with you.
One more day,

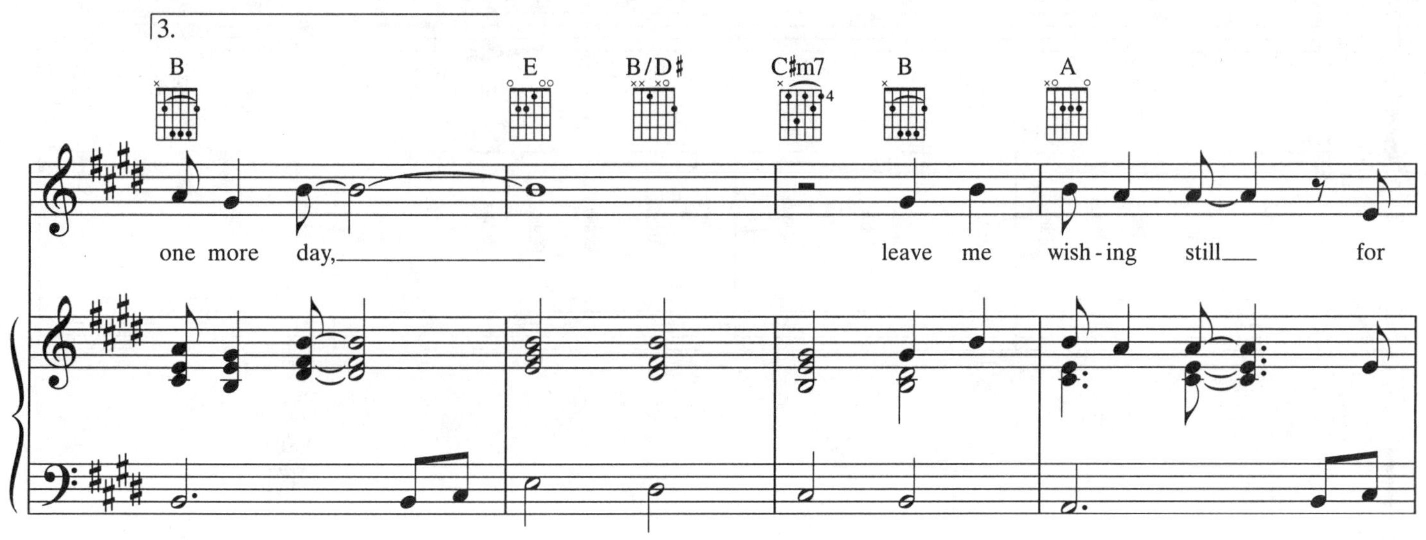
3.
B
E
B/D♯
C♯m7
B
A
one more day,
leave me wish-ing still for

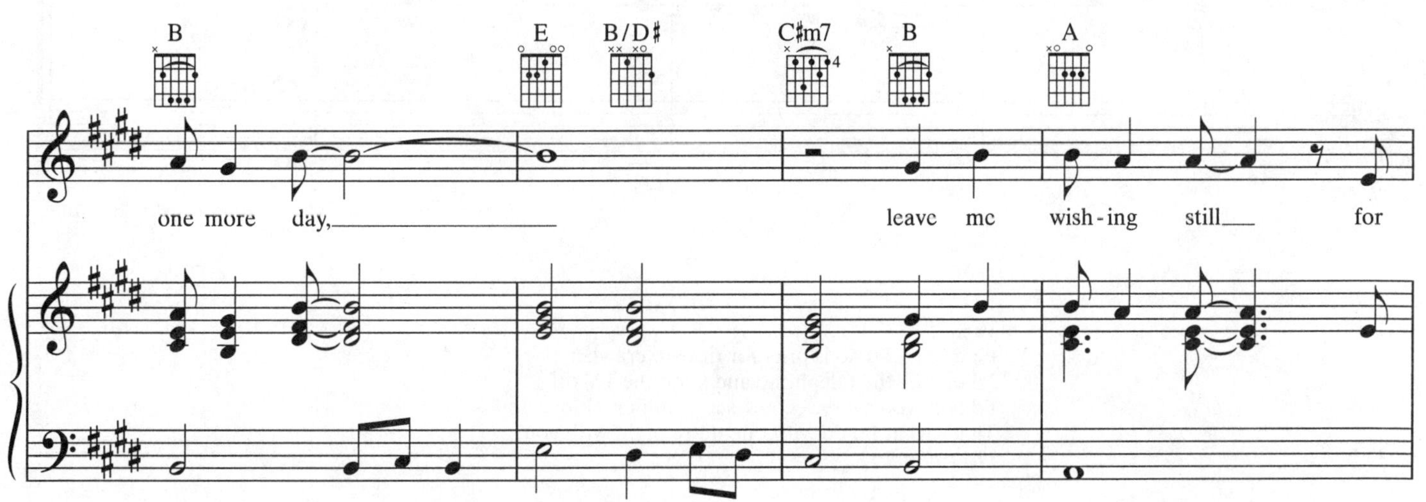
B
E
B/D♯
C♯m7
B
A
one more day,
leave me wish-ing still for

Verse 2:
First thing I'd do is pray for time to crawl.
I'd unplug the telephone and keep the TV off.
I'd hold you every second, say a million "I love you"s.
That's what I'd do with one more night with you.
(To Chorus:)

RHINESTONE COWBOY

Words and Music by
LARRY WEISS

And nice guys get washed a - way like the snow and the rain
C
G
There's been a load of com- pri - mis - in' on the
F
C
F
D (F♯) bass
3
road to my hor - i - zon, but I'm gon-na be where the lights are shin-in' on
3
Dm7 (G bass)
Chorus:
C
F
C
me; Like a Rhine-stone Cow- boy rid - ing out on a horse in a

2. Well, I really don't mind the rain
And a smile can hide the pain;
But you're down when you're riding a train
That's taking the long way . . .
But I dream of the things I'll do
With a subway token and a dollar
Tucked inside my shoe . . .
There's been a load of compromisin'
On the road to my horizon;
But I'm gonna be where the lights are shinin' on me . . .
(Like a) . . .(to Chorus and fade)

PANCHO AND LEFTY

Words and Music by
TOWNES VAN ZANDT

A
G
was gon- na keep you free and clean;
and now you wear your skin
D
A
like iron,
and your breath as hard as ker - o - sene.
G
D
Weren't you ma-ma's on - ly boy?
But her fav - 'rite one it seemed.
G
Bm
G
D
A
She be-gan to cry when you said good-bye,

G
Bm
and sank in - to your dream.
1.
G
A
2.3.4.
A
G
All the Fed - er - al -
(last time) A few gray
D
G
- es say
they could have had him an - y day.
Bm
G
D
A
They on - ly let him slip a - way,
We on - ly let him go so long,

Verse 2:
Pancho was a bandit boy,
His horse was fast as polished steel.
He wore his gun outside his pants,
For all the honest world to feel.
Well, Pancho met his match, you know,
On the deserts down in Mexico.
Nobody heard his dying word,
Ah, but that's the way it goes.

Verse 3:
Lefty, he can't sing the blues,
All night long like he used to.
The dust that Pancho bit down south,
Ended up in Lefty's mouth.
The day they laid poor Pancho low,
Lefty split for Ohio.
Where he got the bread to go,
There ain't nobody know.

Verse 4:
The poets tell how Pancho felt,
And Lefty's living in a cheap hotel;
The desert's quiet, and Cleveland's cold,
And so the story ends we're told.
Pancho needs your prayers, it's true,
And save a few for Lefty, too.
He only did what he had to do,
And now, he's growing old.

PLAYBOYS OF THE SOUTHWESTERN WORLD

Words and Music by
NEAL COTY and RANDY VanWARMER

G C2

(1.) The on - ly two bad ap - ples on our___ fam - 'ly tree,__ kind of
2.3. *See additional lyrics*

G D G

rip - ened and rot - ted in our pu - ber - ty,___ two kin - dred spir - its

C2 D5

bound by___ des - ti - ny. Well, now,

Em D C

I was smart__ but I lacked am - bi - tion. John - ny was wild__ with no__

G
C
G/B
Am7
in - hi - bi - tion. Was a - bout like mix - ing fire and gas - o - line.
D
And he'd say,
Chorus:
"Hey,
Ro - me - o, let's go down to Mex - i - co, chase
se - ño - ri - tas, drink our - selves sil - ly, show them Mex - i - can girls a cou - ple

D G C

real hill - bill - ies. Got - ta pock-et-ful of cash__ and that old____ Ford truck,_ a fuz -

G D C G/B

zy cat hang - in' from the mir - ror for luck."_ Said, "Don't you know_ all those

Am7 G D *To Coda* 𝄌

lit - tle brown - eyed girls____ want play - boys of____ the south -

G C G

west - ern world."_ La la____ la la la la la la la la la la.___

D
G
C
La la la la la la la la la la la
G
1.
D
2.
D
la la la la la.
And I'd say
Bridge:
Am
Em
C
we had a lit - tle change in plans,
like when Paul Mc - Cart - ney got
G
C
G/B
Am7
G
bust - ed in Ja - pan.
And I said we got way - laid when we set foot on Mex - i - can
rit.

Verse 2:
Long around our eighteenth year,
We found two airplane tickets the hell out of here.
Got scholarships to some small town school in Texas.
We learned to drink sangrias 'til the dawn's early light,
Eat eggs rancheros and throw up all night,
And tell those daddy's girls we were majoring in a rodeo.
Ah, but my favorite memory at school that fall,
Was the night John Roy came runnin' down the hall,
Wearin' nothin but cowboy boots and a big sombrero.
And he was yellin'...
(To Chorus:)

Verse 3:
You see, the border guard with the fu manchu mustache
Kind of stumbled on John's pocket full of American cash.
He said, "Doin' a little funny business in Mexico, amigo?"
But all I could think about was savin' my own tail
When he mentioned ten years in a Mexican jail.
So, I pointed to John Roy and said,
"It's all his. Now please, let me go."
I mean, it was your idea, genius, I was just layin' there in bed
When you said...
(To Chorus:)

PRAYIN' FOR DAYLIGHT

Words and Music by
STEVE BOGARD and RICK GILES

Chorus:

Am D D/F♯ G C

Pray-in' for day - light, wait-ing for that morn-ing sun,

D/F♯ G C D/F♯ G

so I can act like my whole life ain't go-ing wrong. Ba-by, come back to me; I

To Coda 𝄌 1.

C G/B C Dsus D

swear I'll make it right. Don't make me wait an-oth - er lone - ly night pray-in' for day -

G C Am D 2. Dsus D

light. night pray-in' for day -

G C Am D G C

light, Pray-in' for day - light.

Bridge:
Am
D
Bm7
Em7
Pray - in' for day - light, hop - in' that I did - n't wait too long,
Bm7
C
D
D.S. 𝄋 al Coda
N.C.
that this is just the dark be - fore the dawn.
⊕ Coda
Dsus
D
D/F♯
G
C
night. Pray - in' for day - light, wait - ing for that morn - ing sun,
D/F♯
G
C
D/F♯
G
so I can act like my whole life ain't go - ing wrong. Ba - by, come back to me; I
C
G/B
C
Dsus
D
swear I'll make it right. Don't make me wait an - oth - er lone - ly night pray - in' for day -

Verse 2:
I made a bad miscalculation, betting you would never leave.
'Cause if you're getting on with your new life, then where does that leave me?
(To Chorus:)

Verse 3:
Deep in my heart I know that you love me as much as I love you.
And that you must be lying somewhere looking up to heaven too.
(To Chorus:)

RAINING ON SUNDAY

Words and Music by
DARRELL BROWN and RADNEY FOSTER

Slowly ♩ = 66

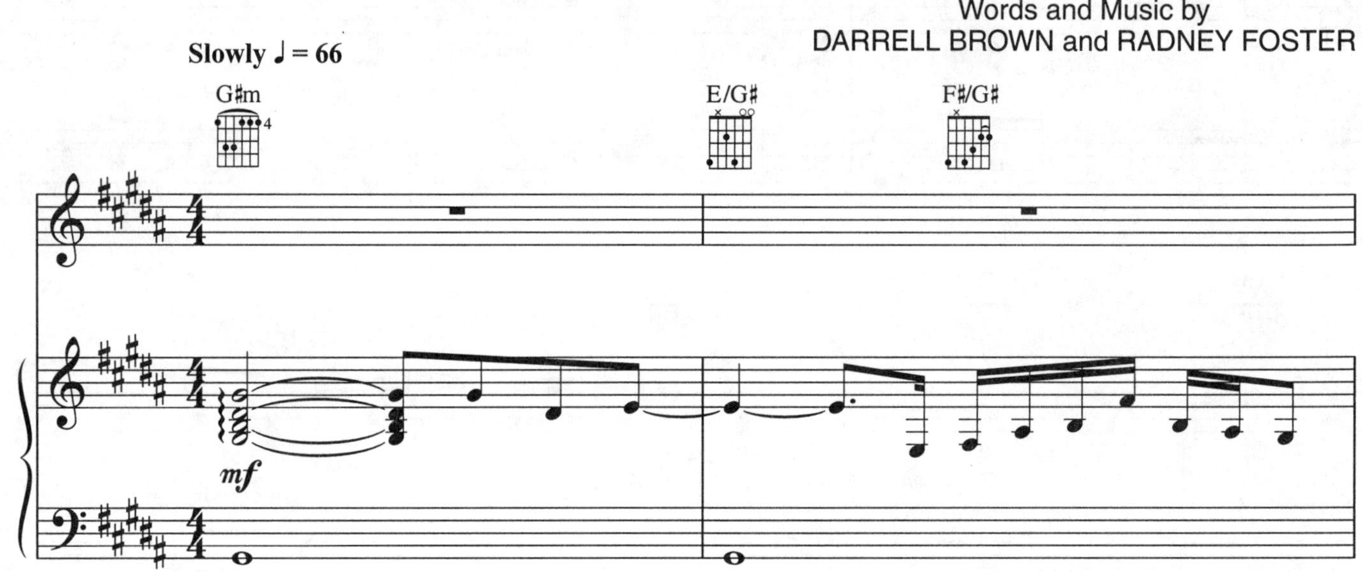

B F♯

Who said life was eas - y? The job is nev - er through. It - 'll

G♯m E(9)

run us till we're rag - ged, it - 'll hard - en our hearts, and

B F♯

love could use a day of rest be - fore we both start fall - ing a - part.

𝄋 *Chorus:*

B

Pray that it's rain - ing on Sun - day,

G♯m7
E
storm - in' like cra - zy.
We'll hide un - der the cov - ers all af - ter - noon.
B
F♯
B
Ba - by, what - ev - er comes Mon - day can take
F♯m7
E
care of it - self, 'cause we got bet - ter things that we can do
B/F♯
F♯
To Coda
B
when it's rain - ing on Sun - day.

Verse 2:
F♯m7
E
G♯m
2. Your love is like re - li - gion, a
E(9)
B
cross in Mex - i - co.
And your kiss is like the in - no-cence of a
F♯/A♯
G♯m
prayer nailed to a door.
Sur - ren - der is much sweet - er when
E(9)
B
we both let go.
Let the wa - ter wash our bod - ies clean and

F♯
C♯9/E♯
D.S. 𝄋 al Coda
love wash our souls.
Pray that it's
⊕ Coda
B
G♯m7
day.
(Inst. solo…
E
C♯9/E♯
…end solo)
Pray that it's
Chorus:
B
G♯m7
rain - ing on Sun - day,
storm - in' like cra - zy.

E
B
F♯
We'll hide un - der the cov - ers all af - ter - noon.
Ba - by, what -
B
F♯m7
ev - er comes Mon - day can take care of it - self, 'cause we
E
B/F♯
F♯
got bet - ter things that we can do when it's rain - ing on Sun -
B
F♯m7
E
Repeat ad lib. and fade
day.
When it's rain - ing on Sun -

REAL GOOD MAN

Gtr. tuned "Double Drop D"
⑥ = D ③ = G
⑤ = A ② = B
④ = D ① = D

Words and Music by
RIVERS RUTHERFORD
and GEORGE TEREN

Moderately slow ♩ = 92

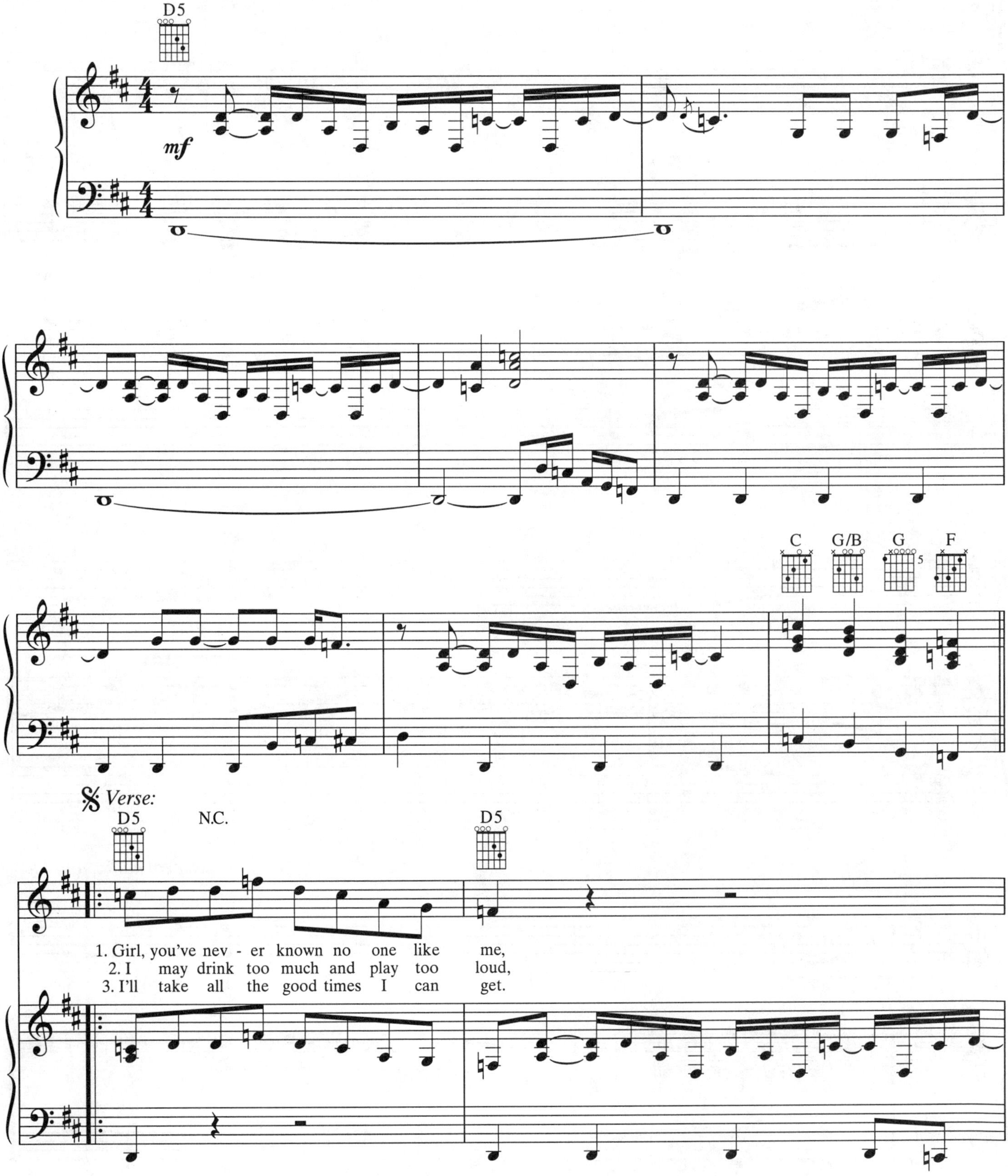

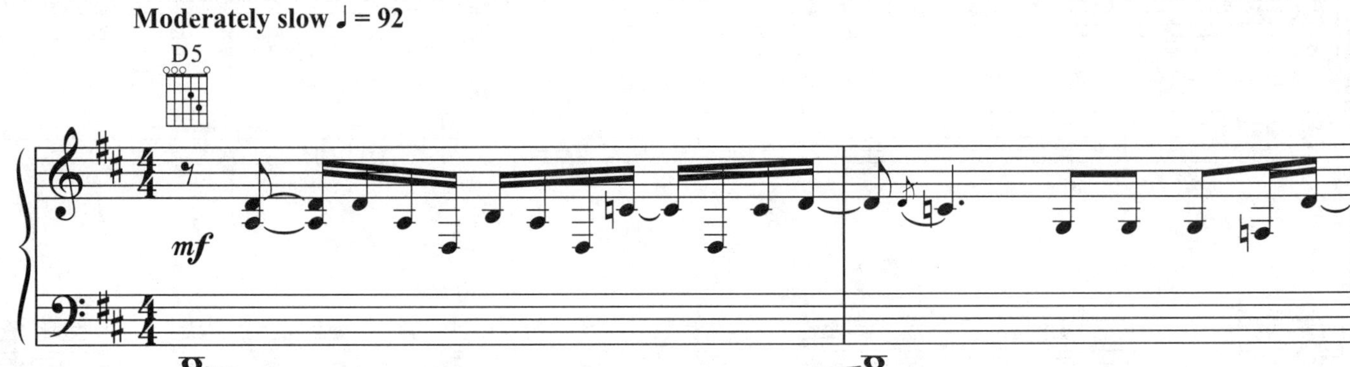

D5
mf
C
G/B
G
F
Verse:
D5
N.C.
D5
1. Girl, you've nev - er known no one like me,
2. I may drink too much and play too loud,
3. I'll take all the good times I can get.

up there in your high so - ci - e - ty.
hang out with a rough and row - dy crowd.
I'm too young for grow - ing up just yet.
G
They might tell you I'm no good. Girl, they need to un - der - stand
That don't mean I dis - re - spect my ma - ma or my Un - cle Sam.
Ain't much I can pro - mise you, ex - cept to do the best I can.
D5
just who I am.
Yes, sir. Yes, ma'am.
I'll be damned.
A7
I may be a real bad boy, but,

To Coda 1.

N.C. D5

ba - by, I'm a real good_ man.______

2. D5

Bridge: N.C. C G/B

I might have a reck - less streak at least a coun - try mile wide

D5 N.C. C G

If you're gon - na run with me, it's gon - na be a wild ride.

Bm
G7
When it comes to lov - in',
I've got vel - vet hands.
D5
C
G/B
I'll show you how a real bad boy
Gm/B♭
Asus
D5
can be a real good man.
G
D5
(Inst. solo ad lib....

D.S. % al Coda
G
A7
C7
C#7
...end solo)
Coda
D5
A7
I may be a real_ bad boy,_ oh, but,
C
G
D5
ba - by, I'm a real good_ man._
Yes, I am.
N.C.
F
D5

Repeat as desired
Last time

ROCKIN' YEARS

Words and Music by
FLOYD PARTON

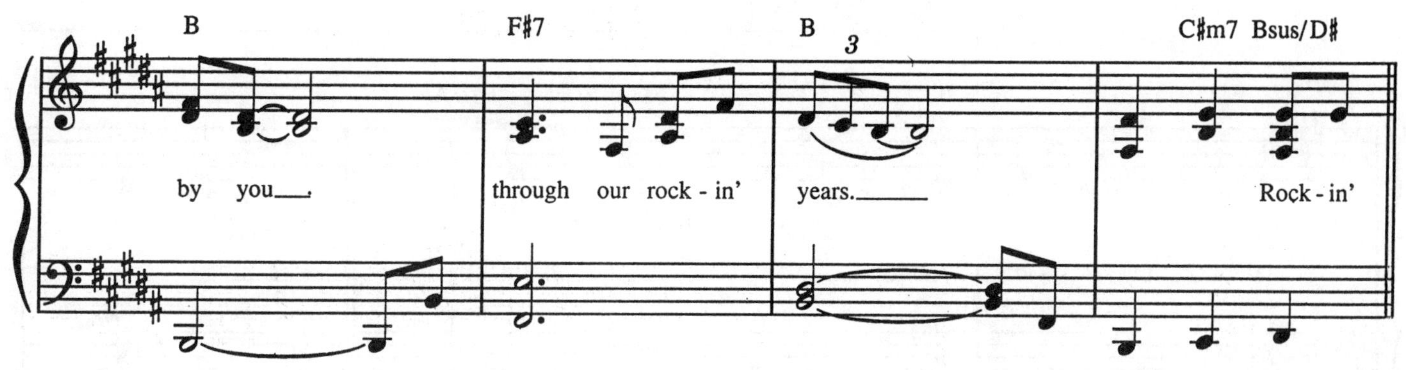
B
F#7
B
C#m7 Bsus/D#
by you
through our rock - in'
years.
Rock - in'

Chorus:
E
B
chairs, rock - in' ba - bies, rock - a - bye, rock of ag - es, side by

F#/A# G#m7 F#7
B
side, we'll be to - geth - er al - ways. And if you'll hold me tight when you

B7
E
B
love me, that's all I'll ask of you. And I'll stand by you

Verse 2:
I'll be your friend, I'll be your lover,
Until the end, there'll be no other,
And my heart has only room for one.
Yes, I'll always love you, and I'll always be here for you.
And I'll stand by you through our rockin' years.
(To Chorus:)

SIMPLE LIFE

Words and Music by
TROY VERGES, CHRISTOPHER LINDSEY,
AIMEE MAYO and HILLARY LEE LINDSEY

Moderately, with a heavy beat ♩ = 102

D5

mf

Da da

G5
D5
noth-ing like com-ing home.
Verses 2 & 3:
N.C.
D
2. I wan-na sit on my front porch and drink my lem-on-ade, cut my
blan-ket down to the creek, let the
grass af-ter church ev-'ry Sun-day. Go out Sat-ur-day night,
wa-ter sing me to sleep. Let go of time,
G
D
live the sim-ple life.
live the sim-ple life.

Bm
A/C♯
D
G(9)
Wake up in the morn - ing to these fields of gold. Take a long walk down a grav -
Late - ly I've seen too man - y cit - y lights. I wan - na go some - where where I can
Chorus:
A
el road.
see the stars at night.
Spend my days in the sweet sun - shine. Rock
Bm7
in my swing and watch my gar - den grow. Know that I'll al - ways have some -
To Coda
1.
one to hold. Oh, I wan - na live the sim - ple life.

D5
Da da da da, da da
da. 2. I wan - na take a
2.
N.C.
wan - na live the sim - ple
D
Bm7
life.
(Inst. solo ad lib....
Asus
G(9)
...end solo)

Bm D/A

Spend my days in the sweet sun - shine. Rock in my swing and watch_ my ba - bies grow.

Gmaj7

D.S.𝄋 al Coda

Know that I'll al - ways have_ some, some - one to hold.________ Oh.__

𝄌 *Coda*

D5

__ wan - na live the sim - ple life.____

Da da da da,__ da da__ da.

SEVEN SPANISH ANGELS

Words and Music by
EDDIE SETSER and TROY SEALS

F7
B♭
hear the ri - ders com - ing, he said, "This is my__ last fight. If they
knew the gun__ was emp - ty and she knew she could - n't win. But her
F
C7
F
take me back__ to Tex - as____ they won't take me back__ a - live."
fi - nal prayer__ was an - swered__ when the ri - fles fired__ a - gain.
There were
F
C7
sev - en Span - ish an - gels at the al - tar of__ the sun.____ They were

F
pray - in' for the lov - ers in the val - ley of the guns. When the
F7
Bb
bat - tle stopped and the smoke cleared, there was thun - der from the throne and
F
C7
1. F
sev - en Span - ish an - gels took an - oth - er an - gel home.
2. F
Db7
She reached home. There were
mf

Repeat and fade
Gb
Db7
sev - en Span-ish an - gels at the al - tar of the sun. They were
ff
pray-ing for the lov - ers in the val-ley of the guns. When the
bat - tle stopped and the smoke cleared, there was thun-der from the throne and
Gb7
Cb
sev - en Span - ish an - gels took an - oth - er an - gel home. There were

SHE AND I

Words and Music by
DAVE LOGGINS

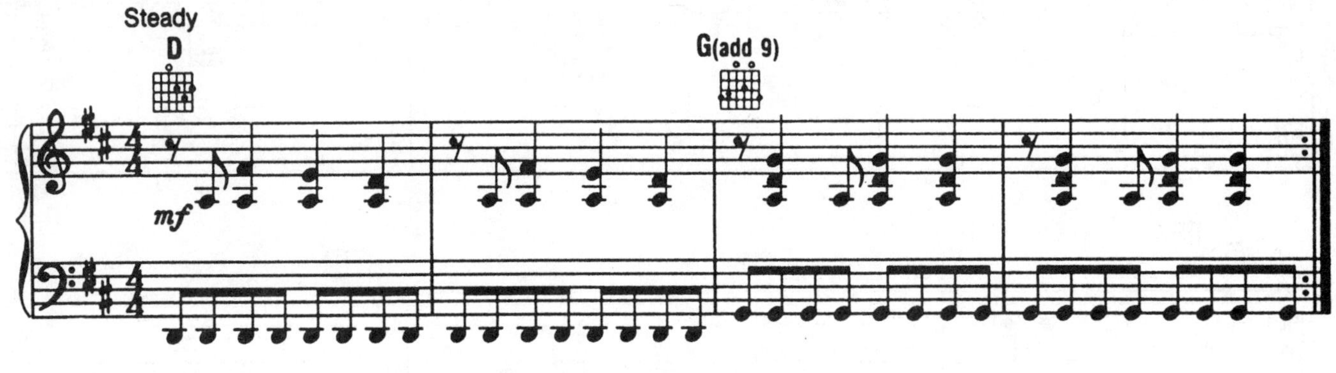

she and I lead a per - fect - ly nor - mal life.
she and I pay on ev - 'ry - thing we ac - quire.
D
D7/A
Ah, but just be - cause we aren't of - ten seen so - cial - ly,
Ah, but just be - cause we aren't of - ten seen sep - 'rate - ly,
Gmaj9
E7
D
peo - ple think we've some - thing to hide.
peo - ple think we live one life.
But all our friends know we're
It's hard for them to see how
A
D
just a lit - tle old fash - ioned, she and I.
an - y - one could be as close as she and I.
Oh, ain't it

G
great (ain't it great), ain't it fine (ain't it fine) to have a love (a love), some-one (some-one) that
D
E7
oth - ers can't find? Ain't it won - der - ful to know all we
G
G/A
1 D
ev - er need is just the two of us, she and I. So
G(add 9)
won - der - ful, she and I. Ah,

2
D
She and I live in our own lit - tle world, ain't it won - der -
G(add 9)
D
ful?
She and I live in our
G
Gmaj9
G6
own lit - tle world, ain't it won - der - ful, ain't it fine, fine, fine?
D
G(add 9)
Repeat and Fade
with improvisation

SHE BELIEVES IN ME

Words and Music by
STEVE GIBB

Bb
Bb7/D
Eb
Bb/D
dream - ing I try to get un - dressed with - out the light. Then
Cm7
F7
F/Eb
Dm7
Gm7
qui - et - ly she says, "How was your night?" And I come to her and say it was all
Cm
F7
Bb
F7sus
right. And I hold her tight. And she be -
Bbsus
Bb
Bbsus
Bb
Am7-5
lieves in me. I'll nev - er know just what she sees in me.

D7
Gm
Gm(+7)
Gm7
Gm6
I told her some-day if she was my girl I could change the world with my
Cm7
F7sus
B♭sus
B♭
lit-tle songs, I was wrong. But she has faith in me,
B♭sus
B♭
Am7-5
D7
And so I go on try-ing faith-ful-ly, And who knows, may-be on some
Gm
Gm(+7)
Gm7
Gm6
Cm7
spe-cial night If my song is right I will find a way,

F7sus
Bb
Bb/D
find a way. While she lays wait-ing I stum-ble to the kit - chen for a
Eb
Cm7
F7
F/Eb
Dm7
bite. Then I see my old gui-tar in the night, just
Gm7
Cm7
F7sus
wait-ing for me like a sec-ret friend, And there's no end. While she lays
Bb
Bb7/D
Eb
Bb/D
cry - ing I fum-ble with a mel - o-dy or two, Then I'm

Cm7
F7
Dm7
Gm7
torn be - tween the things that I should do. Then she says to wake her up when I am
Cm7
F7
Bb
F7sus
Bbsus
Bb
through God, her love is true And she be - lieves in me,
Bbsus
Bb
Am7-5
D7
I'll nev - er know just what she sees in me. I told her some - day if she
Gm
Gm(+7)
Gm7
Gm6
Cm7
was my girl I could change the world with my lit - tle songs, I was

F7sus
Bbsus
Bb
Bbsus
Bb
wrong. But she has faith in me, And so I go on try-ing
Am7-5
D7
Gm
Gm(+7)
faith - ful-ly, And who knows, may-be on some spe-cial night If my
Gm7
Gm6
Cm7
F7sus
song is right I will find a way, while she
Bb
Eb/Bb
Ebm
Bb
waits, while she waits, for me.

SHE THINKS I STILL CARE

Words and Music by
DICKEY LEE

E7
A
F♯7
B
just be - cause I spoke her name some - where, just be -
mem - 'ry of her lin - gers ev - ery - where, just be -
just be - cause I spoke her name some - where, just be -
A7
D
B7
E
cause I dialed her num - ber by mis - take to - day,
cause I'm not the hap - py guy I used to be,
cause I saw her and went to pie - ces,
A
E7
1.
A
E
To Coda
B
F♯7
B
F♯
she thinks I still care. And
she thinks I still
she thinks I still

2.
A
B
D
E
care.
Then if she's hap-py think-ing I still
A
B
need her then let that fool - ish
E7
F#7
B7
C#7
E7
F#7
E
F#
Eb
F
4 fr.
no-tion bring a tear.
But
D
E
A
B
how could she ev-er be so fool - ish?

B7
C♯7
Tell me where would she get such an i-
E
F♯
B7
C♯7
E
F♯
D.S. al Coda
dea?
Coda
A
B
D
E
A
B
sung freely
care.
She thinks
E7
F♯7
D
E
A
B
I still care.

SIXTEEN TONS

C7
Em
mind — that's — weak — and a back that's strong. You load
straw - boss — said — "Well - a bless my soul." You load
high - toned — wo - man make me walk the line. You load
right one don't - a get you, then the left one will. You load
Chorus
Em
Six - teen Tons, what do you get? — An - oth - er day old - er and deep - er in debt. — Saint
mf
Em
Am
Em
Pe - ter, don't you call me 'cause I can't go — I owe — my soul to the com - pa - ny store. —
1. 2. 3.
4.
Em
Em
2. I was
3. I was
4. If you
f
rit.
f
rit.

SOMEBODY LIKE YOU

Words and Music by
JOHN SHANKS and KEITH URBAN

Amaj9
ev - er done. And it sure feels good to fi - n'lly feel the way I do.
E
Bsus
I wan - na love some - bod - y, love
Amaj9
E
To Coda 1.3.
some - bod - y like you.
2. Well, I'm let - tin'
2.4.
Bridge:
A(9)
Yeah, I wan - na feel sun - shine, shin - ing down on me and you.

E
When you put your arms a -
A(9)
round me, you let me know there's noth - ing in this
1.
D.S.𝄋
C♯m
F♯m7
world I can't do.
3. I used to
2.
D.S.𝄋 al Coda
F♯m7
5. Some -

Coda
Bsus
I'm read - y to love some - bod - y, love
A(9)
some - bod - y like you.
E
Bsus
I wan - na love some - bod - y, love
A(9)
some - bod - y like you.

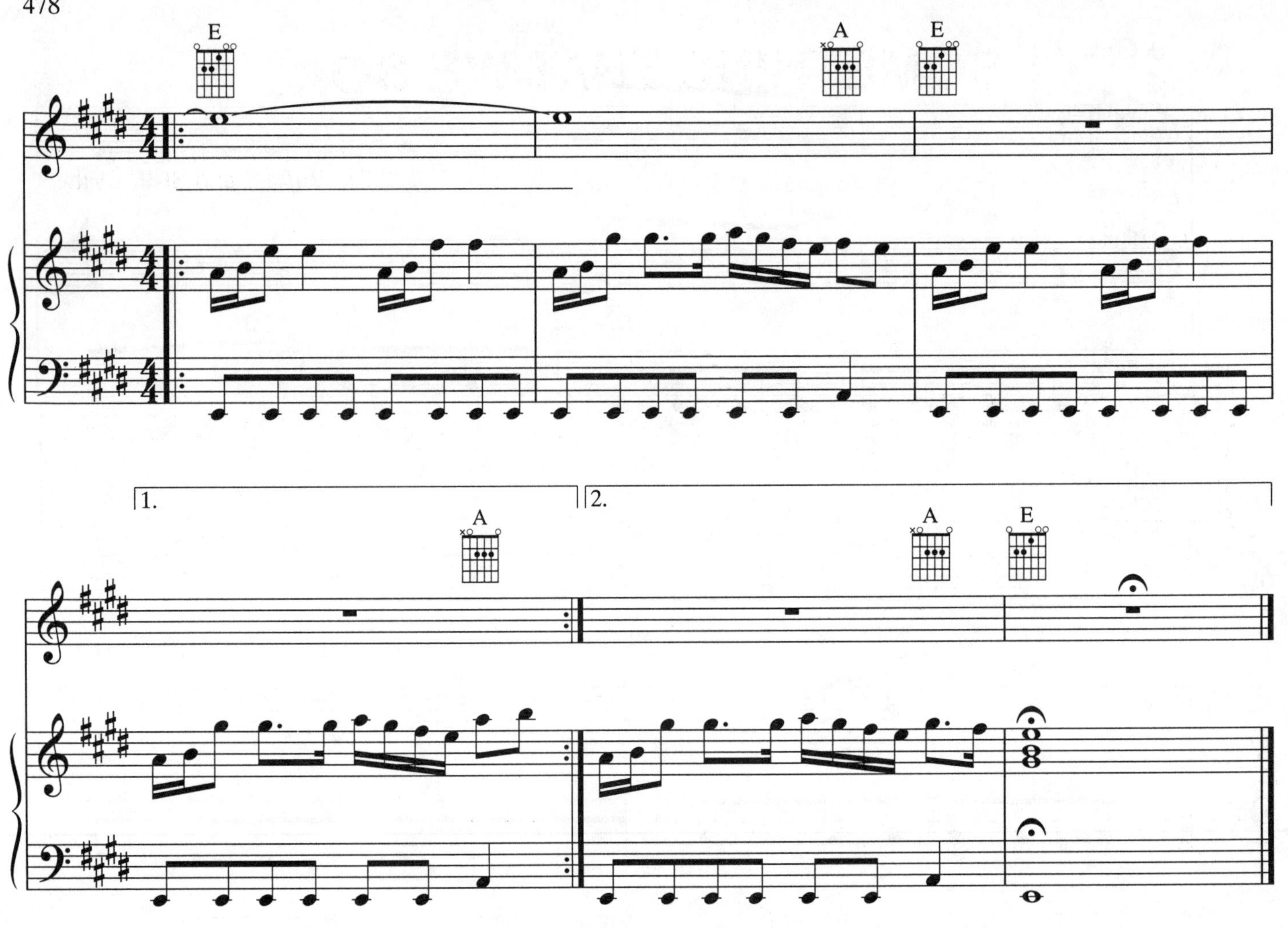

Verse 2:
Well, I'm letting go of all my lonely yesterdays
And forgiving myself for the mistakes I've made.
Now there's just one thing, the only thing I wanna do.
I wanna love somebody, love somebody like you.
(To Bridge:)

Verse 3:
I used to run in circles, goin' nowhere fast.
I'd take one step forward, end up two steps back.
I couldn't walk a straight line even if I wanted to,
But I wanna love somebody, love somebody like you.

Verse 4:
Instrumental solo
(To Bridge:)

Verse 5:
Sometimes it's hard for me to understand,
But you're teachin' me to be a better man.
Don't want to take this life for granted like I used to do.
I wanna love somebody, love somebody like you.
(To Coda)

SOMETHING THAT WE DO

Guitar originally recorded in alternate tuning (open D) w/capo at 5th fret:
⑥ = D ③ = F♯
⑤ = A ② = A
④ = D ① = D

Words and Music by
CLINT BLACK and SKIP EWING

Smoothly ♩ = 66

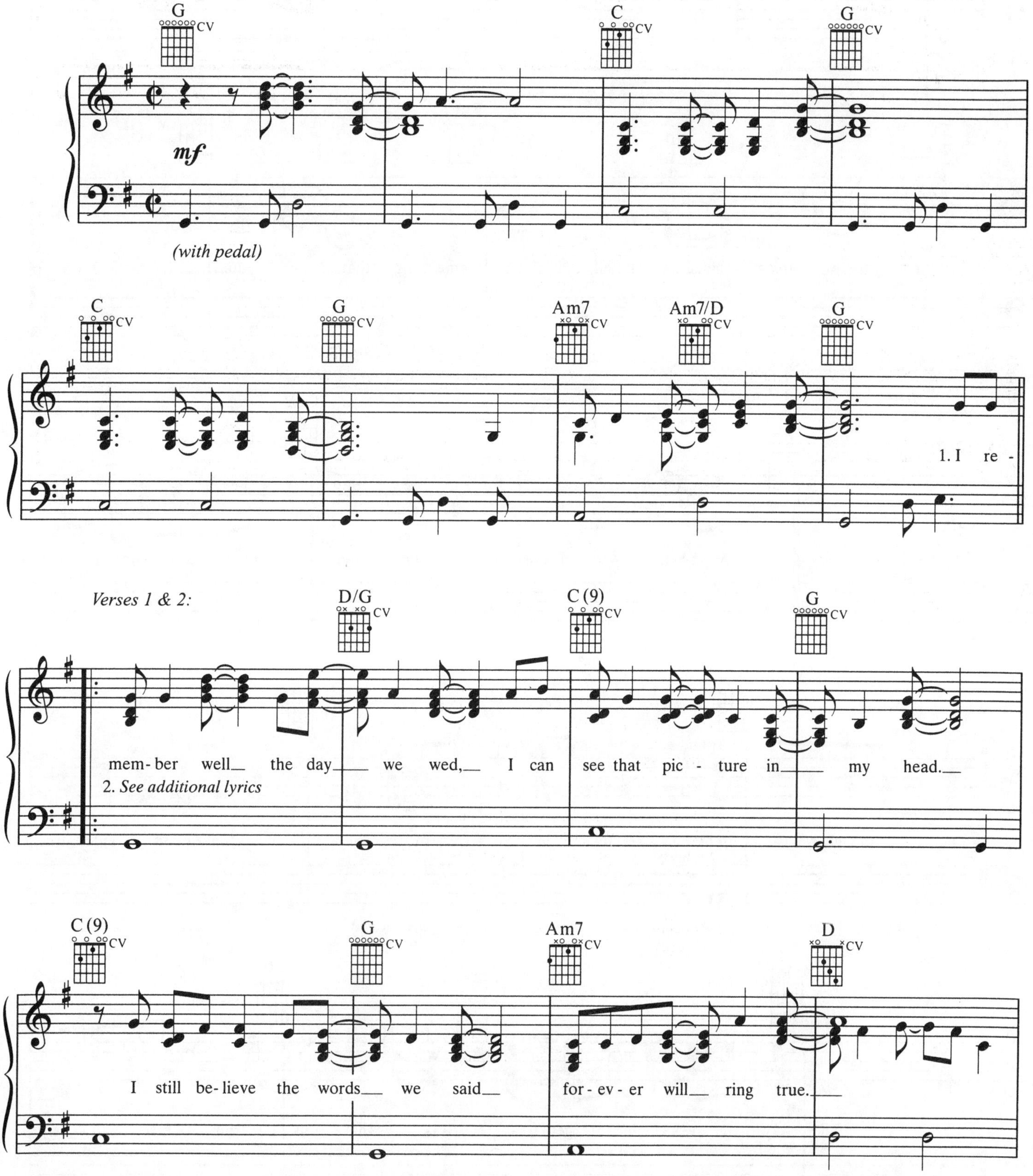

G C G

mf

(with pedal)

C G Am7 Am7/D G

1. I re -

Verses 1 & 2:

D/G C(9) G

mem- ber well__ the day__ we wed,__ I can see that pic - ture in__ my head.__

2. *See additional lyrics*

C(9) G Am7 D

I still be- lieve the words__ we said__ for- ev- er will__ ring true.__

G
D/G
C
G
Love is cer - tain, love is kind, love is yours__ and love is mine.__ But it
C
G
Am7
D7sus
1.
G
is - n't some - thing that__ we find, it's some-thing that__ we do.__ 2. It's
2.
G
Bridge:
C
G/B
__ We help__ to make__ each oth - er all__ that we__ can__
Am7
G
be,__ though we can find our strength and in - spi - ra - tion in - de - pend - ent - ly.__
C
G/B
__ The way we work__ to - geth - er is__ what sets__ our love__ a - part,__

B♭
To Coda
Am7
so close - ly that we can't tell where I
end and where you
rit.
D
Verse 3:
G
D/G
C(9)
start. 3. It
gives me heart, re - mem - b'ring how we start - ed with a sim -
a tempo
G
C(9)
G
Am7
ple vow. There's so much to look back on now.
Still it feels brand new.
D
G
D/G
C
We're on a road that has no end, and each day we be - gin
G
C
G
Am7
D7sus
a - gain. Love's not just some - thing that we're in, it's some - thing that we do.

G
D/G
C
G
CV
D.S. 𝄋 al Coda
C
G
Am7
D7sus
G
G/B
Coda
Am7
D
G
end and where you start.
Love is wide,
rit.
a tempo
D/G
C/G
G
C/G
love is long, love is deep and love is strong. Love is why I love
G
Am7
D
G
this song, I hope you love it, too. I re - mem-ber well the day

Verse 2:
It's holding tight, lettin' go,
It's flyin' high and layin' low.
Let your strongest feelings show
And your weakness, too.
It's a little and a lot to ask,
An endless and a welcome task.
Love isn't something that we have,
It's something that we do.
(To Bridge:)

SONG OF THE SOUTH

Words and Music by
BOB McDILL

Moderately fast Country, with a "2" feel

A
E
Cot- ton on the road - side, cot- ton in the ditch, we
D
A
all picked the cot- ton, but we nev- er got rich. Dad- dy was a vet - 'ran, a
E
D
A
south- ern dem - o - crat, they ought- ta get a rich man to vote like that.
A
E
D
Song, song of the south, sweet po - ta - to pie and I

A
E
shut my mouth. Gone, gone with the wind, there
D
A
A
ain't no - bod - y look - in' back a - gain.
E
D
A
3
E
D

A
Well,
A
E
D
some - bod - y told us Wall Street fell, but we were so poor that we
A
E
couldn't tell. Cot - ton was short and the weeds were tall, but Mis - ter
D
Roo - se - velt's gon - na save us all.
Ped

A
E
Well, Ma - ma got sick and Dad - dy got down, the
D
A
coun - ty got the farm and they moved to town. Pa - pa got a job with the
E
D
T. V. A., he bought a wash - in' ma - chine and then a
A
Chev - ro - let. Sing it: Song,

E
D
A
song of the south,
sweet po - ta - to pie
and I
shut
my
mouth.
E
D
Gone,
gone with the wind,
there
ain't
no - bod - y
look - in'
Dsus2
back
a - gain.
A
E
D
Play it:

A
E
D
Repeat and fade
A
E
Sing it: Song, song of the south,
D
A
sweet po - ta - to pie and I shut my mouth. Gone,
E
D
gone with the wind, ain't no - bod - y look - in' back a - gain.

SPEED

Words and Music by
JEFFREY STEELE and
CHRIS WALLIN

Em7
D
Cmaj9
D
Fm7
E♭
D♭maj9
E♭
I need to get there pret - ty quick.
1.
Em7
D
Cmaj9
Fm7
E♭
D♭maj9
Hey, mis - ter, what you got out on that lot you can sell me
D
Em7
D
E♭
2.
Fm7
E♭
in a pinch?
All that real - ly con - cerns
To Next Strain
3.
Cmaj9
D
Em7
D
D♭maj9
E♭
Fm7
E♭
me is talk on the tail - gate all night

Cmaj9
D
D♭maj9
E♭
long, but now she's gone, and I need to move on, so give me
Chorus:
G
D
C
D
A♭
E♭
D♭
E♭
speed. How fast will it go? Can it get me
o - ver her quick - ly, ze - ro to six - ty? Will it out - run her mem - o -
ry? Yeah, what I real - ly need is an o - pen road
Em
D/F♯
Cmaj9
Fm
E♭/G
D♭maj9

1.
D
Eb
Em7
Fm7
D
Eb
Cmaj9
Dbmaj9
D
Eb
and a whole_ lot-ta___ speed.___
Em7
Fm7
D
Eb
Cmaj9
Dbmaj9
D
Eb
D.S. 𝄋
2.
D
Eb
and a whole_ lot-ta__
Bridge:
Cmaj9
Dbmaj9
__ speed.___
D
Eb
Cmaj9
Dbmaj9
Throw me__ that key__ so I___ can
D
Eb
Cmaj9
Dbmaj9
put some miles be - tween__ us.
Tear off__ that rear__ view mir-ror; there's noth -

D Cmaj9
E♭ D♭maj9

in' left___ to see,___ yeah. Let me lean on that gas; I'll be

Chorus:

D G D
E♭ A♭ E♭

catch - in' up fast.___ Give me speed.___

C D G D
D♭ E♭ A♭ E♭

How fast will it go?___ Can it get me o - ver her quick - ly, ze - ro to six - ty?

C D G D
D♭ E♭ A♭ E♭

Can it out - run___ her mem - o - ry?___ Yeah,

C
D
Em
D/F#
Cmaj9
D♭
E♭
Fm
E♭/G
D♭maj9
what I real - ly need
is an o - pen road
D
Em7
D
E♭
Fm7
E♭
and a whole lot - ta speed.
Cmaj9
D
Em7
D
D♭maj9
E♭
Fm7
E♭
That's what I need.
Cmaj9
D
Em7
D
D♭maj9
E♭
Fm7
E♭
I'm tired of spin - nin' my wheels.

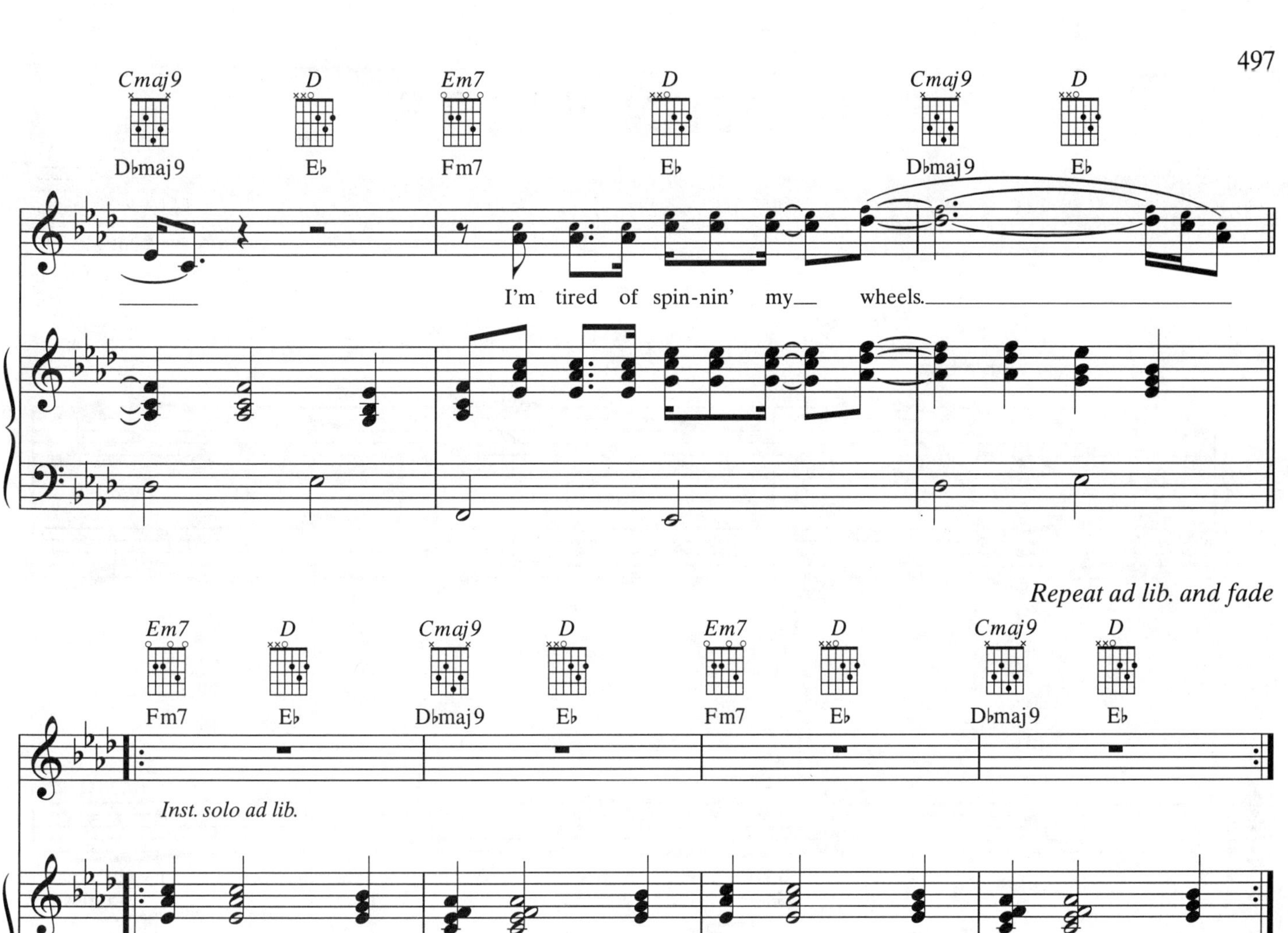

Verse 2:
Maybe one of them souped up muscle cars,
The kind that makes you think you're stronger than you are.
Color don't matter; no, I don't need leather seats.
All that really concerns me is…
(To Chorus:)

Verse 3:
Well, I'd like to trade in this old truck,
'Cause it makes me think of her, and that just slows me up.
See, it's the first place we made love, where we used to sit and talk
On the tailgate all night long, but now she's gone,
And I need to move on, so give me…
(To Chorus:)

SOUTHERN NIGHTS

Words and Music by
ALLEN TOUSSAINT

Am7
men - tion the trees, whis - tling tunes that you know and love so.
just be - yond the eye. It goes run - ning through your soul like the sto -
C7
F
D7
- ries told of old.
South - ern nights, just as good e - ven when
Old man, he and his dog that walked the
G7
Bbmaj7
closed your eyes. I a - pol - o - gize
old land, ev - 'ry flow - er touched
Am7
to an - y - one who can tru - ly say that he has
his cold hand. As he slow - ly walked by, weep - ing

C7
1,2
Guitar Tacet
found a bet - ter way.
wil - lows would cry for joy.
F
D7
G7
Feel so good, feel so good it's fright - 'ning. Wish I could
Bbmaj7
stop this world from fight - ing. La da da da da da la da da da da da

Am7
C7
da da da da da da da da da da da.
F
D7
Mys - ter - ies like this and man - y oth - ers
G7
Bbmaj7
in the trees blow in the night
C7
Guitar Tacet
D.S. (vocal ad lib) and Fade
in the south - ern skies.

STAND BY YOUR MAN

Words and Music by
TAMMY WYNETTE and BILLY SHERRILL

To Coda
A
C♯
D
C♯m
Bm
Stand by your man, Give him two arms to cling to,
Stand by your man, And tell the world you love him,
Stand by your man, And show the world you love him,
1.
A
F♯7
B
E7
And some-thing warm to come to when nights are cold and lone-ly.
2.
A
E7
C♯7
F♯
D
Keep giv-ing all the love you can. Stand
E
A
D
A
E7
D. S. al
Coda
by your man.
Coda
A
E
E7
Keep giv-ing all the love you
C♯7
F♯
D
E
A
D
A
E
A
can; Stand by your man.

SWINGIN'

Words and Music by
JOHN DAVID ANDERSON and
LIONEL A. DELMORE

2,3
CHORUS
A7
love down to my toes. And we was swing - in',
(swing - in';) yes, we was
E7
B7
swing - in'.
(swing - in'.)
Lit - tle Char - lotte, she's as pret - ty as the
Bb7
A7
an - gels when they sing. I can't be - lieve I'm out here on her front porch in the swing, just a
E7
To Coda
D.S. (3rd ending) al Coda
CODA
swing - in'.
(Swing - in'.)
3. Now
Lit - tle

Verse 2.
Her brother was on the sofa
Eatin' chocolate pie.
Her mama was in the kitchen
Cuttin' chicken up to fry.
Her daddy was in the backyard
Rollin' up a garden hose.
I was on the porch with Charlotte
Feelin' love down to my toes,
And we was swingin'. *(To Chorus:)*

Verse 3.
Now Charlotte, she's a darlin';
She's the apple of my eye.
When I'm on the swing with her
It makes me almost high.
And Charlotte is my lover.
And she has been since the spring.
I just can't believe it started
On her front porch in the swing. *(To Chorus:)*

TAKE A LETTER MARIA

Words and Music by
R.B. GREAVES

C
ain't no fool, let me tell you what hap - pened
G
then, I packed some clothes and
C
I walked out and I
ain't goin' back a - gain.
G
So take a
G
let - ter Ma - ri - a,
Ad-
F
dress it to my wife,
C
Say I won't be com - ing home,

EXTRA LYRICS

(Verse 2) You've been many things, but most of all a good secretary to me,
And it's times like this I feel you've always been close to me.
Was I wrong to work nights to try to build a good life?
All work and no play has just cost me a wife.

(Chorus)

(Verse 3) When a man loves a woman, it's hard to understand
That she would find more pleasure in the arms of another man.
I never really noticed how sweet you are to me,
It just so happens I'm free tonight, would you like to have dinner with me?

(Chorus)

TAKE ME HOME, COUNTRY ROADS

Words and Music by
JOHN DENVER, BILL DANOFF and TAFFY NIVERT

Take Me Home, Country Roads - 3 - 1

D C G
E D A
young - er than the moun - tains grow - in' like a breeze.
mist - y taste of moon - shine, tear - drop in my eye.
Coun - try
G D
A E
Roads, take me home to the
Em C G
F♯m D A
place I be - long: West Vir - gin - ia,
D C
E D
To Coda
moun - tain mom - ma, take me home, Coun - try
1. 2.
G Em D
A F♯m E
Roads. All my I hear her voice, in the

G C G
A D A
morn - in' hours she calls me, the ra - di - o re - minds me of my
D Em F C
E F♯m G D
home far a - way, and driv - in' down the road I get a feel - in' that I
G D D7
A E E7
D.S. al Coda
should have been home yes - ter - day, yes - ter - day. Coun-try
Coda
G D G
A E A
Roads, take me home, Coun - try Roads,
D G
E A
take me home, Coun - try Roads.

TAKE THIS JOB AND SHOVE IT

Words and Music by
DAVID ALLEN COE

A7
E
A7
walk - in' out the door. Take this job and
E
B7
To Coda
E
No chord
shove it! I ain't work - in' here no more. Well, that
N.C.
I've been work - in' in this fac-t'ry for nigh on fif-teen years.
fore - man, he's a reg-u-lar dog. The line boss, he's a fool.
A
All this time I watched my wom-an drown-in' in a pool of tears. And
Got a brand-new flat - top hair-cut. Lord, he thinks he's cool.

I've seen a lot of good folk die that had a lot of bills to pay.
One of these days I'm gon-na blow my top. That suck-er, he's gon-na pay.
I'd give the shirt right off of my back if
Lord, I can't wait to see their fac-es when I
I had the guts to say:
get the nerve to say:
1.
2.
D. C. al Coda
Coda
A
E
more.
Tacet
N.C.
B7
E
Take this job and shove it!

TELLURIDE

Words and Music by
TROY VERGES and
BRETT JAMES

A/C#
D
A
B♭/D
E♭
B♭
job at this bar sell-in' beer to the lo - cals, just bare-ly get - tin' by, on the
Em7
A
Bm7
Fm7
B♭
Cm7
tips from the rich kids there on Dad-dy's dime. But when I saw
G
Bm7
G
A7sus
A♭
Cm7
A♭
B♭7sus
her walk in one night, I knew that I'd be al - right in...
Chorus:
D
A/C#
Bm7
E♭
B♭/D
Cm7
Tell - u - ride; the snow fall-in' down. I was wak - in' up in that sleep -

G
D
A/C♯
To Coda
A♭
E♭
B♭/D
y lit - tle town.
In her eyes,
my world
came so a - live.
I
1.
Bm7
G
D
Cm7
A♭
E♭
nev-er will for - get
the mo - ment she ar - rived
in
Tell - u - ride.
A
Bm7
G
B♭
Cm7
A♭
2. We
2.
Solo:
Bm7
G
D
Cm7
A♭
E♭
nev-er will for-get
all
those
sleep-less nights
in
Tell - u - ride. (Inst. solo ad lib....

A/C# Bm7 G D
B♭/D Cm7 A♭ E♭

Tell - u - ride,

A/C# Bm7 G
B♭/D Cm7 A♭

oh, woah. *…end solo)* It

Bridge:

A Bm7 G A Bm7 G
B♭ Cm7 A♭ B♭ Cm7 A♭

end - ed just like a mov - ie scene, and I had to play the part

A Bm7 G
B♭ Cm7 A♭

of the lov - er who stood there and watched her leave and

Em7
A
Fm7
B♭
me with a fro - zen heart in
Chorus:
D
A/C♯
Bm7
E♭
B♭/D
Cm7
Tell - u - ride, the snow fall - in' down, stand-in' there a - lone in that
G
D
A/C♯
A♭
E♭
B♭/D
sleep - y lit - tle town. In her eyes, my world came so a - live. I
Bm7
G
Cm7
A♭
D.S. 𝄋 al Coda
nev - er will for - get the day she said good - bye in...

Verse 2:
We spent that whole winter tangled up by a fire.
Castin' shadows on the cabin wall, drownin' in desire,
Confessin' all our secrets and laughin' out loud,
So high up on that mountain, I thought we'd never come down.
It was a dream we were livin' in.
I was the happiest I'd ever been, in...
(To Chorus:)

THANK GOD I'M A COUNTRY BOY

Words and Music by
JOHN DENVER

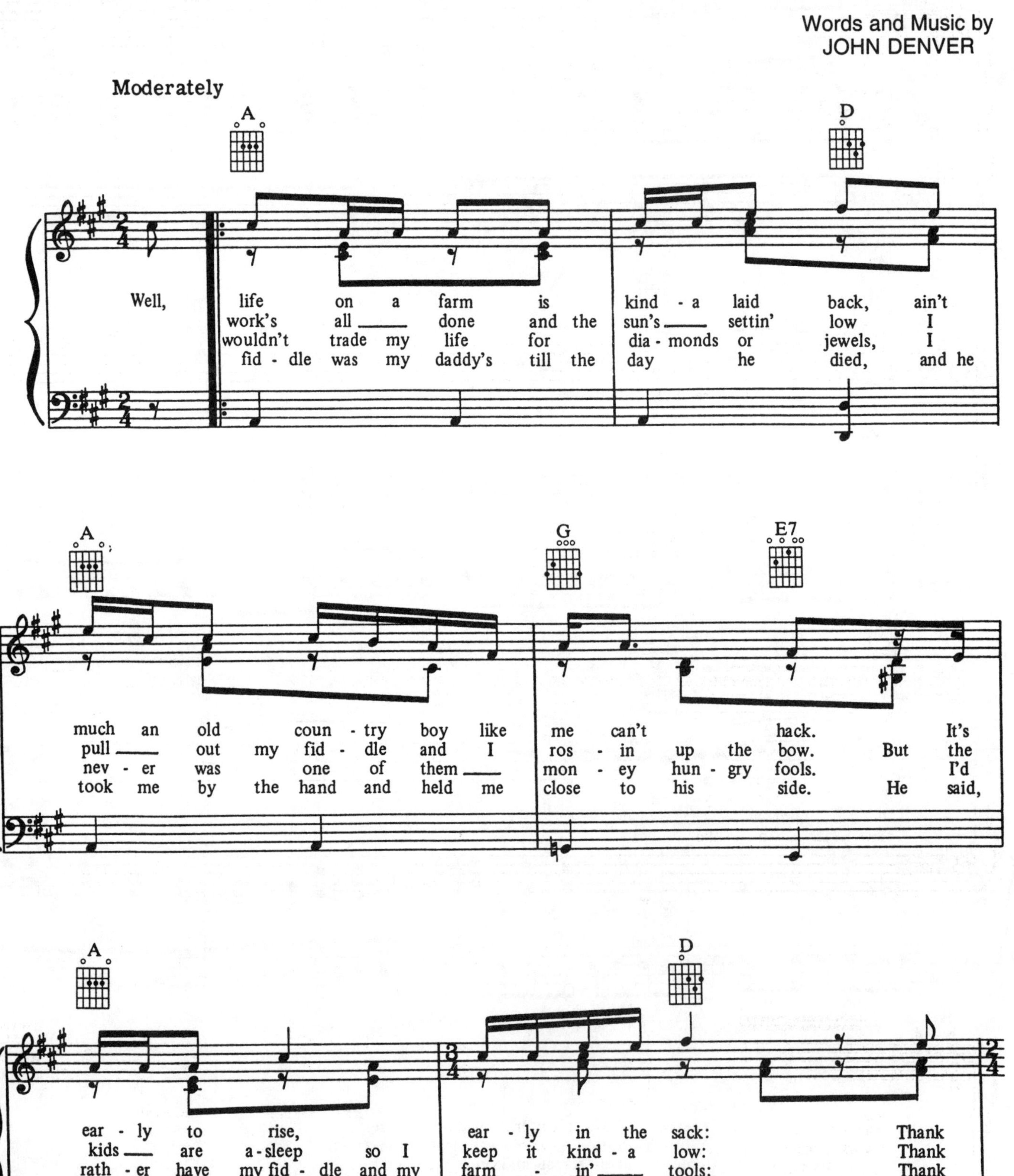

A
E7
A
God I'm a coun - try boy. A sim - ple kind - a life nev - er
God I'm a coun - try boy. I'd play "Sal - ly Goodin'" all
God I'm a coun - try boy. Yeah, cit - y folk drivin' in a
God you're a coun - try boy. My dad - dy taught me young how to
D
A
did me no harm, rais - in' me a fam - i - ly and
day if I could, but the Lord and my wife would - n't
black limou - sine, A lot - ta sad peo - ple think - in'
hunt and how to whittle, He taught me how to work and play a
G
E7
A
work - in' on a farm. My days are all filled with an
take it ver - y good. So I fid - dle when I can and I
that's might - y keen. Well, folks, let me tell you now ex -
tune on the fiddle. He taught me how to love and how to
D
(4th time only)
A
E7
A
eas - y con - try charm: Thank God I'm a coun - try boy.
work when I should: Thank God I'm a coun - try boy.
act - ly what I mean: I thank God I'm a coun - try boy.
give just a little: Thank God I'm a coun - try boy.
Well, I
(4th time)

E
A
got me a fine wife, I got me old fid - dle. When the
sun's com - in' up I got cakes on the grid - dle; And
D
(4th time only)
life ain't noth - in' but a fun - ny, fun - ny rid - dle: Thank
(4th time)
E7
1. 2. 3.
4.
God I'm a coun - try boy.
2. When the
3. I
4. Well, my

TONIGHT I WANNA BE YOUR MAN

Words and Music by
RIVERS RUTHERFORD and TROY VERGES

A(9)
Bsus
To Coda
Ab(9)
Bbsus
week I've been your hus - band, to - night I wan - na be your
1. E
Esus
2. E
Eb
Ebsus
Eb
man. 2. It man. And I'll
Bridge:
A
B/A
A
B/A
Ab
Bb/Ab
Ab
Bb/Ab
al - ways be your cov - er when you're cold, and when the
E
B/E
E
E/G#
Eb
Bb/Eb
Eb
Eb/G
world lines up a - gainst you, I'm the safe place you can go. But

A B/A A E/G#

Ab Bb/Ab Ab Eb/G

now and then we need to find some time to be in

F#m7 Bsus B

Fm7 Bbsus Bb

D.S. 𝄋 al Coda

love, just be in love. 3. Now the

𝄌 *Coda*

E E/G# A B/A

Eb Eb/G Ab Bb/Ab

man.

(Instrumental)

A E/G# F#m7

Ab Eb/G Fm7

F#
F#/A#
E/B
G#/B#
F
F/A
E♭/B♭
G/B
So let me show you who I am.
C#m7
C#m7/F#
F#7
A(9)
Cm7
Cm7/F
F7
A♭(9)
All week I've been your hus - band, to - night I
Bsus
E
B♭sus
E♭
wan - na be your man. Just for -
D
A/C#
Am/C
D♭
A♭/C
A♭m/C♭
get a - bout that wed - ding band. All

Verse 2:
It hit me just this morning
When I passed you in the hall,
I swear I caught you looking
Like you don't know me at all.
Let me show you who I am.
All week I've been your husband,
Tonight I wanna be your man.
(To Bridge:)

Verse 3:
Now the whole world's in bed sleeping,
I think we're finally alone.
And if the telephone starts ringing,
We'll pretend like we're not home.
'Cause any fool would understand
That all week I've been your husband,
Tonight I wanna be your man.
(To Coda)

THAT'D BE ALRIGHT

Words and Music by
MARK D. SANDERS, TIA SILLERS
and TIM NICHOLS

G D G
time was - n't such a lux - ur - y, if love was love - sick o -
D Bm A
ver me, that - 'd be al - right. If I could
D A G
keep the wind in my sails, keep a hold of the ti - ger by
D G D Bm
the tail, a half a ham sand - wich in my lunch pail,

A
D
Chorus:
that - 'd be al - right.
Yeah, that - 'd be al -
A
G
D
right,
that - 'd be al - right.
if ev - 'ry -
G
D
G
bod - y, ev - 'ry - where had a light - er load to bear and a lit - tle big - ger piece of the pie,
D
G
D
Bm
we'd be liv - ing us a pret - ty good life,

1.
A
D
and that - 'd be al - right.
2. Go
2.
D
A
G
D
G
D
Bm
A
D
Yeah, that - 'd be

Chorus:
D
A
G
al - right,
that - 'd be al - right.
D
G
D
if ev - 'ry - bod - y, ev - 'ry-where had a light - er load to bear and a
G
D
G
lit - tle big - ger piece of the pie,
we'd be liv - ing us a pret - ty good life,
1.
D
Bm
A
Bm
A/C♯
that - 'd be al - right.
Yeah, that - 'd be

Verse 2:
Go heavy on the good and light on the bad,
A hair more happy and a shade less sad,
Turn all that negative down just a tad,
That'd be alright.
If my dear ol' dog never got old,
If my family farm never got sold,
If another bad joke never got told,
That'd be alright.
(To Chorus:)

THEN THEY DO

Words and Music by
SUNNY RUSS and JIM COLLINS

D2
E♭2
hang - ing on my shirt tail, an - oth - er's locked up in her room, and I'm
Esus
Fsus
E
F
yell - ing up the stairs, "Stop wor - r'ing a - bout your hair; you look
1.3.
2.4.
A2
A
D/E
E7
D/E
E
D/E
B♭2
B♭
E♭/F
F7
E♭/F
F
E♭/F
fine."
2. Then they're
4. I look
Then they
Chorus:
Bm/A
A
Bm/F♯
F♯m7
Cm/B♭
B♭
Cm/G
Gm7
do, and that's how it is. It's just

E
F
D
E♭
D/E
E♭/F
quiet in the morn - in'. Can't be - lieve how much you miss all they
Bm/A
Cm/B♭
A
B♭
Bm/F♯
Cm/G
F♯m7
Gm7
do and all they did. You want all
the dreams they dreamed of to come true, then they
1.
D.S.𝄋
2.
do.
3. Now, the

Bridge:

D E/D D E/D
E♭ F/E♭ E♭ F/E♭

No more Mon - day P. T. A.'s, no car - pools or soc - cer games;

F♯m7
Gm7

your work is done.

D E/D D E/D
E♭ F/E♭ E♭ F/E♭

Now you've got time that's all your own. You've been wait - in' for so

Bm7 D/E
Cm7 E♭/F

long for those days to come. Then they

rit. *a tempo*

Chorus:
Bm/A
A
Bm/F#
F#m7
Cm/B♭
B♭
Cm/G
Gm7
do, and that's how it is. It's just
E
D
D/E
F
E♭
E♭/F
qui - et in the morn - in'. Can't be - lieve how much you miss all they
Bm/A
A
Bm/F#
F#m7
Cm/B♭
B♭
Cm/G
Gm7
do and all they did. You want all
E
D
E
Bm/A
A
F
E♭
F
Cm/B♭
B♭
the dreams they dreamed of to come true, then they do.

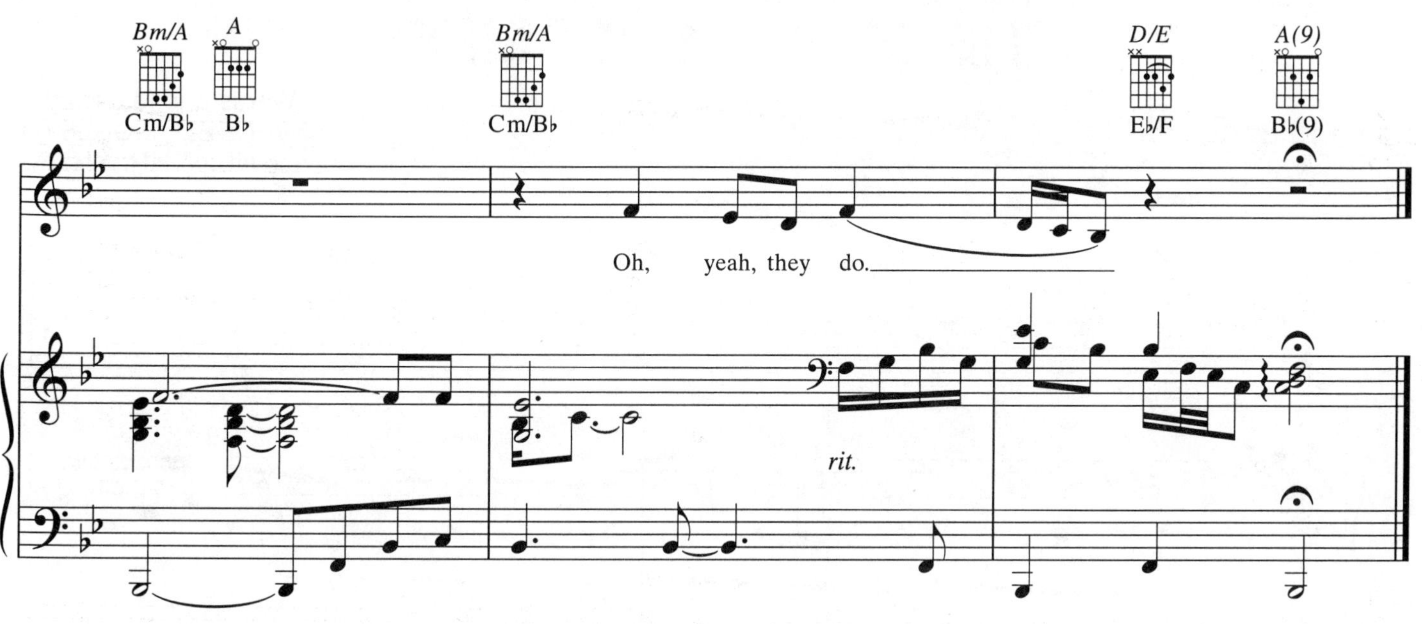

Verse 2:
Then they're fighting in the back seat.
I'm playin' referee.
Now someone's gotta go
The moment that we leave,
And ev'rybody's late. I swear I can't wait
Till they grow up.
(To Chorus:)

Verse 3:
Now the youngest is starting college.
She'll be leaving in the fall.
And Briana's latest boyfriend
Called to ask if we could talk.
And I got the impression
That he's about to pop the question any day.

Verse 4:
I look over at their pictures,
Sittin' in their frames.
I see them as babies;
I guess that'll never change.
You pray all their lives
That someday they will find happiness.
(To Chorus:)

THERE GOES MY LIFE

Words and Music by
WENDELL MOBLEY
and NEIL THRASHER

E A E B

Got my whole life__ a - head.____ Hell, I'm__ just a kid____ my -
So much for ditch - ing this__ town, and hang-ing out on the coast.__ Oh,______

1.
A E A E/G# B

self._ How'm I gon-na raise_ one?________

2.
A B

________ well,_ those plans are long__ gone. And he said...

Chorus:
E B

There goes_ my life.__

A B E B A E/G#

________ There goes__ my fu - ture, my ev - 'ry - thing. Might__

F♯m7
E/G♯
A(9)
E
A
as well kiss it all good - bye. There goes my life.
E/G♯
B
Verses 3 & 4:
E
A
3. A cou - ple years of up all night and a
4. Mom - ma's wait - ing to tuck her in
E
B
E
A
few thou - sand dia - pers la - ter, that mis - take he thought he made, it
as she fum - bles up those stairs. She smiles back at him,
E
B
1.
A
cov - ers up the re - frig - er - a - tor, oh yeah, he loves that
drag - ging that ted - dy bear. Sleep

2.
E
B
A
lit - tle girl.
tight.
Blue eyes and bounc -
Chorus:
B
E
B
A
B
ing curls.
And he smiles.
There goes
my life.
E
B
A
E/G♯
F♯m7
E/G♯
There goes
my fu - ture,
my ev - 'ry - thing.
I love you,
Dad - dy, good - night.
Bridge:
A
B
A
E/G♯
There goes
my life.
She had
that Hon-

F♯m7
E/G♯
A
E/G♯
da load - ed down_ with A - ber - crom - bie clothes_ and fif - teen pairs_ of shoes,_
B
A
E/G♯
and his A - mer - i - can_ Ex - press. He checked_ the oil,_ slammed_ the hood,
F♯m7
E/G♯
A
E/G♯
said you're good_ to go._ She hugged_ them both and head - ed off to the
B2
A(9)
E
B5
west coast. And he cried...
a tempo

Chorus:
E B A B E B
There goes my life. There goes my fu-
A E/G♯ F♯m7 E/G♯
ture, my ev - 'ry-thing. I love you, ba - by, good -
A(9) E A
bye.
a tempo
Repeat ad lib. and fade
E/G♯ B E A E/G♯ B
There goes my life.

THESE DAYS

Words and Music by
JEFFREY STEELE,
DANNY WELLS and STEVE ROBSON

Em7
C(9)
G
D/F♯
it, I real-ly do.
"Nor-ma Jean," ain't that the song we'd sing
in the car driv-ing down-town, top down, mak-in' the rounds, check-in' out the bands
Am7(4)
G/B
on Do-he-ny Av-e-nue.
Yeah, life throws you curves,
Cmaj9
but you learned to swerve.
Me, I swung and I missed, and the next

Em
D
Am7(4)
G/B
thing you know, I'm re - mi - nis - cing, dream - ing old dreams, wish - ing old wish - es, like
C(9)
N.C.
Chorus:
D(9)
C(9)
you would be back a - gain.
I wake up in tear-
G/B
Dsus
C(9)
Em7
drops that fall down like rain.
I put on that old
C(9)
Dsus
D(9)
C(9)
song we danced to, and then
I head off to my

G/B
Dsus
C(9)
Em
job. Guess not much has changed. Punch the clock, head for home,
C(9)
Dsus
C(9)
G/B
check the phone just in case, go to bed, dream of you:
1.
Am7(4)
G
D/F♯
that's what I'm do - in' these days.
Em7
C(9)
G/B
D7sus
G
D/F♯
Yeah, that's what I'm do - in'.

2.
Em7
C(9)
D7sus
Am7(4)
Em
that's_ what I'm do - in'_ these_ days.
(Inst. solo ad lib....
Cmaj9
Em
C2
Ba - by._
D.S.
3.
Am7(4)
that's_ what I'm do - in'_ these..._
...end solo)
Chorus:
D(9)
C(9)
G/B
Dsus
I wake_ up in tear - drops that fall_ down like rain._

C(9) Em7 C(9) Dsus

— I put_ on that old_ song we danced_ to,_ and then..._

D(9) C(9) G/B Dsus

— I wake_ up in tear - drops that fall_ down like rain._

C(9) Em7 C(9) Dsus *Repeat ad lib. and fade*

— I put_ on that old_ song we danced_ to_ and then..._

Verse 2:
Someone told me, after college
You ran off to Vegas.
You married a rodeo cowboy.
Wow, that ain't the girl I knew.
Me, I've been a few places,
Mostly here and there once or twice.
Still sorting out life, but I'm doing alright.
Yeah, it's good to see you, too.
Well, hey girl, you're late,
And those planes, they don't wait.
But, if you ever come back around
This sleepy old town,
Promise me you'll stop in
To see an old friend,
And until then...
(To Chorus:)

THIS KISS

Words and Music by
ROBIN LERNER, ANNIE ROBOFF
and BETH NIELSEN CHAPMAN

B G♯m7 A F♯m7

But you got me like a rock - et shoot - ing straight a - cross the sky.
Ride me off in - to the sun - set, ba - by, I'm for - ev - er yours.

Chorus:

E E/G♯ A B

It's the way you love me. It's a feel - ing like this.

E E/G♯ A B

It's cen - trif - u - gal mo - tion. It's per - pet - u - al bliss.

E E/G♯ A B

It's that piv - ot - al mo - ment. It's, *ah,* {im - pos - si - ble. / un - think - a - ble.}

E E/G♯ A C♯m7 B

This kiss, this kiss, {un - stop - a - ble. / un - sink - a - ble.}

E
E/G♯
1.
A
C♯m7
B
2.
A
C♯m7
B
This kiss, this kiss.
Bridge:
C
Am7
D/F♯
G
You can kiss me in the moon-light, on the roof-top, un-der the sky, oh.
C
Am7
D/F♯
G
You can kiss me with the win-dows o-pen while the rain comes blow-in' in-side, oh.
C
C/B
Am7
G
D/F♯
G
Kiss me in sweet, slow mo-tion. Let's let ev-'ry-thing slide.
F♯m7
F♯m7/B
You got me float-ing, you got me fly-ing.

F♯
F♯/A♯
B
C♯
It's the way you love me. It's a feel-ing like this.

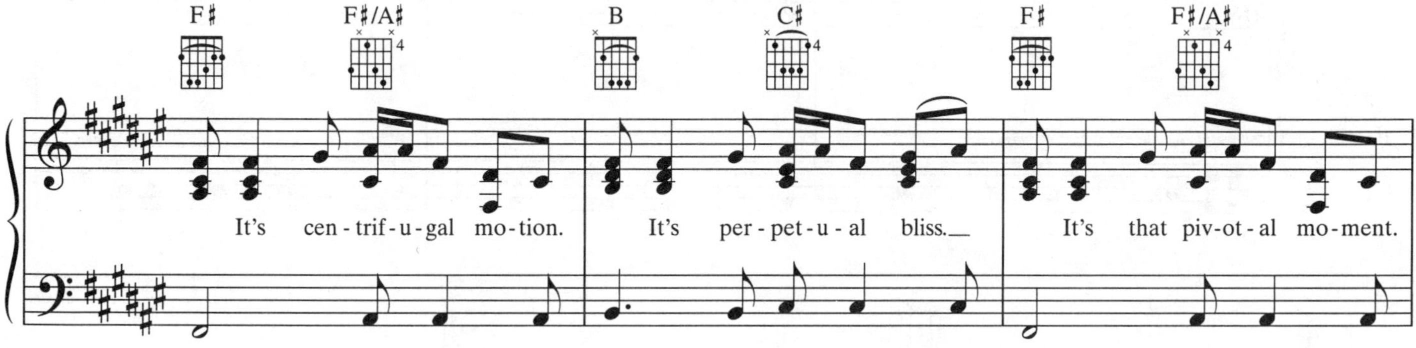
F♯
F♯/A♯
B
C♯
F♯
F♯/A♯
It's cen-trif-u-gal mo-tion. It's per-pet-u-al bliss. It's that piv-ot-al mo-ment.

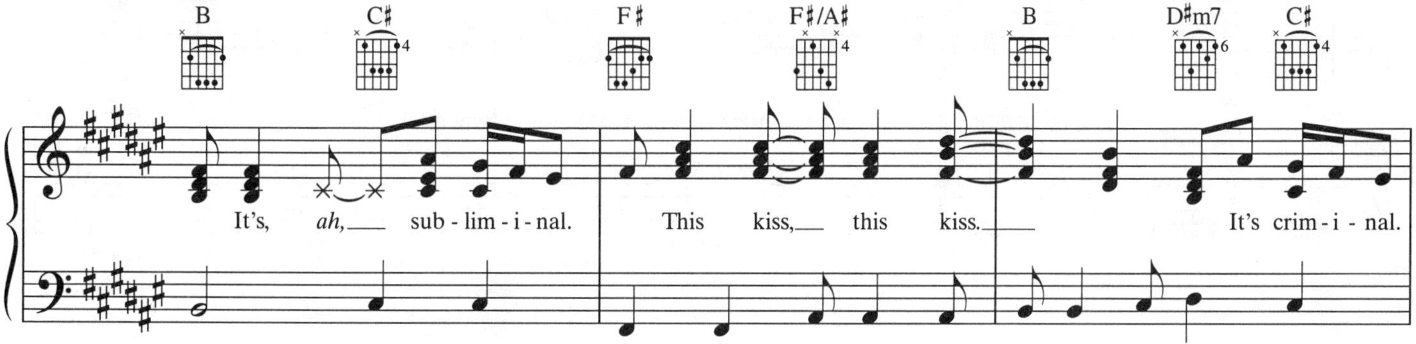
B
C♯
F♯
F♯/A♯
B
D♯m7
C♯
It's, ah, sub-lim-i-nal. This kiss, this kiss. It's crim-i-nal.

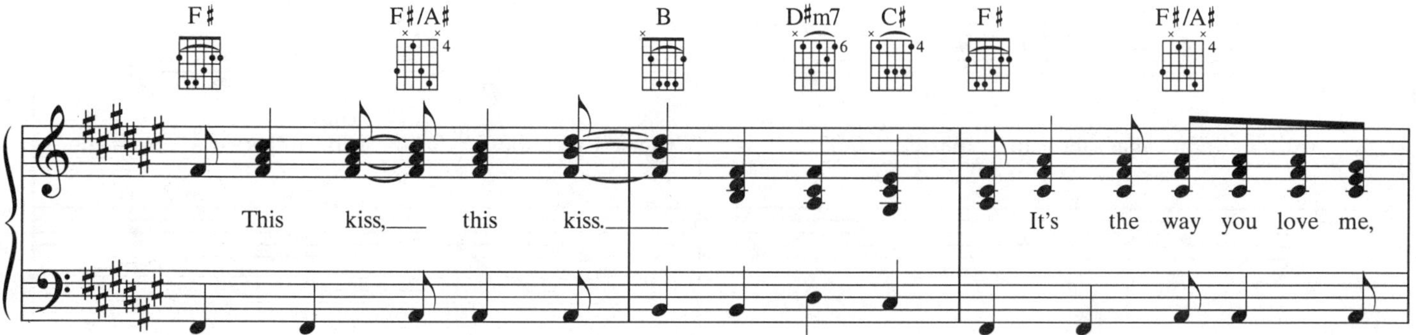
F♯
F♯/A♯
B
D♯m7
C♯
F♯
F♯/A♯
This kiss, this kiss. It's the way you love me,

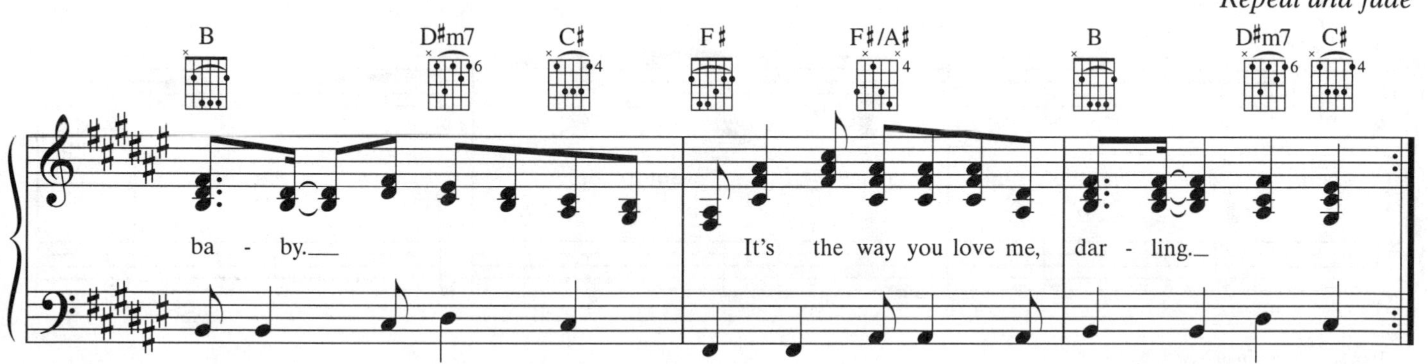
Repeat and fade
B
D♯m7
C♯
F♯
F♯/A♯
B
D♯m7
C♯
ba - by. It's the way you love me, dar - ling.

A THOUSAND MILES FROM NOWHERE

Words and Music by
DWIGHT YOAKAM

C
Am
I got heart-aches in my ___ pock - et, I got
(See additional lyrics)
C
Am
C
ech - oes ___ in my ___ head ___ and all that I ___ keep ___ hear -
Am
F
G
ing are the cruel, ___ cruel things ___ that you said. ___
C
Am
I'm a thou - sand miles ___ from no - where,
C
Am
C
time don't mat - ter to me. ___ 'Cause I'm a thou - sand miles ___ from no -

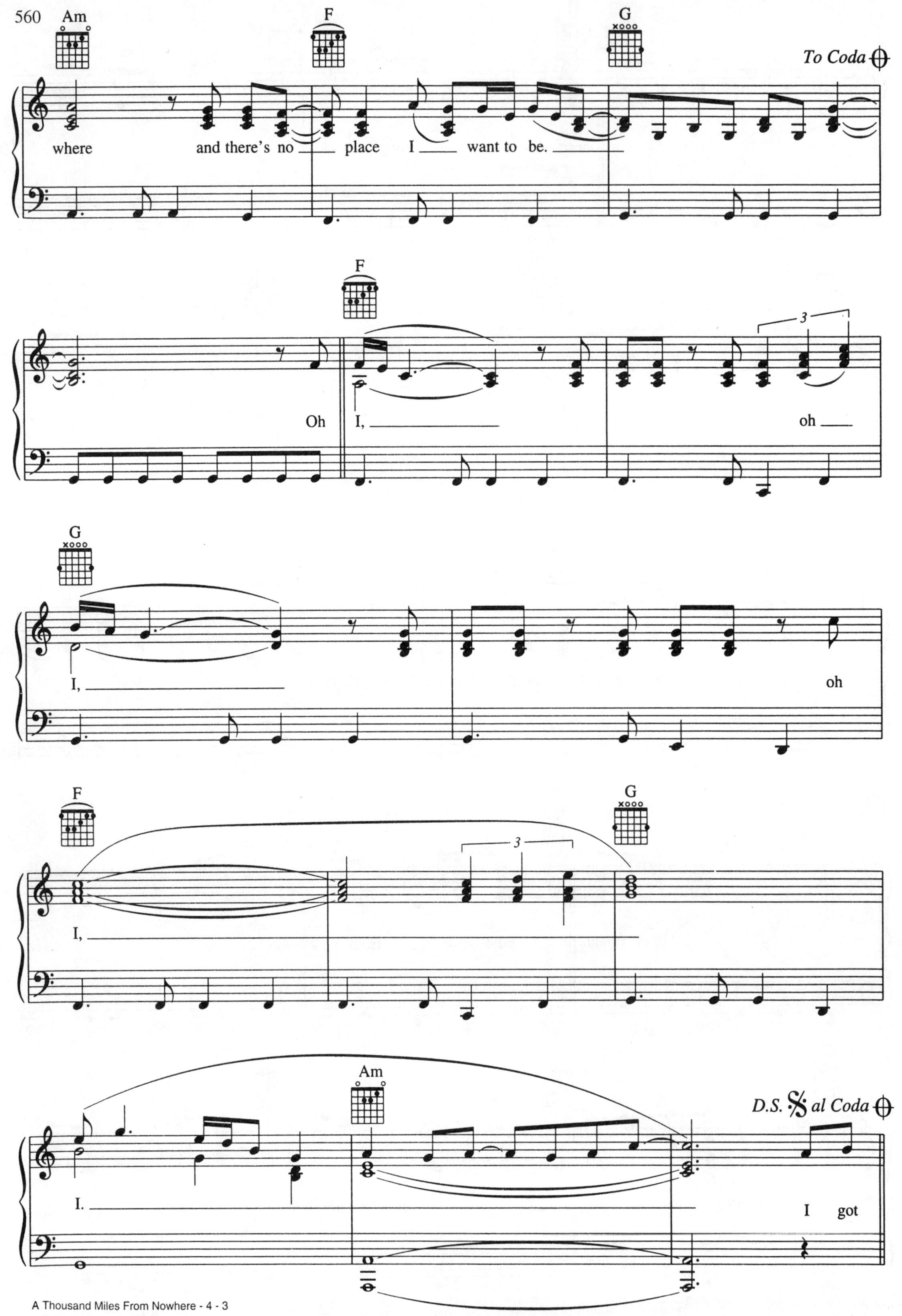
Am
F
G
To Coda
where and there's no place I want to be.
F
Oh I,
oh
G
I,
oh
F
G
3
I,
Am
D.S. al Coda
I. I got

Additional lyrics

2. I got bruises on my memory
I got tear stains on my hands
And in the mirror there's a vision
Of what used to be a man.

TOUGH LITTLE BOYS

Words and Music by
HARLEY ALLEN and DONALD SAMPSON

Em7/A
A
D
Dmaj7
him. So, I did - n't cry when I got a black eye. As
me. If you we're to ask, my wife would just laugh. She'd
D7
G
Gm6
bad as it hurt, I'd just grin. But when tough lit - tle boys grow
say, "I know all a - bout men, and how tough lit - tle boys grow
D
A/C#
Bm7
A
Em7
A
D
A/C#
up to be dads, they turn in - to big ba - bies a - gain. It
up to be dads, they turn in - to big ba - bies a - gain."
Chorus:
Bm7
G
D
A
scared me to death when you took your first steps. I'd fall ev - 'ry time you fell
I know one day, I'll give you a - way and I'm gon - na stand there and

D
A/C♯
Bm7
G
D/F♯
down. Your first day of school, I cried like a fool and
smile. But when I get home and I'm all a - lone, I'll
Em7
Em7/A
A
D
fol - lowed your school bus to town.
sit in your room for a while.
I did - n't cry when
Dmaj7
D7
G
Old Yell - er died, at least not in front of my friends. But when
Gm6
D
A/C♯
Bm7
A
Em7
A
tough lit - tle boys grow up to be dads, they turn in - to big ba - bies a - gain.

1.
G
D
F♯m
Bm7
A
G
Em7
A7sus
D
G/D
2.
D
D/F♯
G
D
A/C♯
When tough lit - tle boys grow up to be dads,
Bm7
Em7
A7sus
Freely
G
they turn in - to big ba - bies a - gain.
a tempo
D
F♯m7
Bm7
A
G
Em7
A7sus
D
rit.

TRAVELIN' SOLDIER

Words and Music by
BRUCE ROBINSON

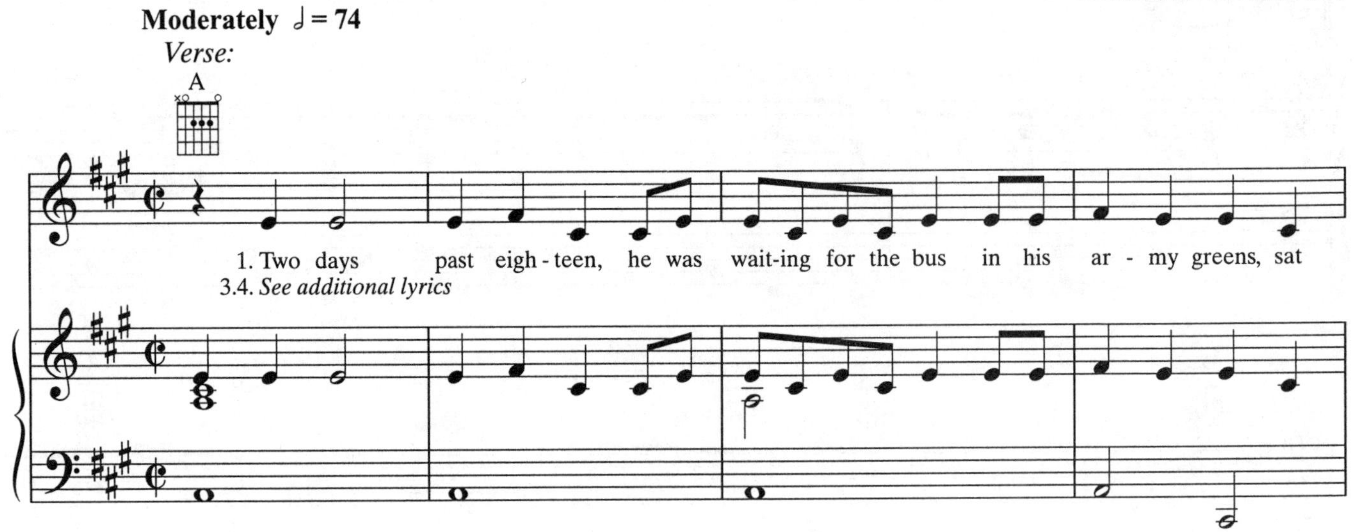

D
down_ for a while_ and talk - in' to me, I'm feel - in' a lit - tle low.___
A
G
1.
D
She said I'm off in an ho - ur and I___ know where we can go._
A
2. So, they
2.3.4.
D
A
E/G♯
___ back here___ to you?___

Chorus:
F♯m
D
I cried, never gonna hold the hand of another guy.
A
E
Too young for him, they told her, waitin' for the love of a traveling soldier.
F♯m
D
Our love will never end, waitin' for the soldier to come back again.
A
E
1.2.
A
Nevermore to be alone, when the letter said a soldier's comin' home.

Verse 2:
So, they went down and they sat on the pier.
He said, I bet you got a boyfriend, but I don't care.
I got no one to send a letter to,
Would you mind if I sent one back here to you?
(To Chorus:)

Verse 3:
So the letters came from an army camp,
In California, then Vietnam.
And he told her of his heart:
It might be love and all the things he was scared of.
He said when it's getting kinda rough over here,
I think of that day, sittin' down at the pier.
And I close my eyes and see your pretty smile.
Don't worry, but I won't be able to write for a while.
(To Chorus:)

Verse 4:
One Friday night at a football game,
The Lord's prayer said and the Anthem sang,
A man said, folks would you bow your head
For a list of the local Vietnam dead.
Crying all alone underneath the stands
Was a piccolo player in the marching band.
And one name read and nobody cared
But a pretty little girl with a bow in her hair.
(To Chorus:)

TWO OF A KIND, WORKIN' ON A FULL HOUSE

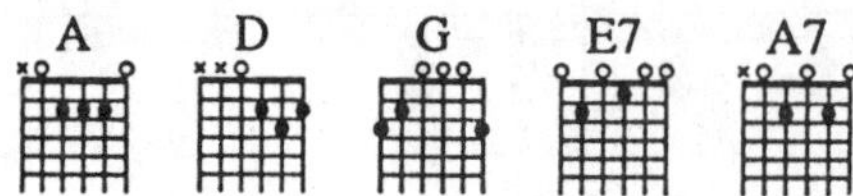

Words and Music by
BOBBY BOYD, WARREN DALE HAYNES
and DENNIS ROBBINS

Moderate country two-beat ♩ = 63

A

mf

D

Verse:

1. Yeah, she's my la - dy luck, hey I'm her wild card man. To - geth - er we're build - in' up a real hot hand. We live out in the coun - try. Hey, she's my lit - tle queen of the south.

G

3

Two of a Kind, Workin' on a Full House - 3 - 1

To Coda
A
Yeah, we're two of a kind,
work - in' on a full

1.
D
2.3.
D
house.
2. She wakes
house.
1. Yeah, a pick -

Bridge:
G
D
- up truck is
her lim - ou - sine. And her
fa - vor - ite dress is her

E7
fad - ed blue jeans. She
loves me ten - der when the
go - in' gets tough. Some-times

Verse 2:
She wakes me every mornin'
With a smile and a kiss.
Her strong country lovin' is hard to resist.
She's my easy lovin' woman,
I'm her hard-workin' man, no doubt.
Yeah, we're two of a kind
Workin' on a full house. *(To Bridge:)*

Verse 3:
Lord, I need that little woman
Like the crops need rain.
She's my honeycomb, and I'm her sugar cane.
We really fit together
If you know what I'm talkin' about.
Yeah, we're two of a kind
Workin' on a full house. *(To Bridge 2:)*

Bridge 2:
This time I found a keeper, I made up my mind.
Lord, the perfect combination is her heart and mine.
The sky's the limit, no hill is too steep.
We're playin' for fun, but we're playin' for keeps.

Verse 4:
So draw the curtain, honey.
Turn the lights down low.
We'll find some country music on the radio.
I'm yours and you're mine.
Hey, that's what it's all about.
Yeah, we're two of a kind
Workin' on a full house.
Lordy mama, we'll be two of a kind
Workin' on a full house.

UP!

Words and Music by
SHANIA TWAIN and R.J. LANGE

F
Dm7
me.
Like noth - in' wants to go my way; yeah, it just ain't been my
G7sus
G
Am
C
N.C.
day. Noth - in's com - in' eas - i - ly.
2. E - ven my skin is act - in'
Verses 2 & 3:
weird.
I wish that I could grow a beard.
(3.) as
for - get - tin' to fill up on gas.
Then I could cov - er up my spots, not play con - nect the dots. I just wan - na dis - ap -
There ain't no ex - pla - na - tion why; things like that can make you cry. Just got - ta learn to have a

Chorus:

Am G F Bb C

pear. Up, up, up, can on - ly go up___ from here,___
laugh. (Up, up.)

F Bb C F

___ up, up, up___ where the clouds_ gon - na clear.___ Up, up; there's no___
(Up, up.) (Up, up.)

Bb C 1. F Bb C N.C.

___ way but up___ from here.___ 3. E - ven some - thin' as sim - ple

2. F Bb C N.C. *Bridge:* F

___ Oh,___ e - yeah,_ yeah,_

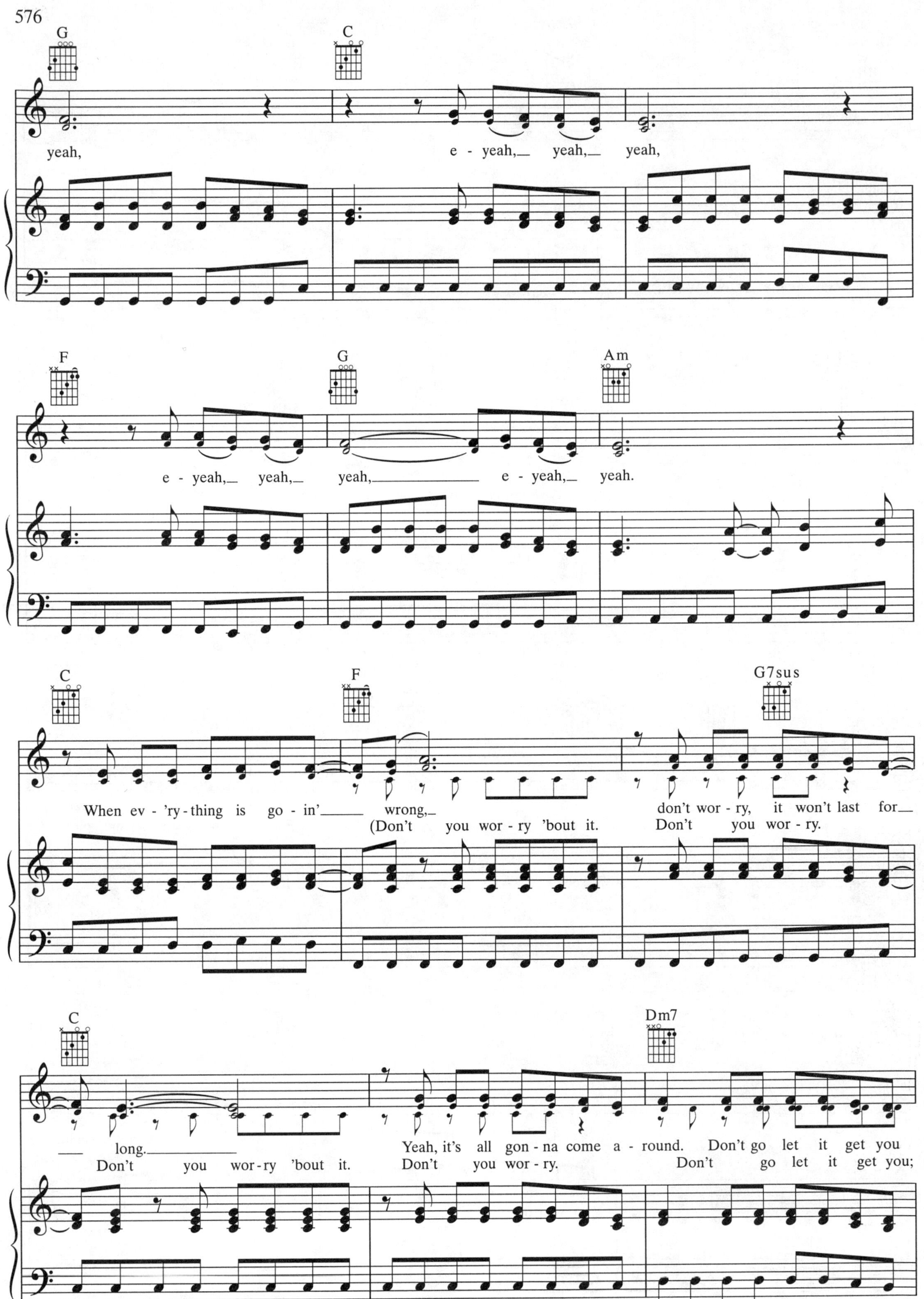
G
C
yeah,
e - yeah, yeah, yeah,
F
G
Am
e - yeah, yeah, yeah, e - yeah, yeah.
C
F
G7sus
When ev - 'ry - thing is go - in' wrong, don't wor - ry, it won't last for
(Don't you wor - ry 'bout it. Don't you wor - ry.
C
Dm7
long. Yeah, it's all gon - na come a - round. Don't go let it get you
Don't you wor - ry 'bout it. Don't you wor - ry. Don't go let it get you;

G7sus
G
Am
G/B
C
N.C.
down. You got - ta keep on hold - in' on.
Got - ta keep on hold - in'.)
4. It's 'bout as bad as it could
Verse 4:
C
F
be.
(Bad as it can be.)
Seems ev - 'ry - bod - y's bug - gin' me.
(Ev - 'ry - bod - y's bug - gin' me.
Dm7
G7sus
G
Like noth - in' wants to go my way; yeah, it just ain't been my day. Noth - in's com - in' eas - i -
)
Chorus:
Am
F
ly, oh, oh, oh, oh.
Up, up, up; can on -
(Up, up.)

Bb
C
F
Bb
C
ly go up from here, up, up, up where the clouds gon-na clear.
(Up, up.)
F
Bb
C
Up, up; there's no way but up from here.
(Up, up.)
F
Bb
C
F
Up, up, up. Oh, I'm go - in' up. I'm
(Up, up.) (I'm go - in' up.
Bb
C
F
go - in' up. I'm go - in' up, bom, bom.
I'm go - in', go - in', I'm go - in' up.

B♭
C
F
B♭
C N.C.
I'm go - in' up.
Oh,
I'm go - in',
I'm go - in' up.)
Bridge:
F
G
e - yeah, yeah, yeah,
C
F
e - yeah, yeah, yeah,
e - yeah, yeah,
G
Am
C
yeah, e - yeah, yeah.

THE VOWS GO UNBROKEN

(Always True to You)

Words and Music by
GARY BURR and ERIC KAZ

1 Asus
A
2 Asus
A
To next strain
feet. And to way. The
3 A
D
A
D
made. The vows go un - bro - ken. And
G
A
D
D/F#
G
A
you still know I do love keep and
D
G
D/A
A
To Coda
D
D.C. al Coda
hon - or, al - ways true to you.

CODA
D
Bm
E/G#
you. I knew from the first that for
A
D/F#
Bm
E7
bet - ter or worse I'd stand by you all my life.
Asus
A
D
A
And the vows go un -
D
G
A
bro - ken. And you still know I

D
D/F#
G
A
do
love
keep and
D
G
D/A
A
D
hon - or,
al - ways true to
you.
G
D
G
D/A
A
Love
keep and
hon - or,
al ways true to
D
A/D
G/D
D
A/D
G/D
D
you.

WALK A LITTLE STRAIGHTER

Words and Music by
BILLY CURRINGTON, CARSON CHAMBERLAIN
and CASEY BEATHARD

G
G/B
C(9)
A♭
A♭/C
D♭(9)
mem - ber most the time he was - n't there. I'd be
could - n't help but feel so a - shamed. And I
Em
D
C(9)
Fm
E♭
D♭(9)
wait - ing at the door when he got home at night. He'd
was - n't sur - prised a bit that he did - n't stay. He
Am7
G/B
D
B♭m7
A♭/C
E♭
pass me by to go pass out in his chair. And I'd say…
stum - bled out be - fore they called my name. And I thought…
Chorus:
G
Em7
C(9)
D
A♭
Fm7
D♭(9)
E♭
1.3. Walk a lit - tle straight - er, Dad - dy, you're sway - ing side to side.
2. Walk a lit - tle straight - er, Dad - dy, you're sway - ing side to side.

G
Em7
C(9)
D
Ab
Fm7
Db(9)
Eb
Your foot - steps make me diz - zy and no mat - ter how I try, I keep
It's not just me who's watch - ing, you've caught ev - 'ry - bod - y's eye. And you're
Am7
G/B
C
Bbm7
Ab/C
Db
trip - ping and stum - bling. If you'd look down here, you'd see. Walk a lit - tle
trip - ping and stum - bling and, e - ven though I've turned eigh - teen, walk a lit - tle
To Coda
1.
Am7
C
D
Bbm7
Db
Eb
straight - er, Dad - dy, you're lead - ing me.
straight - er, Dad - dy,
G
G/B
C(9)
Ab
Ab/C
Db(9)
2. He

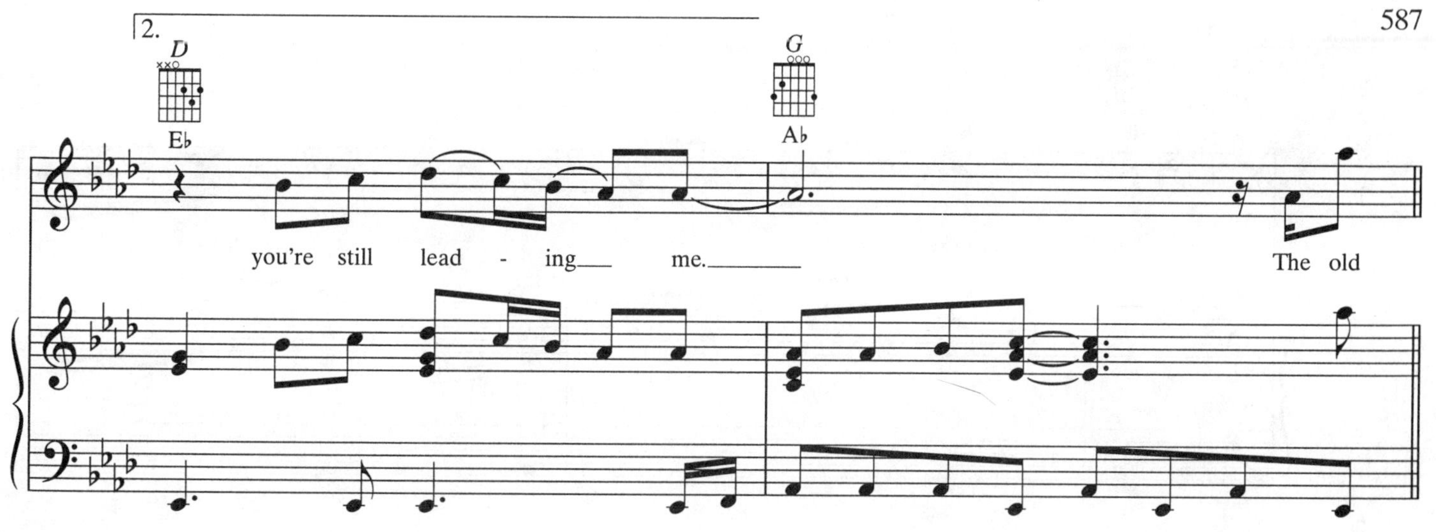
2.
D
E♭
G
A♭
you're still lead - ing me.
The old

Bridge:
C
D♭
G/B
A♭/C
man's still like he al - ways was, but I love him an - y - way. If I've

Am7
B♭m7
C
D♭
D
E♭
D.S. 𝄋 al Coda
learned one thing from him, it's my kids will nev - er have to say…
8va

Coda
D
E♭
G
A♭
you're lead - ing me.
Yeah, walk a lit - tle

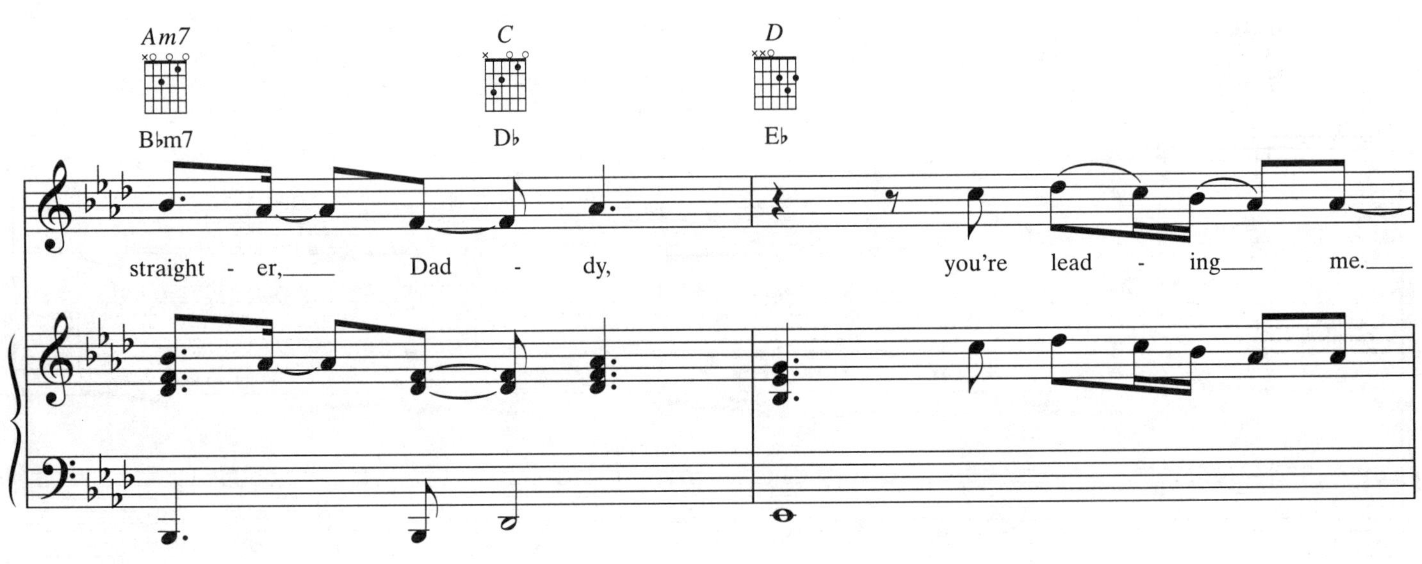
Am7
B♭m7
C
D♭
D
E♭
straight - er, Dad - dy,
you're lead - ing me.

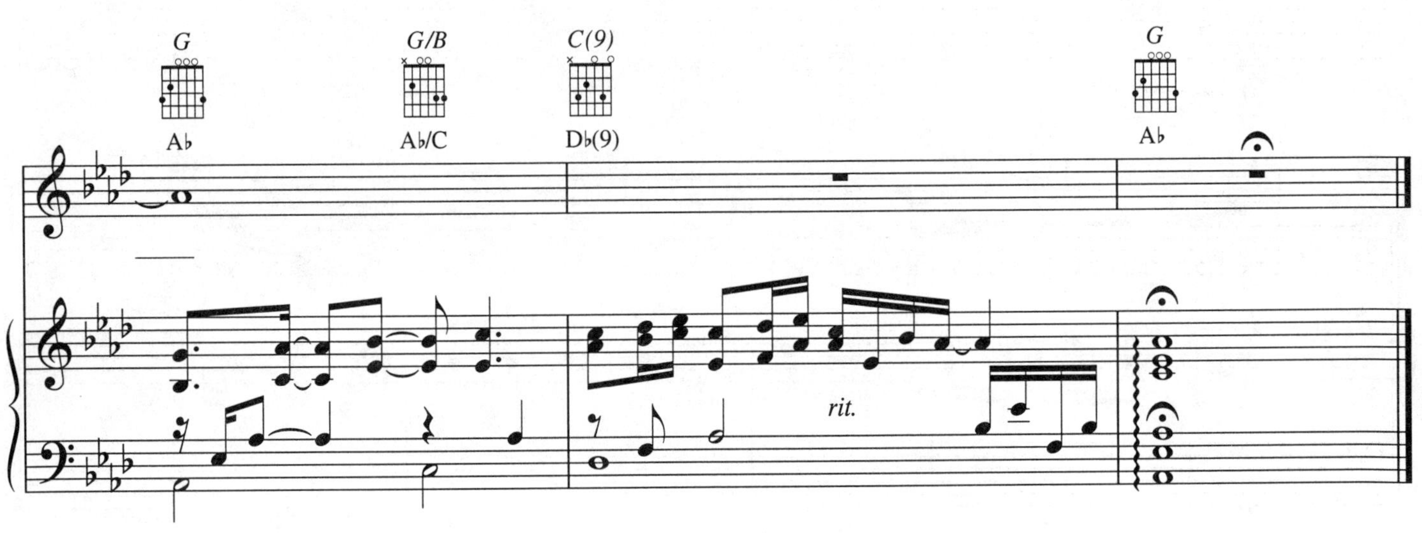
G
A♭
G/B
A♭/C
C(9)
D♭(9)
G
A♭
rit.

WHEN YOU SAY NOTHING AT ALL

Words and Music by
PAUL OVERSTREET and DON SCHLITZ

Ab
Bb
Ab
Bb
Try as I may, I could nev - er ex-plain
Old Mis-ter Web - ster could nev - er de-fine
Eb
Bb
Ab
Bb(addC)
what I hear when you don't say a thing.
what's be - ing said be- tween your heart and mine.
The
Eb
Bb
Ab
Bb
Eb
Bb
smile on your face lets me know that you need me. There's a truth in your eyes say - ing you'll
f
Ab
Bb
Eb
Bb
Ab
never leave me. A touch of your hand says you'll catch me if ev - er I fall.
Bb
To Coda
Ab/C
Bb/D
Eb/G
Ab
Yeah, you say it best

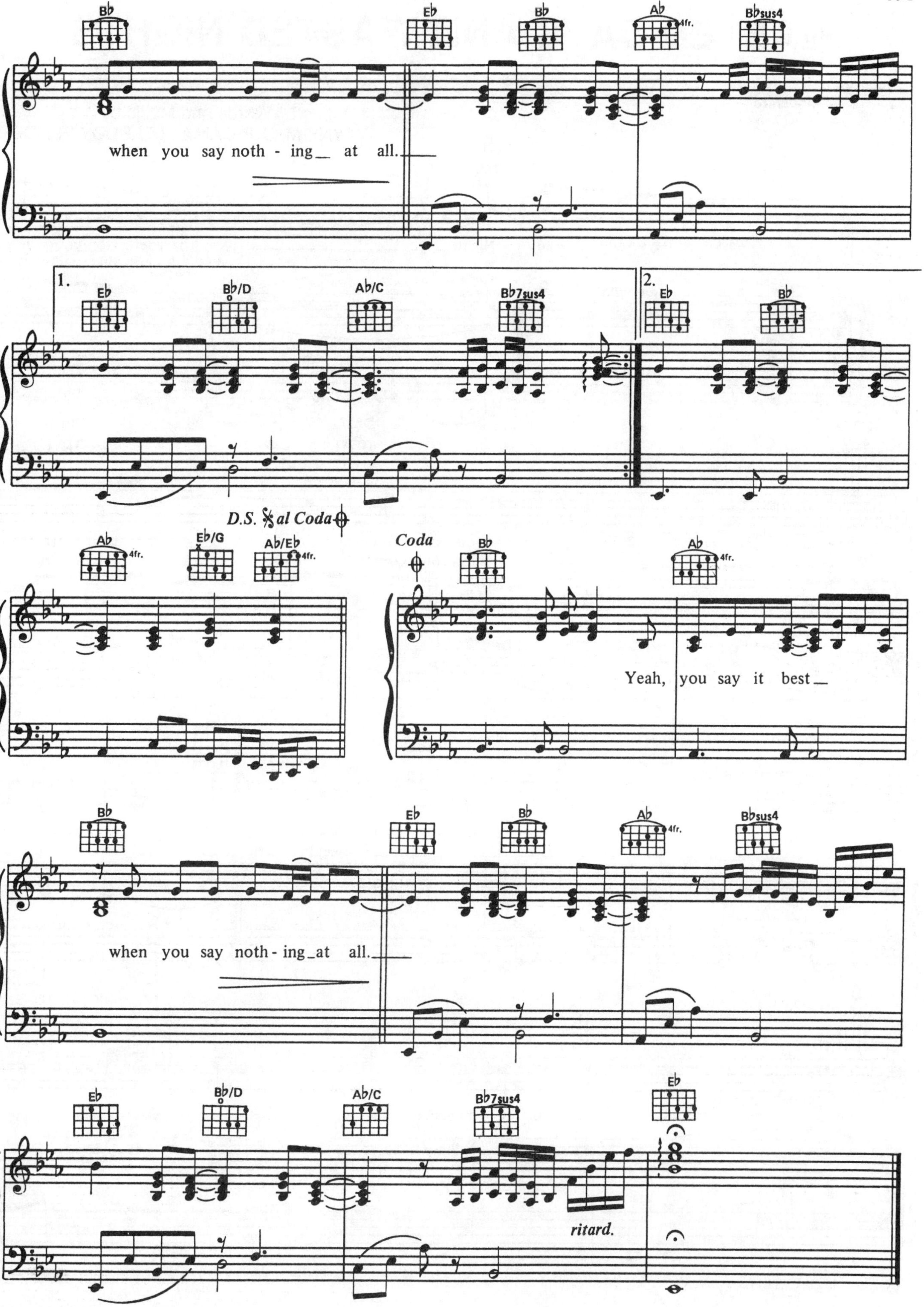

B♭ E♭ B♭ A♭ 4fr. B♭sus4

when you say noth - ing_ at all.__

1. E♭ B♭/D A♭/C B♭7sus4

2. E♭ B♭

D.S. 𝄋 al Coda ⊕

A♭ 4fr. E♭/G A♭/E♭ 4fr.

Coda ⊕ B♭ A♭ 4fr.

Yeah, you say it best_

B♭ E♭ B♭ A♭ 4fr. B♭sus4

when you say noth-ing_at all.__

E♭ B♭/D A♭/C B♭7sus4 E♭

ritard.

WASTED DAYS AND WASTED NIGHTS

Words and Music by
WAYNE M. DUNCAN and FREDDY FENDER

C
D7
left_ me.
I was so lone-ly
prayed for you on-ly,
my
G7
Tacet
C
love.
Why should I keep lov-ing you
G7
Dm7
when I know that you're not true,
And why should I call your
G7
Dm7
G7
C
F
C
name
when you're the blame
for mak-ing me blue.

WHAT A BEAUTIFUL DAY

Words and Music by
MONTY POWELL and CHRIS CAGLE

C(9)
G/B
C
B(9)
F♯/A♯
B
Av - e - nue.
Day two:
rest of my life.
Day one-eight-y -
Em7
D
D♯m7
C♯
nine:
We grabbed a bite to eat and talked
I al - most lost that girl to my
C(9)
G/B
C
B(9)
F♯/A♯
B
all af - ter - noon.
fool - ish pride.
Am7
D
G♯m7
C♯
Caught a mov - ie on day four - teen
She said I do on day four-eight-y - two

C(9)
D
B(9)
C♯
and day six - ty - sev - en she said I love you to me.
and gave me a son on day sev - en - six - ty - one.
Oh, what a feel -
Chorus:
G
Bm7
C(9)
F♯
A♯m7
B(9)
ing. What a won - der - ful e - mo - tion.
D
G
C♯
F♯
Yeah, what a life,
Bm7
C(9)
D
A♯m7
B(9)
C♯
count - ing my bless - ings and know - ing; oo, we

C(9) D
B(9) C♯

had our ups__ and downs__ all a - long__ the way.__ She

To Coda 𝄌

C(9) D
B(9) C♯

had a chance__ to leave,__ but chose to stay. What a beau - ti - ful

1.

G/B C(9) D/F♯ G
F♯/A♯ B(9) C♯/E♯ F♯

day.__ What a beau - ti - ful__

G/B C(9) D/F♯ G
F♯/A♯ B(9) C♯/E♯ F♯

__ day. 2. Day one - six -

2.
G/B
C(9)
D/F#
G
F#/A#
B(9)
C#/E#
F#
day.
G/B
C(9)
D/F#
G
F#/A#
B(9)
C#/E#
F#
3
Bridge:
Bm7
C(9)
A#m7
B(9)
Day eight - teen thou - sand, two hun-dred and fif - ty three: Well, hon-ey,
Bm7
C(9)
D
D.S. 𝄋 al Coda
A#m7
B(9)
C#
that's fif - ty years. Yeah, here's to you and me. Oh, what a feel -

Coda
D
C♯
to stay.
What a beau - ti - ful
G/B
C(9)
D/F♯
G
F♯/A♯
B(9)
C♯/E♯
F♯
day.
What a beau-ti - ful
G/B
C(9)
D/F♯
G
F♯/A♯
B(9)
C♯/E♯
F♯
day.
Day one:
Em7
D
C(9)
D♯m7
C♯
B(9)
I thank God I said hel-lo on Fifth Av-e - nue.

WHEN I SAID I DO

Words and Music by
CLINT BLACK

A
B♭
E
F
We take 'em all the way that we should. To -
D
E♭
geth - er, you and me, for - sak - ing them all.
F♯m
Gm
E
F
Deep in the night and by the light of day, it
D
E♭
al - ways looks the same. True love al - ways does.
A
B♭
E/G♯
F/A
And here by your side, we're a mil - lion miles a - way. Noth - ing's

D
E♭
ev - er gon - na change the way I feel. The way it is is the way that it
Chorus:
A
B♭
E
F
Bm7
Cm7
was. When I said I do, I meant that I will,
D
E♭
Bm7/E
Cm7/F
A
B♭
'til the end of all time, be faith - ful and
E
F
G
A♭
D
E♭
true, de - vot - ed to you. That's what I had in mind when
1.
A
B♭
D/A
E♭/B♭
I said I do.
2. Well, this

Verse 2:
Well, this old world keeps changin'
And the world stays the same
For all who came before.
And it goes hand in hand,
Only you and I can undo
All that we became.
That makes us so much more
Than a woman and a man.
And after everything that comes and goes around
Has only passed us by,
Here alone in our dreams,
I know there's a lonely heart in every lost and found.
But forever you and I will be the ones
Who found out what forever means.
(To Chorus:)

WHEN YOU LIE NEXT TO ME

Words and Music by
KELLIE COFFEY, TRINA HARMON
and J.D. MARTIN

C Gsus G C

time___ to feel;___ I don't want to miss_ the chance_ to be so___
time___ to love,___ 'cause you nev - er know_ when life___ will leave_

F2 Dm Am7 G

___ real._ The days all fly a - way, and I for - get the truth,_
___ us.___ I want to take in all the beau - ty here;_

Dm Am7 B♭ C/B♭ B♭ B♭/C

Chorus:

F

ev - 'ry - thing_ that mat - ters___ *is* in this room._
let the world_ a - round us___ *just* dis - ap - pear.__

When you_ lie next to me,__ breath - ing the

C Dm B♭ C/B♭ B♭ B♭/C

air I breathe,_ we don't have to speak, just___ be. Love is a

F C C7/E F F/A
pre-cious thing. Don't want to waste a day, one more min - ute with-out you
1.
F/B♭ Dm9 Csus C F
in it. Life is so sweet when you lie next to me.
B♭2
2. My
2.
F/B♭ Dm9 Csus C
in it. Life is so sweet when you lie
F B♭2 C/B♭ B♭ B♭2 N.C.
next to me, oh, lie next to me, oh. When you

Chorus:
G
D
Em
lie next to me, breath-ing the air I breathe, we don't have to speak, just
C
D/C
C
D
G
D
D7/F♯
be. Woah, love's a pre-cious thing. Don't want to waste a day, one more
G
G/B
G/C
Em9
min - ute with-out you in it. Life is so
Dsus
D
C2
G(9)
sweet when you lie next to me, when you lie next to me.
rit.

WHEN YOU THINK OF ME

Words and Music by
TROY VERGES and BRETT JAMES

B♭
C/B♭
B♭
C/B♭
my best to beat 'em, but in my head, the de - mons said, "Move
F
F2
F
F2
on."
Am7
Gm7
When you wake up, you're gon - na curse my name.
Am7
B♭(9)
But as some time goes by, I hope and pray. When you
3
3
3

Chorus:
Dm7
B♭
F
C
think of me,
re-mem-ber the way that I used
to be.
Re-mem-ber the times I held you ten-
der-ly.
Re-mem-ber the way that I
C/B♭
B♭
1.
B♭2
loved you.
2. I think a-

2.

B♭2 B♭ Dm7 B♭

Oh, when you think of me. *(Inst. solo ad lib....*

F C Dm7 B♭

F C Am7

Bridge:

...end solo) As I pick up these bags and turn

Gm7 G7/B

a - round, I say a lit - tle prayer and

Chorus:
B♭
Dm7
B♭
hope some - how. When you think of me,
F
C
Dm7
B♭
re - mem - ber the way that I used to be.
F
C
Dm7
B♭
Re - mem - ber the times I held you ten - der - ly.
F
C
1.
C/B♭
B♭
Re - mem - ber the way that I loved you. When you

Verse 2:
I think about the night I met you.
I swore I'd never forget you.
Well, I won't.
I think about the way you'll live
And breathe inside my dreams forever.
You'll be better when I'm gone.
You'll be better when I'm gone.
'Cause I know you're gonna fall in love again.
I'm sorry, this is how it has to end.
But…
(To Chorus:)

WHERE THE BLACKTOP ENDS

Words and Music by
STEVE WARINER and
ALLEN SHAMBLIN

Moderate two-beat ♩ = 80

Chorus:
A
G
D
kick off my shoes and run___ in bare feet where the grass and the dirt and the
G
D
A
G
grav - el all meet. Go - in' back to the well, gon - na vis - it old friends, and
D
N.C.
A
feed my soul___ where the black - top___ ends.
1. I'm

Verse:
D G D A
look-in' down the bar-rel of Fri - day night, and rid - in' on a riv - er of free-
2. Work-in' in the grind is an up - hill road. I'm punch - in' that clock and
D G D
way lights. Good-bye, cit - y; I'm coun - try bound 'til
car - ry'n' that load. I bust it all week and then I'm free. The
B E
Mon - day rolls a - round.
week - end be - longs to me.
Gon - na
Chorus:
A G D
kick off my shoes and run in bare feet where the grass and the dirt and the

G
D
A
G
grav - el all meet. Go - in' back to the well, gon - na vis - it old friends, and
To Coda
1.
D
N.C.
A
feed my soul where the black - top ends.
3
3
3
3

2.
To Next Strain
A
where the black - top ends.
So, come on.
3.
D.S. 𝄋 al Coda
Bridge:
C
You bet.
Gon - na
Give me that fresh air;
G
D
A
give me that farm.
Give me some time with you in my arms.
C
G
E
Far a - way from the hus - tle and the pres - sure and the noise.

N.C.
D.S. 𝄋
Gon - na
𝄌 Coda
A
where the black - top___ ends,
3
3
where the black - top___ ends.
3
Repeat ad lib. and fade
Where the black - top___
3
3

WHO WOULDN'T WANNA BE ME

Words and Music by
MONTY POWELL and KEITH URBAN

Moderately fast ♩ = 120

Verse 1:
1. I got no mon-ey in my pock-ets.
I got a hole in my jeans.
I had a job__ and I lost it,

but it won't get to me.
2. 'Cause I'm
Verses 2 & 3:
rid - ing with my ba - by
strum - ming on my six string
and it's a brand new day.
a - cross her pret - ty knees.
We're on the wheels of an an - gel,
She's stomp - ing out a rhy - thm
fly - ing a -
and sing - ing to
Chorus:
D
way.
me
the sweet - est song.
And the sun is shin -

Em7
ing and this road keeps wind - ing through the pret -
G
D
ti - est coun - try from Geor - gia to Ten - nes - see.
And I got the one I love be - side me, my trou -
To Coda 1.
Em7
G
bles be - hind me. I'm a - live and I'm free. Who

D5
would-n't wan-na be me?
2.
G
3. Now, she's and I'm free. Who
D
would-n't wan-na be me?
(Inst. solo ad lib….
Em7
G

D.S. 𝄋 al Coda
D
...end solo) And the
Coda
G
D5
and I'm free.
Who would-n't wan-na be me?
Repeat ad lib. and fade
D
Em7
F♯m7
Em7
1. Got no mon-ey in my pock-et.
2. I got a hole in my jeans.
3. etc.

WHY THEY CALL IT FALLING

Words and Music by
ROXIE DEAN and DON SCHLITZ

A
B7sus
B7
feel - ing that can take you an - y - where. So
Chorus:
E
E/G♯
A
A/C♯
B
C♯m
why they call it fall - ing, why they call it fall - ing, why
To Coda
1.
A
Bsus
E
E/G♯
A
A/C♯
B7sus
B
they call it fall - ing, (1.2.) I don't (3.) now I know.
2. There was
2.
Bridge:
E
D
A/C♯
know. But you can't live your life walk - ing in the clouds.
C
E/B
B
A
Soon - er or lat - er, you have to come down.

Verse 2:
There was passion, there was laughter
The first morning after.
I just couldn't get my feet to touch the ground.
Everytime we were together
We talked about forever.
I was certain it was heaven we had found.
(To Chorus:)

Verse 3:
It's like a knife through the heart
When it all comes apart.
It's like someone takes a pin to your balloon.
It's a hole, it's a cave,
It's kinda like a grave
When he tells you that he's found somebody new.
(To Chorus:)

WIDE OPEN SPACES

Words and Music by
SUSAN GIBSON

F♯m7
E/G♯
Who's nev - er left home, who's _ nev - er struck out to find a
A
E
A
dream and a life _ of their own, a place _ in the clouds, _ a foun - da -
A/B
B
E
F♯m7
tion of stone? _
Man - y pre - cede and man - y will
She trav - eled this road _ as _ a
E
F♯m7
fol - low, a young girl's dreams no long - er
child, _ wide - eyed and grin - ning, she nev - er
3

E
A
E
hol - low. It takes the shape of a place out west.
tired. But now she won't be com - ing back with the
A
rest. But what it holds for her she has - n't yet
If these are life's les - sons, she'll take this
A/B
B
E
F♯m7
guessed.
test.
She needs wide o - pen spac -
A
B
E
F♯m7
- es, room to make her big mis -

A
B
E
F#m7
takes. She needs new fac
es. She knows the high stakes.
stakes. She know the high stakes.

F♯m7
E
F♯m7
E
F♯m7
A/B
E
A/C♯
E
As her folks drive a-way, her dad yells, "Check the oil."
A/C♯
E
Mom stares out the win-dow and says, "I'm leav-in' my girl." She said, "It

A
E
A
did-n't seem like that long a - go,"
when she stood _ there
and let her own
A/B
B
E
F#m7
A
B
folks know _ she need - ed
wide o - pen spac - es,
E
F#m7
A
B
room to make _ her big _ mis - takes.
She needs _
E
F#m7
A
B
new _ fac - es.
She knows the high

E
F#m7
A
B
E
F#m7
stakes. She knows the high stakes, she knows the high stakes. Wide o - pen spac -
A
B
E
F#m7
- es, she knows the high stakes,
A
B
E
F#m7
A
B
she knows the high stakes, wide o - pen spac - es.
E
F#m7
A
A/B
E

WINGS OF A DOVE

Words and Music by
BOB FERGUSON

Eb
Bb
Eb
us. He sends down His love On the Wings Of A Dove.
ten. He sent Him His love On the Wings Of A Dove.
He sent Him His love On the Wings Of A Dove.
Ab
Eb
Chorus
(Tacet)
(Tacet)
Eb
On the wings of a snow white dove He sends His
mp
Ab
Eb
Bb7
pure sweet love, A sign from a - bove On the Wings Of A
1,2 Eb
Ab
Eb
(Tacet)
3 Eb
Ab
Eb
Dove. 2. When No - ah had
3. When Je - sus went
Dove.

WWW.MEMORY

Words and Music by
ALAN JACKSON

WWW.Memory - 4 - 1

F
B♭
C
write. You made your mind up; you're gone to - night.
F
Gm
C
If some rain - y day you're all a - lone,
Gm
C
N.C.
you feel like talk - in' you can log me on.
At W W W .
Chorus:
B♭
F
mem - o - ry
I'll be wait - in' for you pa - tient - ly.
B♭
C
If you feel the need, just click on me at W W W .

B♭
F
To Coda
N.C.
memory.
F
C
Bridge:
You won't even have to hold me or
look into my eyes. You can tell me that you love me through
E♭

B♭
F
B♭
C
your key - board and wires. No, you won't have to touch me or e - ven take my hand. Just
E♭
C
N.C.
D.S. 𝄋 al Coda
slide your lit - tle mouse a - round un - til you see it land. At W W W .
Coda
B♭
C
If you feel like love, just click on me at W W W .
B♭
F
N.C.
B♭
mem - o - ry.
C
B♭
F

WITHOUT YOU

Moderately
Words and Music by
NATALIE MAINES
and ERIC SILVER
D
mf
D
A7
I've sure en - joyed the rain, but I'm
nev - er thought I'd be ly - ing
D
look - in' for - ward to the sun. You have to feel the pain
here with - out you by my side. It seems un - real to me
A7
D
when you lose the love you gave some - one. I
that the life you prom - ised was a lie. You

Bm
D/A
G
thought by now the time would take a-way these lone-ly tears. I
make it look so eas-y mak-ing love in-to mem-o-ries. I
D
A
D
hope you're do-in' fine all a-lone, but where do I go from here?
guess you got what you want-ed, but what a-bout me?
'Cause
A
D
A
with-out you I'm not o-kay. And with-out you I've lost
D
Bm
Bm/A
my way. My heart's stuck in sec-ond place, ooh,

1
2
G
A
D
To Coda
Em7
D/F#
ooh,
with - out
you.
Well, I
3

A
C
G
Some-bod - y tell my head to try to tell my heart
D
E
A
that I'm bet - ter off with - out you. 'Cause, ba - by,
D.S. al Coda
I can't live. With - out you I'm not
CODA
D
With-out you.

YOU CAN'T HIDE BEAUTIFUL

Words and Music by
MICHAEL DULANEY and JASON SELLERS

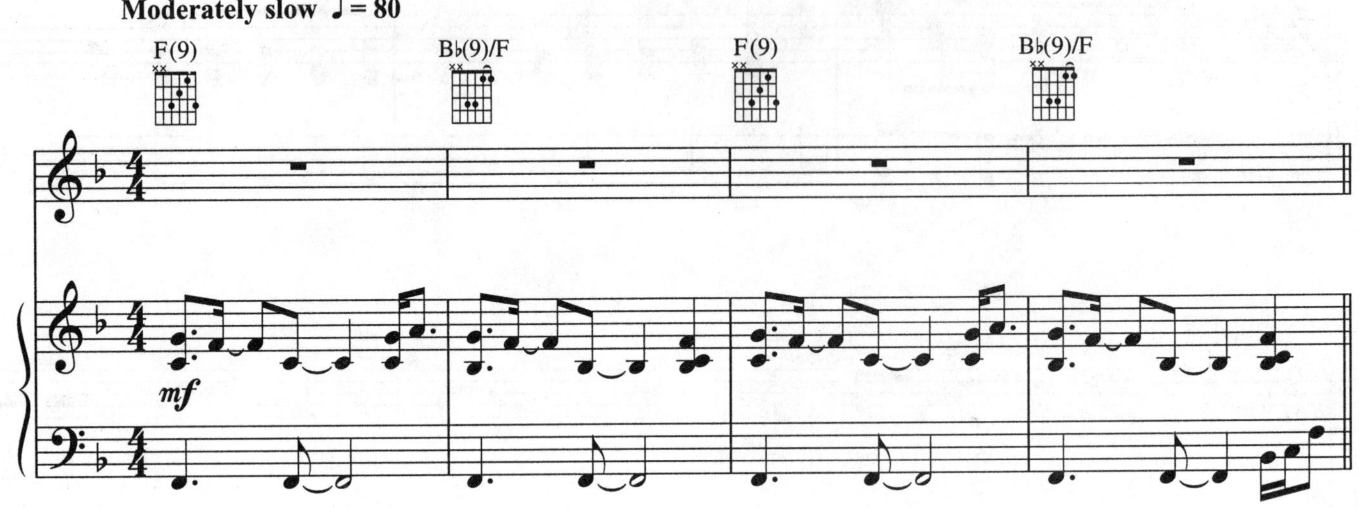

C2
She looks through mag - a - zines,
with ev - 'ry page, she dreams of
B♭2
look-ing like some-bod-y else
I wish she was-n't so hard on her-self.
Gm7
F/A
B♭(9)
Then she falls a - sleep with just my T shirt on,
Gm7
F/A
B♭
but e - ven when her hair's messed up and her make-up's gone...

Chorus:
Csus
C
F(9)
You can't hide beau - ti - ful. You can't hide
C
B♭(9)
won - der - ful. There's noth - ing that she has to do, it just comes
Dm7
Csus
F(9)
nat - u - ral. She makes it look eas - y. I love what she
C
B♭
C
does to me. No way to dis - guise the way

Bb/D
C/E
Gm7
that she shines. You can't hide beau - ti - ful.
1.
Bb2
2.
Bb
C
You can't hide
F(9)
C
beau - ti - ful.
Bb(9)
Bb/D
C/E
She makes it look eas -

F(9)
C
y.
I love what she does to me.
No way
B♭
C
B♭/D
C/E
to dis - guise the way that she shines.
You can't hide beau -
Gm7
B♭2
ti - ful.
You can't hide
F(9)
B♭(9)/F
beau - ti - ful

F(9) Bb(9)/F

F(9) Bb(9)/F

F(9) Bb(9)/F

Repeat ad lib. and fade

Verse 2:
She can take a simple dress,
Put it on and turn some heads.
Man, every time she moves, she gets me.
She doesn't even know she's sexy.
And the way she thinks sometimes
Out of nowhere blows my mind.
She makes me laugh and makes me dream.
I love the way she looks at things.
A little piece of heaven, God gave to this world.
She might think she's just an ordinary girl but…
(To Chorus:)

YOU CAN'T TAKE THE HONKY TONK OUT OF THE GIRL

Words and Music by
BART ALLMAND and BOB DiPIERO

E
B
A
F
C
B♭
Just in time for the re-hears-al din-ner, that cra-zy Con-nie was-n't
Con-nie said, "Hey, girls, let's hud-dle up a-round some-thin' 'bout a
wear-in' an-y shoes. Yeah, she lives in
hun-dred proof." She lives in
Chorus:
L. A., she flies to
New York Cit-y, that wom-an's been a-round the world.
You can take that
girl out of the hon-ky-tonk, but you can't take the hon-ky-tonk,

To Coda
1.
E
F
take the hon - ky - tonk out of the girl.
(Ooh,
B
C
A
B♭
ooh.)
2. Well, that
2.
E
F
B
C
A
B♭
E
F
B
C

Bridge:
A
B♭
E
F
Well, at nine A. M., out in front
B
C
A
B♭
of that church, people go - in' nuts, look - in' for the groom.
E
F
B
C
Some - bod - y says, "Hey, by the way, where's Con - nie?"
A
B♭
B
C
D.S. 𝄋 al Coda
She's run off with that boy to Can - cun. Yeah, she lives in

Coda
E
F
Vocal 1st time only
B
C
A
B♭
E
F
B
C
A
B♭
Repeat and fade

YOU LIGHT UP MY LIFE

Words and Music by
JOE BROOKS

G
B♭
Cm7
B♭/D
lone in the dark,
now you've come a - long.
Nev - er a - gain
to be all a - lone.
And
E♭
E♭maj7
E♭7
C7
you light up my life.
You give me hope
Fm
Fm7
B♭7
To Coda
to car - ry on.
You light up my days
and fill my
1.
E♭
B♭/D
Cm7
Fm
Fm7
B♭
nights
with
song.

D.S. 𝄋 al Coda
2.
E♭
B♭/D
Cm7
Fm
Fm7
B♭
Cm7
B♭/D
nights with song. 'Cause
𝄌 Coda
G7
G7/B
Cm
F7
E♭/B♭
nights with song. It can't be wrong when
G7/B
Cm7
F9
E♭/B♭
B♭7sus
it feels so right, 'cause you,
B♭7
A♭
E♭
B♭7
A♭(9)
E♭/G
Fm7
E♭
you light up my life.
rit.
a little slower

YOU LOOK SO GOOD IN LOVE

Words and Music by
RORY BOURKE, KERRY CHATER
and GLEN BALLARD

C
G
more than the wine.
wear in your eyes.
And he must do
I had my
Am
some - thing that I did-n't do.
chan - ces but I set you free,
What
D
C
ev - er he's do - ing it looks good on
and now I won - der why I could - n't
D
G
Bm7
you.
see.
You look so good in
3

Am
D
love.
You want him
that's
ea - sy
to see.
G
D
You look
G
Bm7
Am
so
good
in love.
D
I wish
you still want - ed
3
3

G
D
Bm
Am
me.
D
G
Eb7
Ab
Cm7
(spoken:) Darling I've wasted alot of
so good in
Bbm
Eb
years not seeing the real you. but
love. You want him that's

Ab
Eb
tonight your beauty is shining through.
ea - sy to see.
You look
Ab
Cm7
Bbm
3
And I never took the time to let you know.
so good in love.
3
Eb
So before he takes you away, please let me
I wish you still want - ed
Ab
1 Eb
2 Eb
D.S. and Fade
say
me.
(Sung:) You look
You look

YOU NEEDED ME

Words and Music by
RANDY GOODRUM

F
D7
G
back for me, and held it up and gave it dig- ni- ty. Some-how you
C
F/C
need- ed me. You gave me strength to stand a- lone a-gain, to face the
G7/C
C
Em
world out on my own a-gain. You put me high up- on a
F
F♯dim
C/G
E/G♯
Am
D7
ped- es-tal, so high that I can al- most see e- ter- ni-ty. You

G7
C
E/G♯
Am
C/G
need-ed me.
You need-ed me.
And I can't be-lieve it's you, I can't be-lieve
mf
F
C/E
Dm7
Dm7/G
C
E7
it's true.
I need-ed you
and you were there.
And I
Am
C/G
F
C/E
nev- er leave, why should I leave, I'd be a fool,
'cause I've
D7/F♯
D7
G7sus
G7
fin- 'lly found some- one who real- ly cares.
You held my
smoothly
mp

C
F/C
G7/C
hand when it was cold. When I was lost you took me
C
Em
F sus
F
home. You gave me hope, when I was at the end,_ and turned my
D7
G sus
G
lies back in- to truth a-gain._ You e- ven
C
F/C
called me friend. You gave me strength to stand a- lone a-gain,_ to face the
mf

G7/C
Csus
C
Em
world out on my own a-gain.
You put me high up- on a
Fsus
F
F♯dim
C/G
E/G♯
Am
D7
ped- es- tal,
so high that I can al- most see e- ter- ni- ty.
You
G7
C
A7
D7
G7
need- ed me.
You need- ed me.
You need- ed me.
You
mp
C
A7
Dm
G7
C
need- ed me.
rit.

YOU WERE MINE

Written by
MARTIE SIEDEL and EMILY ERWIN

E/G#
E
F#m7
D
to hang on.
What went wrong can be for-giv - en.
With-out
have be - gun to fade.
Please tell me she's not real
and that you're
F#m7
D
A
you, it ain't worth liv - in' a - lone.
real - ly com - in' home to stay.
Some - times
E
D
A
D
I wake up cry - in' at night.
And some - times
E
D
A
I scream out your name.
What right

E
D
A
does she have to take { you a - way / your heart a - way } when for so
Bm7
2fr
D
1
E
2
E
D
long you were mine?
I
G
D/F#
I can give you two good rea - sons to
F
C
show you love's not blind.
He's

A
E/G♯
F♯m
D
A/C♯
two and she's four and you know they a - dore you. So,
Bm7
2 fr
A/C♯
D
E
how can I tell them you've changed your mind? Some - times
F♯
E
B
E/G♯
I wake up cry - in' at night and some - times
F♯
E
B
I scream out your name. What right

F♯
E
B/D♯
4fr
B
does she have to take your heart a - way when for so
C♯m7
4fr
E
F♯
long you were mine?
I re - mem -
C♯m7
4fr
E
F♯
B
E
ber when you were mine.
Gm7
Esus2
Emaj7
B

YOU'RE STILL HERE

Words and Music by
AIMEE MAYO and
MATRACA BERG

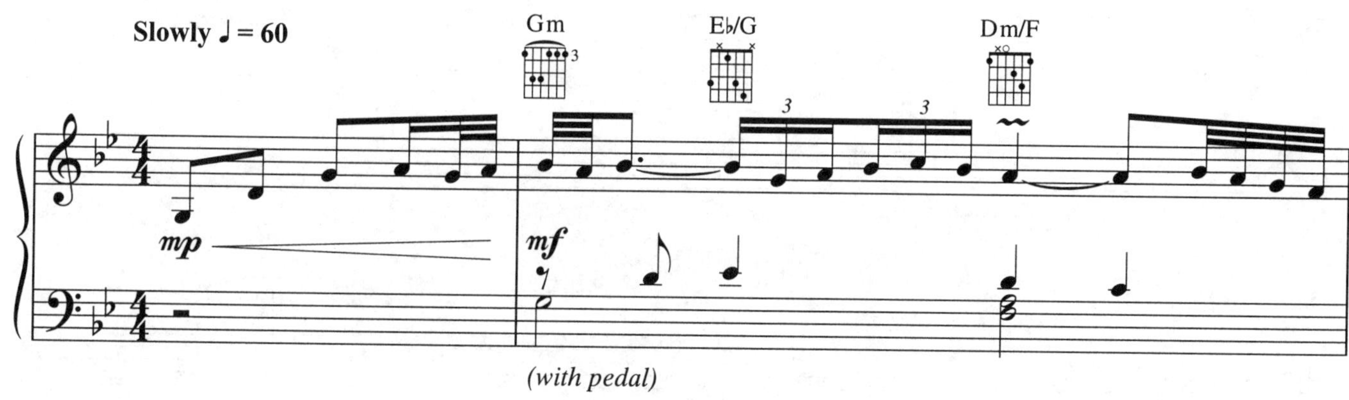

E♭(9)
B♭
F7sus
And I knew it could - n't be but my heart be -

B♭
Gm
Dm/F
E♭
lieved. Oh, it seems like there's some-thing ev - 'ry day. How

Gm
F
E♭
B♭
B♭/D
could you be so far a - way? When you're still here,
cresc.

Chorus:
E♭
F/E♭
E♭
F/E♭
E♭
Gm
when I need you you're not hard to find. You're still
mf

E♭ F/E♭ E♭ F/E♭ E♭

here. I can see you in my ba - by's eyes, and I laugh and

F7sus F7 B♭ F7sus F7

cry. You're still__ here. 2. I had a dream last

dim. *mp*

Verse 2:

B♭ Gm Dm/F E♭

night that you came to me on sil - ver wings__ and I, I

B♭ F7sus F7 B♭ F/A

flew a - way with you__ on a paint - ed sky. And I

Gm
Dm/F
E♭(9)
E♭
F
woke up won - d'rin' what was real. Is it
Gm
Dm/F
E♭
B♭(9)
B♭/D
what you see and touch or what you feel? 'Cause you're still
cresc.
Chorus:
E♭
F/E♭
E♭
F/E♭
E♭
here. oh, you're ev - 'ry - where we've ev - er been.
mf
Gm
E♭
F/E♭
E♭
F/E♭
E♭
You're still here. I heard you in a strang-er's laugh and I

Eb
F/Eb
Eb
Bb(9)
Bb
F7sus
F7
hung a - round__ to hear him laugh a - gain, just once a-gain.
rit. e dim.
Bb
F7sus
F7
Freely
Oh.______
Thought I saw you to -
mp
a tempo
rit.
Bb
Gm
Dm/F
Eb(9)
F/Eb
day. You were stand - ing in__ the sun,__ then you turned a - way,__
Eb
F/Eb
Bb(9)
a - way.______
molto rit.
p

YOUR CHEATIN' HEART

Words and Music by
HANK WILLIAMS

C
C7
F
C
you
When tears come down
like fall - in' rain
you
When tears come down
like fall - in' rain
D7
G7
You'll toss a - round
and call my name
You'll walk the
You'll toss a - round
and call my name
You'll walk the
C
C7
F
G7
floor
the way I do
YOUR CHEAT-IN' HEART
floor
the way I do
YOUR CHEAT-IN' HEART
1 C
G7
2 C
will tell on you.
2. YOUR CHEAT-IN'
will tell on
you.
3
3

THE DEVIL WENT DOWN TO GEORGIA

Words and Music by
CHARLIE DANIELS, JOHN THOMAS CRAIN, JR.,
WILLIAM JOEL DiGREGORIO, FRED LAROY EDWARDS,
CHARLES FRED HAYWARD and JAMES WAINWRIGHT MARSHALL

Fast hoedown two-beat ♩ = 132

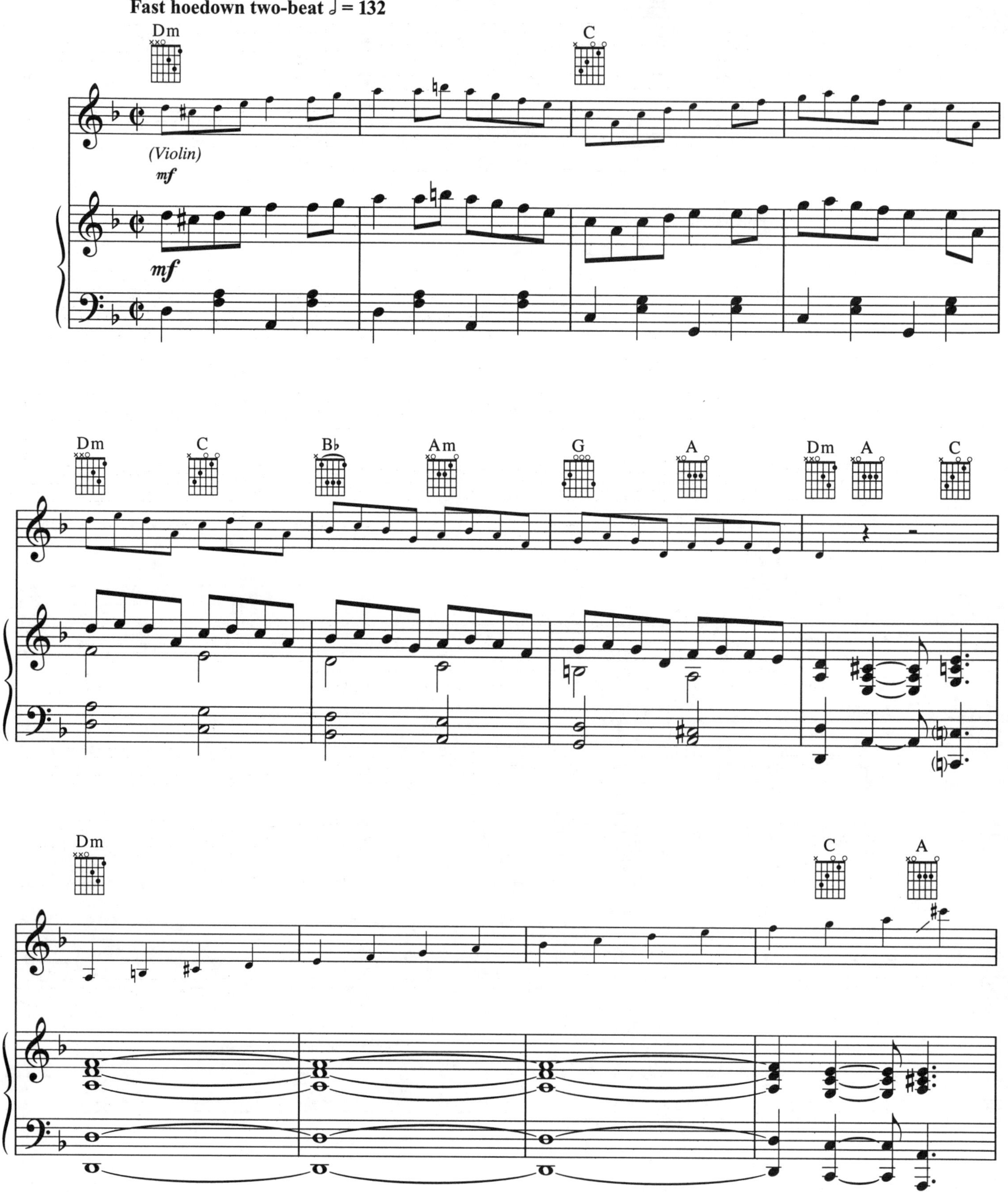

Dm
1. The
17
Verse 1:
D5
dev - il went down to Geor - gia. He was look-in' for a soul to steal.
He was in a
8vb
bind 'cause he was way be - hind, and he was will-in' to make a deal,
when he
(8vb)
came a - cross this young man saw-in' on a fid - dle and play-in' it hot.
And the

A
C
dev - il jumped_up on a hick - o - ry stump. and said, "Boy, let me tell you what.
2. I
33
Verse 2:
Dm
guess you did - n't know it but I'm a fid - dle play - er, too.
And
if you'd care to take a dare,_ I'll make a bet__ with you.
Now,
you play pret - ty good fid - dle, boy,__ but give the dev - il his due.
I'll bet a

A
C
fid - dle of gold a - gainst your soul, 'cause I think I'm bet - ter than you."
3. The
49
Verse 3:
Dm
boy said, "My name's John - ny, and it might be a sin,
but I'll
N.C.
take your bet, you're gon - na re - gret, 'cause I'm the best that's ev - er been."
57
Chorus:
Dm
C
John - ny, ros - in up your bow and play your fid - dle hard, 'cause

Gm
Dm
hell's broke loose in Geor - gia and the dev - il deals the cards. And
Gm
G♯dim7
if you win, you get this shin - y fid - dle made of gold. But
A
if you lose, the dev - il gets your soul.
73
Solo:
Dm
C
(Violin)

Dm
C
B♭
Am
G
A
Dm
A5
C5
4. The
81
Verse 4:
D5
dev - il o - pened up his case and he said, "I'll start this show." and fire
flew from his fin - ger - tips as he ros - ined up his bow. And he
pulled the bow a - cross the strings and it made an e - vil hiss. Then a

A5
C5
band of de - mons joined in___ and it sound - ed some-thin' like this:
97
Interlude:
Dm
F/D
Em/D
Dm
(Violin tacet)
F/D
Em/D
Dm
105
F/D
Em/D
Dm
1. 2.
3.
(Violin solo ad lib....

Gm
Am
B♭
C
Dm
A
C
Dm
...end solo)
5. When the
122
Verse 5:
D5
dev - il fin - ished, John-ny said, "Well, you're pret - ty good, old son, but

sit down in that chair right there and let me show you how it's done."
130
Bridge:
D
Fire on the moun - tain; run, boys, run. (Violin)
The
C
dev-il's in the House of the Ris - ing Sun. (Violin)
D
Chick-en in the bread-pan, pick-in' out dough. (Violin)

To Coda 

C

Gran-ny, does your dog bite? No, child, no. *(Violin)*

146 *Solo:*

Dm C

1. 2.

3.

A

C

Dm
6. The
8vb
161
Verse 6:
dev - il bowed his head be-cause he knew that he'd been beat. And he
(8vb)
laid that gold - en fid - dle on the ground at John - ny's feet.
(8vb)
John-ny said, "Dev-il, just come on back if you ev - er want to try a - gain. 'Cause I

D.S.% al Coda
told you once, you son-of-a-gun, I'm the best that's ev-er been." He played:
Coda
Solo:
Dm
(Violin)
C
Dm

N.C.
184
Dm
C
B♭
Am
Dm
C
B♭
Am
Dm
C
B♭
Am
Dm
C
B♭
Am
Gm
3
F
Dm

The Collection Series

BIG BAND & BEYOND MUSIC
(MFM0406)

If you love that big band, can't get enough of that swing, and like to lounge around with the blues, this is *The Collection* for you. *Titles include:* Artistry in Rhythm • Drumboogie • Hallelujah! • I Gotta Right to Sing the Blues • It Don't Mean a Thing • The Lady Is a Tramp • Love Walked In • The Man I Love • Oh, Lady Be Good! • Swing Is Back in Style • This Can't Be Love • What's New, and many more.

BROADWAY MUSIC
(MFM0407)

All the best Broadway tunes are covered in this show-stopping collection. *Titles include:* And All That Jazz (*Chicago*) • Dancing Queen (*Mamma Mia!*) • Don't Rain on My Parade (*Funny Girl*) • Grease (*Grease*) • I Don't Know How to Love Him (*Jesus Christ Superstar*) • I Got Plenty o' Nuttin' (*Porgy and Bess*) • I Honestly Love You (*Boy from Oz*) • I've Got a Crush on You (*Strike Up the Band*) • People (*Funny Girl*) • Sunrise, Sunset (*Fiddler on the Roof*), and many more.

CLASSIC ROCK MUSIC
(MFM0402)

Get ready to rock with songs from the Eagles, Lynyrd Skynyrd, Van Morrison, and many more favorites. *Titles include:* After Midnight • Blinded by the Light • Dancing in the Dark • Go Your Own Way • Hotel California • I've Gotta Get a Message to You • Locomotive Breath • Moondance • Old Time Rock & Roll • Rock and Roll All Nite • Shake It Up • Sweet Home Alabama, and many more.

COUNTRY MUSIC
(MFM0403)

It's time to play your favorite country hits. *Titles include:* Amazed • Because You Love Me • Breathe • How Do I Live • I Like It, I Love It • I Will Always Love You • I'm Gonna Getcha Good! • It's Five O'Clock Somewhere • There's Your Trouble • Two Sparrows in a Hurricane • You're Still the One, and many more.

JAZZ MUSIC
(MFM0405)

In the mood for some jazz? This book's what you need! *Titles include:* As Time Goes By • Autumn Nocturne • Come Rain or Come Shine • 500 Miles High • Love for Sale • Lover Man (Oh, Where Can You Be?) • South Beach Mambo • That's All • Trav'lin Light • Witchcraft, and many more.

MOVIE MUSIC
(MFM0404)

Bring home the magic of the movies with this assortment of blockbusters. *Titles include:* Across the Stars (*Star Wars*®: Episode II *Attack of the Clones*) • All for Love (*The Three Musketeers*) • Because You Loved Me (*Up Close & Personal*) • Gollum's Song (*The Lord of the Rings: The Two Towers*) • How Do I Live (*Con Air*) • I Don't Want to Miss a Thing (*Armageddon*) • I Will Always Love You (*The Bodyguard*) • James Bond Theme (*Die Another Day*) • Stayin' Alive (*Saturday Night Fever*) • Theme from *Jurassic Park* • There You'll Be (*Pearl Harbor*), and many more.

ROCK & ROLL MUSIC
(MFM0408)

If you love that good old rock & roll, this collection has your favorite tunes. *Titles include:* Be My Baby • California Dreamin' • Da Doo Ron Ron • Great Balls of Fire • Hurt So Bad • I Want to Hold Your Hand • Itsy Bitsy Teenie Weenie Yellow Polka Dot Bikini • Let's Twist Again • (We're Gonna) Rock Around the Clock • Runaround Sue • Shake Rattle and Roll, and many more.

TV MUSIC
(MFM0409)

This book has all your new and old TV favorites. More than 90 of television's best themes including: 24 • Batman • Bonanza • Charlie's Angels • Everybody Loves Raymond • Hawaii Five-O • I'll Be There for You • Law and Order • The Pink Panther • The Rockford Files • Sex and the City • Song from M*A*S*H • The West Wing • Whose Line Is It Anyway, and many more.

WEDDING MUSIC
(MFM0401)

All the classical music favorites for the ceremony and popular love songs for the reception are in this great collection of wedding music. *Titles include:* Ave Maria (Bach/Gounod) • The Wedding March (from *A Midsummer Night's Dream*) • All the Way • Butterfly Kisses • Could I Have This Dance • Forever and for Always • From This Moment On • Here and Now • I Believe in You and Me • I Finally Found Someone • I Swear • I'll Always Love You • When I Fall in Love • With This Ring, and many more.

THE SHEET MUSIC HITS SERIES

All Your Favorite Songs in Seven Music-Packed Volumes!

Popular Sheet Music Hits
(MFM0324)

Titles include: As Time Goes By • Back at One • Because You Loved Me • Foolish Games • God Bless the U.S.A. • Greatest Love of All • I Could Not Ask for More • I Turn to You • I Will Always Love You • Lean on Me • My Way • Now and Forever • Over the Rainbow • The Prayer • The Rose • Somewhere Out There • Theme from New York, New York • There You'll Be • A Thousand Miles • Time to Say Goodbye • To Where You Are • Un-Break My Heart • The Wind Beneath My Wings • You Needed Me • Your Song.

Country Sheet Music Hits
(MFM0322)

Titles include: Amazed • Because You Love Me • Breathe • Come On Over • Concrete Angel • The Dance • The Devil Went Down to Georgia • From This Moment On • Go Rest High on That Mountain • Holes in the Floor of Heaven • How Do I Live • I Could Not Ask for More • I Cross My Heart • I Hope You Dance • I Swear • I'll Be • I'm Already There • I'm Movin' On • The Keeper of the Stars • On the Side of Angels • Something That We Do • There You Are • This Kiss • When You Say Nothing at All • You're Still the One.

Classic Rock Sheet Music Hits
(MFM0323)

Titles include: After Midnight • American Pie • Aqualung • Bad Moon Rising • Black Water • Brown Eyed Girl • Down on the Corner • Drive • Europa • Free Bird • Gimme Some Lovin' • Go Your Own Way • Heart of Gold • Higher Love • Hotel California • Layla • Long Train Runnin' • Lyin' Eyes • Maggie May • Money • More Than a Feeling • Old Time Rock & Roll • Open Arms • Proud Mary • Sister Golden Hair • Someone Saved My Life Tonight • Truckin' • What a Fool Believes.

Movie Music Sheet Music Hits
(MFM0325)

Titles include: Somewhere Out There • Power of Love • The Entertainer • Stayin' Alive • It Might Be You • Because You Loved Me • That's What Friends Are For • As Time Goes By • How Do I Live • I Don't Want to Miss a Thing • A Fool in Love • There'll You'll Be • Come What May • Hedwig's Theme • In Dreams • Across the Stars • Fawkes the Phoenix • Gollum's Song • James Bond Theme • I Move On • Somewhere, My Love (Lara's Theme) • Over the Rainbow • Arthur's Theme • Eye of the Tiger • Wind Beneath My Wings.

TV Sheet Music Hits
(MFM0326)

Titles include: Batman • Boss of Me Now • ER (Main Theme) • Everybody Loves Raymond • Flying Without Wings • Hawaii Five-O • High Upon This Love • I'll Be There for You • Law and Order • Miami Vice • Mr. Ed • Nine to Five • The Pink Panther • Searchin' My Soul • Sex and the City • Song from M*A*S*H • Theme from Family Guy • Theme from Futurama • Theme from Magnum, P.I. • Theme from NYPD Blue • Theme from the Simpsons • This Is the Night • The West Wing • Where There Is Hope • Whose Line Is It Anyway? • Woke Up This Morning • Scooby-Doo (Main Theme) • Twilight Zone • Charlie's Angels • Theme from the X-Files.

Broadway Sheet Music Hits
(MFM0327)

Titles include: Almost Like Being in Love • And All That Jazz • Anything Goes • Beautiful City • Big Spender • Corner of the Sky • Dancing Queen • Don't Cry for Me Argentina • Embraceable You • Forty-Second Street • Good Morning Starshine • Heart • Hey There • I'll Never Fall in Love Again • I've Got a Crush on You • I've Gotta Be Me • Mack the Knife • New York, New York • On a Clear Day You Can See Forever • Ragtime • Send in the Clowns • Suddenly, Seymour • Summertime • Sunrise, Sunset • Thoroughly Modern Millie.

Wedding Sheet Music Hits
(MFM0328)

Titles include: All I Have • Always • Amazed • Because of You • Ave Maria (Schubert) • Endless Love • Bridal Chorus • At Last • Forever and for Always • From This Moment On • Here and Now • How Deep Is Your Love • I Swear • Love Like Ours • In Your Eyes • Once in a Lifetime • This Magic Moment • Tonight I Celebrate My Love • Wedding Song (There Is Love) • The Wedding March (from "A Midsummer Night's Dream") • With This Ring • Years from Here • You Light Up My Life • Your Love Amazes Me • You're the Inspiration.

Collect them all!

AD1132 11/03